Rome of the Caesars

NEW DIMENSIONS IN HISTORY

Historical Cities

Series Editor: Norman F. Cantor

John Wiley & Sons, Inc., New York · London · Sydney

ROME
OF THE CAESARS

THOMAS W. AFRICA

Library of Congress Catalog Card Number: 65–24285
Printed in the United States of America

"Was there ever a city like the great city?"

Rev. 18:18

PREFACE

While there are many histories of imperial Rome and excellent studies of the city itself, the present book is based on the premise that the Roman world is best seen through Roman eyes. In the first and second century A.D., Rome was no longer an overgrown Italian town—it was the capital of a vast empire which included a great variety of nations. From the provinces and from Italy as well, able men came to Rome to further their careers, others to preach a message, and a few to seize a throne. The vitality and major themes of Roman life are well reflected in the lives of individuals who were drawn to the capital. To mirror the times, a selection of representative Romans may suffice—the ambitious politician Sejanus, the wily prince Herod Agrippa, the Christian missionary Paul, the troubled courtier Seneca, the Jewish apologist Josephus, the Asian wizard Apollonius, the gentleman scholar Pliny the Younger, the grim historian Tacitus, the cosmopolitan ruler Hadrian, the philosopher king Marcus Aurelius, and the great physician Galen. Only one of these men, Marcus Aurelius, was born in the capital, but all were caught up in the life of the world city. As individuals they were unique, but together they made up the kaleidoscopic Rome of the Caesars.

While the focus of attention is on eleven men, the political history of the era is provided for continuity and background. Genealogical charts of the Julio-Claudian, Herodian, and Antonine families are included, as is a note on sources and problems of interpretation. Throughout the book administrative titles have been simplified and technical terminology has been held to a minimum. The prominence of religious and philosophical thought in these sketches reflects the importance of intellectual anxiety and personal religion in the Roman world. It is hoped that modern readers will find interpretations of the men of the imperial era more meaningful than improbable anecdotes about the mad, bad Caesars.

All quotations from the New Testament are from *The New English Bible: New Testament,* copyrighted by the Delegates of the Oxford University Press and the Syndics of the Cambridge University Press, 1961. They are reprinted with permission.

As usual, my wife Ursula has provided constant encouragement and invaluable editorial aid.

THOMAS W. AFRICA

Los Angeles, California
July, 1965

CONTENTS

The Roman Emperors
In the First and Second Centuries A.D.

The Julio-Claudian Dynasty

Augustus	30 B.C.–14 A.D.
Tiberius	14–37
Caligula	37–41
Claudius	41–54
Nero	54–68

The Year of the Four Emperors

Galba	68–69
Otho	69
Vitellius	69

The Flavian Dynasty

Vespasian	69–79
Titus	79–81
Domitian	81–96

The Adopted Emperors

Nerva	96–98
Trajan	98–117
Hadrian	117–138
Antoninus Pius	138–161
Lucius Verus	161–169
Marcus Aurelius	161–180
Commodus	180–192

Interregnum

Pertinax	193
Didius Julianus	193

The Severan Dynasty

Septimius Severus	193–211
Caracalla	211–217
Elagabalus	218–222
Severus Alexander	222–235

LIST OF ILLUSTRATIONS

LIST OF MAPS

Maps by Theodore R. Miller.
    *These are original maps and may not be reproduced without
    permission.*

Rome of the Caesars

ONE

The City of Rome

The first glimpse of the city of Rome has often overwhelmed visitors. In 357 A.D. the Christian emperor Constantius II entered Rome for the first time and was dazzled by the physical appearance of the Eternal City. The historian Ammianus Marcellinus described the scene and its effect on the imperial tourist:

> Wherever he looked, Constantius was awed by the variety of impressive sights. . . . As he gazed at the sections of the city lying within the crests of the seven hills . . . whatever first caught his eye seemed larger than all the rest—the holy temple of Jupiter . . . the baths as big as provinces; the great Colosseum . . . rising almost beyond human sight; the high and beautiful vault of the Pantheon . . . the lofty columns which . . . are topped with images of former emperors; the Temple of Venus and Rome, the Forum of Peace, the Theater of Pompey, the Odeum, the Stadium of Domitian, and . . . the other ornaments of the Eternal City. However, when he saw the Forum of Trajan which is unique under the heavens . . . Constantius stood amazed and stared at the gigantic complex which is simply indescribable and will never again be imitated by mortal men.[1]

Most of these impressive structures were built in the first two centuries A.D. to adorn the Rome of the Caesars.

Even the shattered relics of Rome hold a fascination for visitors. In the fall of 1764 young Edward Gibbon first viewed the city which would obsess the rest of his life. In middle age, Gibbon recalled the experience:

> My temper is not very susceptible of enthusiasm, and the enthusiasm which I do not feel I have ever scorned to affect. But at the distance

of twenty-five years, I can neither forget nor express the strong emotions which agitated my mind as I first approached and entered the Eternal City. After a sleepless night I trod with a lofty step the ruins of the Forum; each memorable spot where Romulus stood, or Tully spoke, or Caesar fell, was at once present to my eye, and several days of intoxication were lost or enjoyed before I could descend to a cool and minute investigation. . . . It was at Rome, on the 15th of October, 1764, as I sat musing amid the ruins of the Capitol, while the barefooted friars were singing vespers in the temple of Jupiter, that the idea of writing the decline and fall of the city first started to my mind.[2]

The Rome which wove its spell about Gibbon was a city of the mind, a ghost of imperial splendor conjured up by a glimpse of broken columns in the twilight.

A century later, Henry Adams also found the city a challenging enigma:

No doubt other young men, and occasionally young women, have passed the month of May in Rome since then, and conceive that the charm continues to exist. Possibly it does—in them—but in 1860 the lights and shadows were still medieval, and medieval Rome was alive; the shadows breathed and glowed, full of soft forms felt by lost senses. No sand-blast of science had yet skinned off the epidermis of history, thought, and feeling. . . . To a young Bostonian, fresh from Germany, Rome seemed a pure emotion, quite free from economic or actual values. . . . Rome could not be fitted into an orderly, middle-class, Bostonian, systematic scheme of evolution. No law of progress applied to it. Not even time-sequences—the last refuge of helpless historians—had value for it. The Forum no more led to the Vatican than the Vatican to the Forum. Rienzi, Garibaldi, Tiberius Gracchus, Aurelian might be mixed up in any relation of time, along with a thousand more, and never lead to a sequence. . . . Adams more than once sat at sunset on the steps of the Church of Santa Maria di Ara Coeli, curiously wondering that not an inch had been gained by Gibbon—or all the historians since—towards explaining the Fall. The mystery remained unsolved; the charm remained intact. Two great experiments of Western civilization had left there the chief monuments of their failure, and nothing proved that the city might not still survive to express the failure of a third.[3]

The ruins of Rome were tidied up by Mussolini, and tourists today may view more of the ancient city than could Gibbon or Adams, but the historical problem of survival and collapse still nags thoughtful men.

In the first two centuries A.D. the rulers of Rome maintained order from Scotland to the Euphrates. As the capital of the Western world, Rome was the brain and stomach of a vast organism, the Roman empire. The city consumed large amounts of grain which the provinces furnished as tribute, and in return Rome guaranteed peace and security for the subject peoples. The population of the capital was large and probably exceeded a half million permanent residents. With the fragmentary nature of ancient statistics, demographic certainty is impossible, but perhaps a third of the inhabitants of imperial Rome were slaves and many of the free population were descended from slaves. In the heyday of Roman imperialism, hordes of captives had been dragged from Greece, the Balkans, Asia Minor, Syria, Spain, Africa, and Gaul to labor in the shops, factories, and homes of their conquerors. By the first century A.D. many of these aliens had been emancipated for faithful service, and a few clerical slaves had purchased freedom with their life savings. Though some Italian aristocrats despised Greeks and Semites, the lower and middle classes of Rome attached little stigma to men with a servile background. The poet Horace freely boasted that his father was a freedman, and in time Pertinax, the son of a former slave, would occupy the imperial throne.

Many provincials moved to the capital of their own volition. The Spanish intellectual Seneca described the variety of men who had followed the roads which led to Rome:

Behold this concourse of men, for whom the houses of huge Rome scarcely suffice. . . . From their towns and colonies, from the whole world in fact, hither have they flocked. Some have been brought by ambition; some by the obligation of a public trust; some by an envoy's duty having been laid upon them; some, seeking a convenient and rich field for vice, by luxury; some by a desire for the higher studies; some by the public spectacles; some have been drawn by friendship; some, seeing the ample opportunity for displaying energy, by the chance to work; some have presented their beauty for sale; some their

eloquence for sale—every class of person has swarmed into the city
that offers high prizes for both virtues and vices.[4]

In many respects, imperial Rome was New York on the Tiber.
A center of international finance, the city attracted enterprising
businessmen and speculators. For artists and writers, Rome provided many opportunities to display their talents and snare
wealthy patrons. Since the city was also the seat of government,
ambitious politicians from the provinces visited Rome to win
or buy favors from influential members of the imperial court.
To countless people throughout the empire, the capital was a
symbol of worldly success and conspicuous consumption, a distant
scene of glamor, wealth, and power. The residents of Rome
relished the excitement of life in the city and enjoyed a sense of
proximity to the rulers of the world.

    Under the emperors, Rome was a vast melting pot of many
ethnic groups, but the common use of Latin prevented the city
from becoming a polyglot babel. In the crowded streets of the
capital, Berbers and Negroes jostled Greeks and Sicilians, and
Spaniards, Germans, and Celts might idly watch a snake-charmer
from Egypt or a fire-eater from Syria. In the markets, which
resembled oriental bazaars, Italian farmers haggled with Jewish
merchants, and African grain importers often bargained with
bakers of Balkan origin. The cosmopolitan complexion of the
city reflected the international society which the Roman empire was becoming. Though conservatives complained that the
minorities had become the majority, the city was enriched by its
variegated population. With the sincere bias of a small-town Italian, the emperor Augustus tried to slow the alien tide and limited
the freeing of slaves, but his efforts were in vain and even emperors would soon be drawn from the provinces. The Augustan
attempts to revive the ancestral religion of Rome were also largely
abortive. Ancient temples were restored and splendid new edifices
rose in the capital, but the religious temper of the city was
eclectic and both Isis and Yahweh were worshiped by the banks
of the Tiber. In a venerable temple on the Capitol hill, Jupiter
was honored as the head of the Roman pantheon. At Rome and
elsewhere in the empire, all citizens and subjects offered sacrifices
to the spirit (*genius*) of the reigning emperor and his deified

Imperial Rome in the time of Constantius II, featuring the Capitol hill

ancestors.* To the emperor in his palace on the Palatine hill, worship of the state and obedience to the laws were always more important than traditional prayers to the gods.

To the modern tourist or antiquarian, Rome is a city of stately ruins—the Colosseum, the Forum Romanorum, Hadrian's Tomb, the Pantheon, Trajan's Column, the Arch of Titus, and the Baths of Caracalla. However, imperial Rome was not just a collection of public buildings and monuments—it was also a city of homes, most of them shabby. Though handsome villas graced the suburbs and many mansions lay within the city itself, Rome was essentially a great slum, congested, foul-smelling, and noisy. Hundreds of thousands of human beings were crowded into an area of about six square miles, where real estate was expensive and considerable space was occupied by public buildings and thoroughfares. Unable to expand horizontally, Rome swelled upward and became a city of tenements, many of which towered six and seven stories over the narrow twisting streets. In comfortable homes facing inward on courts and light wells, the rich could ignore the noise and commotion of street life, but only one building in every twenty-six was a private dwelling. The overwhelming majority of the urban population lived in huge, ugly apartment houses. As a rule, an entire family occupied one dingy room off a common balcony which ran about the building and was connected to the lower floors by a steep staircase. Since living space in the city was at a premium, landlords charged tenants outrageous rents for the tiny rooms. Jerry-built by unscrupulous contractors, the tenements were enormous firetraps, and the city was often swept by disastrous fires. So crowded were the streets of Rome that vehicular traffic was forbidden in the city during daylight hours. An exception was made for the carts of contractors who were working on new buildings or tearing down condemned tenements. At night the city was plunged in darkness and the side streets became a jungle of crime. Families huddled behind locked doors and only hardy souls ventured out into the dangers of the night. The main thoroughfares were crowded with commercial vehicles, and the night was

---

*Though Jews were exempted from the imperial cult, the priests of the Jerusalem Temple made sacrifices to Yahweh on behalf of the Roman rulers.

filled with the din of creaking axles and cursing drivers. When dawn came, the city was revealed as a drab collection of wooden and brick buildings. Though Augustus bragged that he had found Rome a town of brick and made it a city of marble, his boast could literally apply to only a few temples and public buildings. More likely, the emperor implied a symbolic permanence in his overall accomplishments rather than an elaborate urban renewal.

Though not an industrial center in the modern sense, Rome was a busy city and most of its inhabitants worked hard for meager incomes. The needs of the urban population were served by thousands of small shopkeepers, from the exclusive jeweler and perfumer to the corner shoemaker and neighborhood baker. Less reputable were street vendors, ragpickers, and the streetwalkers who loitered near the Circus Maximus. Roman industry was limited to the production of tools, furniture, and houseware by a few slaves or free laborers in small factories. Smoky olive-oil lamps made all interiors dim, and the working day was restricted to seven hours in the summer and six in the winter. Many wealthy homes were heated by steampipes in the floor, but the poor huddled near charcoal braziers or small brick stoves which filled their tiny flats with smoke. The basic Roman diet consisted of bread, olive oil, and wine and was augmented by a few vegetables or a bit of salted fish. The average man rarely saw meat on his table and eagerly looked forward to the sacrifice of a pig at a temple feast.* Figs and honey provided sweetening, and garlic and salt spiced an otherwise dull diet. Wealthy Romans ate a greater variety of foods, but only a few gourmands indulged in excessive oral gratification. According to the historian Tacitus, high society imitated the simple eating habits of the middle-class emperor Vespasian, whose successors also dined with taste and moderation.

Grain fleets from Africa and Egypt kept Rome supplied with wheat for bread and mush, and the emperors made sure that the flow of grain was constant and plentiful, for even a brief shortage could bring the city to the brink of famine and riot. The government also provided water for the capital and an

---

*Happily, the gods preferred bones and fat, and the priests divided the choicer parts of the animal among the worshipers.

excellent sewer system. Each day great aqueducts brought more than 222 million gallons of water into the city, but only the rich had running water piped into their homes.* The tenement dwellers had to fetch their water from public fountains or buy the liquid from water carriers. Since only the homes of the rich were equipped with toilet facilities, the poor used slop jars which were later emptied into cesspools. Too often tired apartment tenants dumped their jars off the balcony to the discomfort of pedestrians below. Away from home, Romans of all classes patronized large public toilets. The city boasted huge public baths with exercise halls, steam rooms, and swimming pools. Though the streets of Rome were dirty, the inhabitants were clean and bathed with more regularity than any people in European history. The Roman baths were a triumph of hygiene and sane living, compared to which the Middle Ages were a thousand-year stench.

Under the Republic, the city of Rome had lacked an adequate municipal administration and its residents were unprotected from fire and disorder. As emperor, Augustus organized the government of the city with efficiency and practicality. By 7 B.C. he had divided Rome into fourteen regions, each of which was administered by a magistrate who served for one year. The emperor also established about 265 wards which were headed by supervisors elected by the residents of the ward. The supervisors performed official religious functions and were also responsible for the gangs of public slaves who served as firefighters. However, the problem of fires was too great for the supervisors, who were stripped of all but religious duties in 6 A.D. when Augustus set up a force of 7,000 nightwatchmen and firemen under the control of a prefect. The emperor also appointed an urban prefect as the police chief of the city. The urban prefect was usually a senator and commanded a riot squad of 3,000 soldiers. Another imperial prefect was responsible for procuring grain for the city, but the distribution of free grain to authorized citizens was supervised by a commission of four senators. A board of three senators had control of the water supply for Rome, and other senatorial

---

*Lead poisoning from water pipes may have contributed to the gout which afflicted some wealthy Romans.

commissions were responsible for flood control of the Tiber and for the repair of temples and public buildings. By ancient standards, Rome was a well-run city under the benevolent despotism of the emperors. Originally, Augustus used the municipal offices as patronage for his friends in the Senate, but in time imperial aides absorbed many of the functions of city officials. Whether directly through the prefects or indirectly through the senatorial commissions, the emperors governed the capital of the empire. Except for palaces and public buildings, the city was allowed to grow without organized planning, and imperial regulations provided only minimal safety for its residents. Only Nero seemed to grasp the concept of urban planning, and even he could not adjust the size of the city to its sprawling population.

As in any crowded city, the noise in Rome was deafening. The writer Seneca recalled the noises which assailed him when he lived above a public bath:

So picture to yourself the assortment of sounds which are strong enough to make me hate my very powers of hearing! When your strenuous gentleman, for example, is exercising himself by flourishing leaden weights; when he is working hard or else pretends to be working hard, I can hear him grunt; and whenever he releases his imprisoned breath, I can hear him panting in wheezy and high-pitched tones. Or perhaps I notice some lazy fellow content with a cheap rub-down, and hear the crack of the pummeling hand on his shoulder, varying in sound according as the hand is laid on flat or hollow. Then, perhaps, a professional [athlete] comes along, shouting out the score; that is the finishing touch. Add to this the arresting of an occasional roisterer or pickpocket, the racket of the man who always likes to hear his own voice in the bathroom, or the enthusiast who plunges into the swimming-tank with unconscionable noise and splashing. Besides all those whose voices, if nothing else, are good, imagine the hair-plucker with his penetrating, shrill voice—for purposes of advertisement—continually giving it vent and never holding his tongue except when he is plucking the armpits and making his victim yell instead. Then the cake-seller with his varied cries, the sausageman, the confectioner, and all the vendors of food hawking their wares, each with his own distinctive intonation. . . . Among the sounds that din round me without distracting, I include passing carriages, a machinist in the same block, a saw-sharpener nearby, or some fellow who is demon-

strating with little pipes and flutes at the Trickling Fountain, shouting rather than singing.[5]

Although he insists that the commotion did not distract him from
his reading, Seneca paid more attention to the noise than he
admits.

While satirists are rarely unprejudiced witnesses, the complaints of the poet Juvenal vividly portray the daily life of Rome,
the teeming streets and rickety apartment houses of the great
city:

Who, on Tivoli's heights, or a small town like Gabii, say,
Fears the collapse of his house? But Rome is supported on pipestems,
Matchsticks; it's cheaper, so, for the landlord to shore up his ruins,
Patch up the old cracked walls, and notify all the tenants
They can sleep secure, though the beams are in ruins above them.
No, the place to live is out there, where no cry of *Fire!*
Sounds the alarm of the night, with a neighbor yelling for water,
Moving his chattels and goods, and the whole third story is smoking.
This you'll never know: for if the ground floor is scared first,
You are the last to burn, up there where the eaves of the attic
Keep off the rain, and the doves are brooding over their nest eggs. . . .

Death in a flaming tenement was not the only disadvantage to
urban life:

Here in town the sick die from insomnia mostly.
Undigested food, on a stomach burning with ulcers,
Brings on listlessness, but who can sleep in a flophouse?
Who but the rich can afford sleep and a garden apartment?
That's the source of infection. The wheels creak by on the narrow
Streets of the wards, the drivers squabble and brawl when they're
    stopped,
More than enough to frustrate the drowsiest son of a sea cow.
When his business calls, the crowd makes way, as the rich man,
Carried high in his car, rides over them, reading or writing,
Even taking a snooze, perhaps, for the motion's composing.
Still, he gets where he wants before we do; for all of our hurry
Traffic gets in our way, in front, around and behind us.
Somebody gives me a shove with an elbow, or two-by-four scantling.
One clunks my head with a beam, another cracks down with a beer
    keg.

Mud is thick on my shins, I am trampled by somebody's big feet.
Now what?—a soldier grinds his hobnails into my toes.

The unwary pedestrian might also be trampled by a crowd of
dinner guests hurrying to their patron's feast:

Don't you see the mob rushing along to the handout?
There are a hundred guests, each one with his kitchen servant.
Even Samson himself could hardly carry those burdens,
Pots and pans some poor little slave tries to keep on his head, while
    he hurries
Hoping to keep the fire alive by the wind of his running.
Tunics, new-darned, are ripped to shreds; there's the flash of a fir
    beam
Huge on some great dray, and another carries a pine tree,
Nodding above our heads and threatening death to the people.
What will be left of the mob, if that cart of Ligurian marble
Breaks its axle down and dumps its load on these swarms?

At night a stroller in Rome was in peril from thugs, drunks, and
careless householders:

Look at other things, the various dangers of nighttime.
How high it is to the cornice that breaks, and a chunk beats my brains
    out,
Or some slob heaves a jar, broken or cracked, from a window.
Bang! It comes down with a crash and proves its weight on the side-
    walk.
You are a thoughtless fool, unmindful of sudden disaster,
If you don't make your will before you go out to have dinner.
There are as many deaths in the night as there are open windows
Where you pass by; if you're wise, you will pray, in your wretched
    devotions,
People may be content with no more than emptying slop jars.
There your hell-raising drunk, who has had the bad luck to kill no one,
Tosses in restless rage, like Achilles mourning Patroclus,
Turns from his face to his back, can't sleep, for only a fracas
Gives him the proper sedation. But any of these young hoodlums,
All steamed up on wine, watches his step when the crimson
Cloak goes by, a lord, with a long, long line of attendants,
Torches and brazen lamps, warning him, *Keep your distance!*
Me, however, whose torch is the moon, or the feeblest candle
Fed by a sputtering wick, he absolutely despises.

Here is how it all starts, the fight, if you think it is fighting
When he throws all the punches, and all I do is absorb them.
He stops. He tells me to stop. I stop. I have to obey him.
What can you do when he's mad and bigger and stronger than you
    are?
"Where do you come from?" he cries, "you wino, you bean-bloated
    bastard?
Off what shoemaker's dish have you fed on chopped leeks and boiled
    lamb-lip?
What? No answer? Speak up, or take a swift kick in the rear.
Tell me where you hang out—in some praying-house with the Jew-
    boys?"
If you try to talk back, or sneak away without speaking,
All the same thing: you're assaulted, and then put under a bail bond
For committing assault. This is a poor man's freedom.
Beaten, cut up by fists, he begs and implores his assailant,
Please, for a chance to go home with a few teeth left in his mouth.[6]

Surely, every day at Rome was not so hazardous or exciting, but
Juvenal's humorous lines bared the grotesque reality which only
cartoons can reveal.

Perhaps Juvenal's most familiar line is the quip that the
residents of imperial Rome were interested only in "bread and
circuses." Though Juvenal was exaggerating as usual, "bread and
circuses" often heads the indictment which moralists raise against
the city of the Caesars. The games in the circus were elaborate
and costly, and the Circus Maximus held 250,000 spectators
who were fanatic devotees of chariot racing. Begun by Vespasian
and completed by Titus, the Colosseum seated 50,000 and fea-
tured the slaughter of wild animals, the execution of criminals,
and fierce combats between gladiators. The gladiatorial games
had originally been funeral sacrifices but had evolved into
spectacles of bloodshed which revolted sensitive men. Like many
moderns, most Romans had brutal tastes and flocked to scenes
of death and violence, but the circus and amphitheater also
displayed pageants and feats of skill by acrobats, athletes, and
animal trainers—the emperor Galba, for example, exhibited
tightrope-walking elephants. In the Roman theater, Greek tragedy
became Italian opera and ballet, and pantomime was raised to a
high art by great mimes. Heavy with slapstick, comedy was

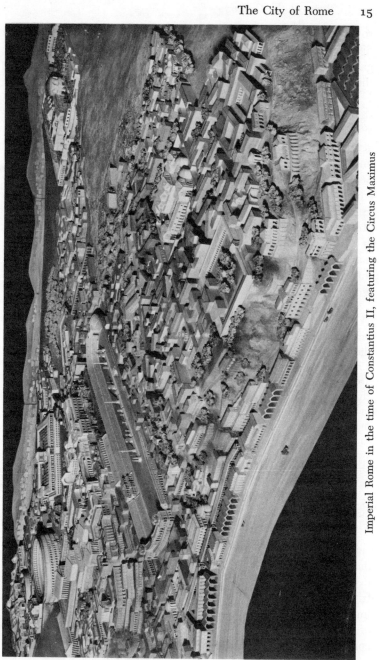

Imperial Rome in the time of Constantius II, featuring the Circus Maximus

rowdy and ribald, for the Romans enjoyed burlesque and bawdiness. During the first century, the state provided free public games on about ninety-three days per year, which is less than the time devoted today to free radio and television.

In supplying free entertainment and also grain, the Roman state acted from motives of self-interest and civic responsibility. When a theater crowd split into noisy factions over two rival actors, Augustus expressed his displeasure, but one of the actors imprudently rebuked the emperor: "Be glad, Caesar, that the people quarrel about us and not about you!" The rule of the emperors deprived the Roman commons of the stimulation and excitement of political life. For centuries, the masses had been absorbed with elections and legislation and had played the game of politics in deadly earnest. The Caesars removed decision making from the Senate and the popular assemblies and substituted the diversions of the circus and arena. The second-century writer Fronto praised the sagacity of the emperor Trajan:

For the arts of peace, scarcely anyone has excelled if indeed anyone has equalled Trajan in popularity with the people. . . . The emperor did not neglect even actors and the other performers of the stage, the circus, or the amphitheater, knowing as he did that the Roman people are held fast by two things above all, the corn-dole and the shows, that the success of a government depends on amusements as much as more serious things; neglect of serious matters entails the greater loss, neglect of amusements the greater discontent. Food largess is a weaker incentive than shows; by largesses of food, only the proletariat on the corn-register are conciliated singly and individually, whereas by the shows the whole populace is kept in good humor.[7]

It is noteworthy that Fronto considered entertainment the opiate not only of the masses but of the entire citizenry.

The grain dole benefited about 200,000 Romans who received a grain allotment from the state to augment their meager incomes. Since the state did not supply clothing, rent, or other necessities, no one could live on the dole alone. A hang-over from the political bribery of the Republic, the grain dole in imperial Rome was an attempt to alleviate the crushing poverty of the urban poor. To recipients and donors alike, the dole was considered a just reward for the descendants of men who had conquered the nations of the Mediterranean. With the grain dole, the rulers of Rome diverted a portion of the enormous revenues of the empire to relieve want in the capital. The city of Rome was made up of a handful of millionaires, a tiny middle class, and an overwhelming majority of poor workers. A better life could be had in the provinces, but it was not easy for city dwellers to tear up roots and take up rural ways. In the excitement at the circus and in the fast pace of urban life, the Roman masses could forget their poverty as long as the grain dole was forthcoming.

The city of Rome was one gigantic mouth, the largest center of consumption in the Mediterranean world. Most grain entered the city as tribute, but other commodities were purchased and

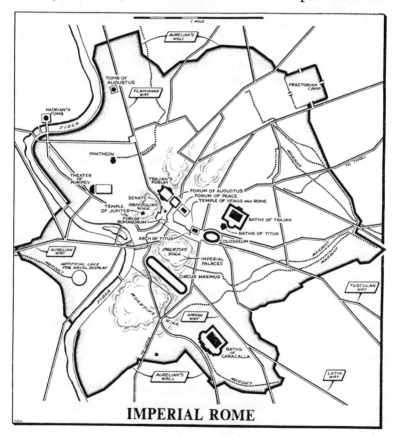

IMPERIAL ROME

brought wealth to producers and transporters. The great social historian Jérôme Carcopino summarized the variety of goods which flowed into the imperial city:

Into her three ports of Ostia, Portus, and the emporium beneath the Aventine poured the tiles and bricks, the wines and fruits of Italy; the corn of Egypt and Africa; the oil of Spain; the venison, the timbers, and the wool of Gaul; the cured meats of Baetica; the dates of the oases; the marbles of Tuscany, of Greece, and of Numidia; the porphyries of the Arabian Desert; the lead, silver, and copper of the Iberian Peninsula; the ivory of the Syrtes and the Mauretanias, the gold of Dalmatia and of Dacia; the tin of the Cassiterides, now the Scilly Isles, and the amber of the Baltic; the papyri of the valley of the Nile; the glass of Phoenicia and of Syria; the stuffs of the Orient; the incense of Arabia; the spices, the corals, and the gems of India; the silks of the Far East. In the city and its suburbs, the sheds of the warehouses stretched out of sight. Here accumulated the provisions that filled Rome's belly, the stores that were the pledge of her well-being and of her luxury.[8]

A complete list of imports would also include slaves. Rich Romans bought up teachers, chefs, business managers, and pretty boys, and many slaves without education or talent became attendants and domestic servants. However, most unskilled slaves were shipped directly to the work-gangs who labored under the lash on the great plantations of Italy. Later, with the establishment of universal peace, the supply of captives diminished and rural slaves were replaced by tenant farmers. However, the incubus of slavery continued to weaken the fiber of Roman society and plagued free labor with servile competition.

By right of conquest, the city of Rome enjoyed a favored position in the economy of the empire. But not all Romans were complacent with the fruits of imperialism. At the court of Nero, the poet Petronius viewed the extension of the empire as a predatory nightmare:

Lord and master of the world, our Roman stood supreme,
on land, on sea, and where the daystar dawned and plunged;
but unappeased. Everywhere his cargoed keels
swirled the marble water white; but if, beyond, unknown,

some landfall lay, some shore touched to amber by the blaze of gold,
Rome called it foe, Rome dealt it fate. Through war to wealth
we hacked our way.
                    Boredom and greed.
                                    Old pleasures palled,
decayed. Attrition of dirty hands, pawing, soiling.
And the savor eroded, the bloom of goodness rubbed away.
Vulgarity by plenty spawned.
                                    Now rarity seemed all,
plunder of boredom born.
                    At Corinth, soldiers of Rome,
gaping, connoisseurs of bronze, collectors of antiques.
And the gashed earth bleeding:
                                    the red rocks ripped away,
the marbles, the rare, the rose, the porphyries pryed up,
peers of ocean's purple.
                    And the plunder:
                                    Numidia a waste;
desert through Cashmere, the splendid fleeces shorn away;
Arabia ravished, the spices scattered.
                                    Rome rampant
on a victim world.[9]

The guilt, which Petronius and other Roman writers expressed,
was accompanied by a chilling fear that one day the captive
nations would rise and Rome would reap a harvest of hate.

As an apparatus for maintaining order and extorting taxes,
the Roman empire was a model of efficiency. However, justice
for provincials only came when political power was no longer
monopolized by Italians. Under Augustus, Roman citizenship was
often granted to provincials. Under his successors, more provincials were allowed into the circle of privilege, and consequently
the empire was disturbed by only a few serious revolts. The
Romans were still not popular in the Hellenistic East where
Greeks, Asiatics, and Egyptians considered them barbarous
upstarts. During the reign of Domitian, a bitter Christian writer
in Asia Minor used veiled apocalyptic images to express hatred
of Roman dominion. The author of the Apocalypse of John
eagerly anticipated the fall of Rome as "Babylon, the harlot of the
seven hills, the great city that holds sway over the kings of the
earth."

In an ecstasy of hate, the prophet portrayed the city of Rome as seen by hostile provincials and persecuted sectarians:

Her sins are piled high as heaven, and God has not forgotten her crimes. Pay her back in her own coin, repay her twice over for her deeds! Double for her the strength of the potion she mixed! Mete out grief and torment to match her voluptuous pomp! She says in her heart, "I am a queen on my throne! No mourning for me, no widow's weeds!" Because of this, her plagues shall strike her in a single day— pestilence, bereavement, famine, and burning. . . . The kings of the earth who committed fornication with her and wallowed in her luxury will weep and wail over her, as they see the smoke of her conflagration. They will stand at a distance, for horror at her torment, and will say, "Alas, alas for the great city, the mighty city of Babylon! In a single hour your doom has struck!" The merchants of the earth also will weep and mourn for her, because no one any longer buys their cargoes, cargoes of gold and silver, jewels and pearls, cloths of purple and scarlet, silks and fine linens; all kinds of scented woods, ivories, and every sort of thing made of costly woods, bronze, iron, or marble; cinnamon and spice, incense, perfumes and frankincense; wine, oil, flour and wheat, sheep and cattle, horses, chariots, slaves, and the lives of men. "The fruit you longed for," they will say, "is gone from you; all the glitter and the glamour are lost, never to be yours again!" The traders in all these wares, who gained their wealth from her, will stand at a distance for horror at her torment, weeping and mourning and saying, "Alas, alas for the great city, that was clothed in fine linen and purple and scarlet, bedizened with gold and jewels and pearls! Alas, that in one hour so much wealth should be laid waste!" Then all the sea-captains and voyagers, the sailors and those who traded by sea, stood at a distance and cried out as they saw the smoke of her conflagration: "Was there ever a city like the great city?" They threw dust on their heads, weeping and mourning and saying, "Alas, alas for the great city, where all who had ships at sea grew rich on her wealth! Alas, that in a single hour she should be laid waste!"

Without compassion, the Christian author gleefully imagined the plight of Rome:

Then a mighty angel took up a stone like a great millstone and hurled it into the sea and said, "Thus shall Babylon, the great city, be sent hurtling down, never to be seen again! No more shall the sound of harpers and minstrels, of flute-players and trumpeters, be heard in

you; no more shall craftsmen of any trade be found in you; no more
shall the sound of the mill be heard in you; no more shall the light of
the lamp be seen in you; no more shall the voice of the bride and
bridegroom be heard in you! Your traders were once the merchant
princes of the world, and with your sorcery you deceived all the nations. . . ." Alleluia! The smoke goes up from her for ever and ever![10]

In his bitterness, the Christian writer had forgotten the moral of
the Book of Jonah in which Yahweh had cautioned another
prophet: "And should not I pity Nineveh, that great city, in
which there are more than a hundred and twenty thousand
persons who do not know their right hand from their left, and also
much cattle?" Despite the hopes of the Apocalypse of John,
Rome did not perish in one awful cataclysmic hour. When at
last the city was sacked by the Goths in 410 A.D., the Roman
empire had been ruled by Christians for a century and Christianity had been the mandatory state religion for a generation. When
the dreadful news reached Bethlehem, Jerome, who was a wiser
Christian than John, groaned: "In one city, the whole world has
perished!" Pagan or Christian, Rome was something which the
world could not afford to lose.

When Augustus held sway in the early first century, no one
anticipated the fall of the city or the empire. The emperor had
restored peace and removed the fear of civil war, but his price
was the termination of the Republic and the establishment of
autocracy. Both the city and the empire willingly paid the
despot's fee and men no longer participated in deciding their own
fates. The individuals who came to the Rome of the Caesars
lived in a world which Augustus had made, a world without
freedom but still filled with fear and inner weariness. In general,
the emperors were benevolent despots, but the weight of the
state increased with the passage of time. Innovations became
precedents and servility a way of life. While some men adapted
themselves readily to the new order and tried to build careers
in the shadow of the despot, others sought escape in ideas or
religion. Ironically, the few who attained the imperial throne
also found that even rulers are not free under despotism.

TWO

The Politician—Sejanus

The career of Sejanus, right-hand man of the emperor Tiberius, was a model for aspiring politicians in any era. With ability, agility, and cunning, he pushed his way through the power structure to a position second only to the emperor himself. Sejanus would have been equally successful under the cold and suspicious Stalin. However, the wily Sejanus succumbed to ambition and was crushed by the master whom he threatened. The ultimate fate of Sejanus had elements of tragedy, and his meteoric fall from power excited Roman moralists of later generations. While the rise and fall of agile schemers is a common theme in world history, the career of Sejanus was conditioned by factors which Augustus had set in motion.

Like any successful revolutionary government, the political apparatus which Augustus imposed on the Roman people reflected the failures of the previous regime. Under the Republic, the entire citizenry had made up the legislative body of Rome, but the propertied classes controlled the election of major magistrates—the consuls and praetors who commanded the Roman armies, and the censors who supervised public morals and voting lists. The legislative and electoral assemblies were subject to the advice, though not the approval, of the Senate, an august body of about 600 former magistrates. The Senate controlled foreign policy, appointed provincial governors, and held the purse strings of the Republic. On most matters of importance, decision making lay in the hands of a senatorial oligarchy of noble families who monopolized major offices and resented the appearance of new names in politics. Since high politics was largely a family affair, alliances between politicians were confirmed by marriages which were broken as soon as the political climate changed. Disregarding the tragic effects of such marriages and divorces on wives and children, the Roman ruling circles undermined the family as an institution while praising the family as an ideal. A similar hypocrisy was applied to the pressing problems which ultimately wrecked the Republic—urban poverty at Rome and corrupt government in the provinces.

In the late Republic, the city of Rome was filled with landless proletarians who lived on the verge of destitution and survived by the grain dole and the sale of their votes in the popular assembly. The nobles, who had incorporated many small farms into their great plantations, were generally hostile to programs for the resettlement of proletarians on public land. Limited by the mental attitudes of a courthouse gang, the nobles freely corrupted the electorate and employed force against their political rivals. The use of armies in politics led to bloody civil wars and the triumph of Gaius Julius Caesar who tried to alleviate the urban crisis by encouraging immigration from the capital to provincial towns where proletarians could become small property owners. Caesar also provided for honest administrations in the provinces where Roman governors had often plundered the subject peoples without restraint. Irritated by his success and stung by his sarcasm, Caesar's former peers murdered the dictator, but the assassination did not remove the decisive role of the military in Roman politics. The men who slew Caesar were soon defeated in battle by Mark Antony and young Octavian, the grand-nephew and adopted son of the late dictator. In time, Octavian crushed Antony and became Augustus in the process. By 30 B.C. all of his rivals were dead and Augustus was the uncontested master of the Roman world. His supremacy was readily acknowledged by the Senate, and the Roman commons welcomed the benevolent despotism of another Caesar.

The system of Augustus was called the Principate, for he was the Princeps or ranking man in the state. In his memoirs, Augustus described his role as he conceived it:

In my sixth and seventh consulships, when I had put out the flames of civil war and after having received absolute power by universal consent, I transferred the state from my own hands to the control of the Senate and the Roman people. For this service, I was given the title of Augustus by order of the Senate; the doorposts of my house were covered with laurels, and a civic crown was placed over my door. In the Curia Julia, a golden shield was set up, inscribed with the testimony of the Senate and the Roman people that they had given it to me for my courage, clemency, justice, and piety. From that time on, I took precedence over all in rank, but I had no more power than my colleagues in any office.[1]

When he wrote this passage, Augustus was a very old man who had never had a high regard for the truth. His very title, Augustus (the Holy One), was religious and distinguished him from lesser mortals. The Princeps did not wish to restore the Republic, for he had struggled too long to win power. When the servile Senate begged him to retain control of the state, Augustus gracefully accepted their flattering pleas. The charade was characteristic of his constant concern for public opinion.

Unlike Caesar, Augustus worried over appearances and deliberately played down the predominant role which he held in the new order. Caesar had sneered that the Republic was only an antiquated formality, but to Marcus Brutus the Republic had been a reality. The murder of Caesar haunted Augustus, who had no intention of suffering a similar fate. The Princeps treated the Senate with calculated respect and often used senators to staff his administration. Though the assemblies continued to legislate and elect officials, Augustus recommended legislation and approved candidates for office. The Republic under Augustus was a state of mind, an illusion that one man embodied the general will of the Senate and the Roman people. The old Republic had relied upon collegiate rule to prevent any politician from abusing authority—every office (except the dictatorship which was authorized only in emergencies) was shared by at least two men who could veto each other. Within the city limits of Rome, any of ten tribunes had the power to veto any act of the Roman state.*
However, Augustus held multiple offices and made a farce of the check and balance system. In order to retain control of the veteran frontier legions, he was permanently invested with

---

*The tribunes were legally sacrosanct and had been instituted to protect the masses from unjust decisions by the nobles.

proconsular military authority (*imperium*).* To keep the Senate and assemblies in line, Augustus also assumed tribunician powers for life. In time, the consulship became a hollow honor for deserving civil servants. While the assemblies eventually disappeared altogether, the Senate evolved into a debating society and a high court for political crimes. Although the Senate was allowed to govern Italy and the quiet provinces, the emperor kept the provinces of Gaul, Spain, Syria, and the northern Balkans under his direct control. Since the death of Cleopatra, Augustus held Egypt as his private estate and forbade senators to set foot in the strategic province. He also commanded Roman troops in the client kingdoms of Morocco, Bulgaria, Judea, and the Crimea. Always wise in money matters, Augustus collected the vast revenues of the empire and kept an eye on most expenditures of public funds. Despite Augustan propaganda, neither the Princeps nor his subjects had any doubts as to the autocratic reality of the Principate.

To complete the totality of despotism, all Roman citizens and every resident of the empire swore a personal loyalty oath to the emperor:

I swear by Jupiter, Earth, Sun, by all the gods and goddesses, and by Augustus·himself, that I will be loyal to Caesar Augustus and to his children and descendants all my life in word, in deed, and in thought, regarding as friends whomever they so regard, and considering as enemies whomever they so adjudge; that in defense of their interests I will spare neither body, soul, life, nor children, but will in every way undergo every danger in defense of their interests; that whenever I perceive or hear anything being said or planned or done against them, I will lodge information about this and will be an enemy to whoever says or plans or does any such thing; and that whomever they adjudge to be enemies I will by land and sea, with weapons and sword, pursue and punish. But if I do anything contrary to this oath or not in conformity with what I swore, I myself call down upon myself, my body, my soul, my life, my children, and all my family and property, utter ruin and utter destruction unto all my issue and all my descendants, and may neither earth nor sea receive the bodies of my family or my descendants, or yield fruits to them.[2]

*Under the Republic, *imperium* was normally held only by consuls, praetors, and provincial governors (proconsuls, propraetors).

In the light of this document alone, it would be difficult to maintain that Augustus preserved the Republic or shared real power with any representative of the old order.

As a system of government, the Principate was a great success and Rome never returned to popular government. The longevity of the emperor contributed to the permanence of the Principate. When his last rival, Antony, was defeated, Augustus was in his early thirties and the Princeps held power until his death at the age of seventy-five. A whole generation grew up in the shadow of the despot, and "few men were left," growled the historian Tacitus, "who could remember the Republic." The long life of Augustus surprised everyone including himself, for he was a chronic invalid who suffered from catarrh and liver trouble. In cold weather, the emperor shuffled about the palace in heavy woolen underwear and no fewer than five layers of clothing. So careful was Augustus with his delicate health that he outlived most of his contemporaries. However, the excessive family pride of the emperor almost wrecked the regime, for he insisted that the imperial power be passed on to his direct descendants. Augustus' only child, Julia, was the product of an unsuccessful early marriage and had been raised with undue severity by his second wife, Livia. In marrying the imperious Livia, Augustus had combined romance with political calculation. He truly loved the beautiful and able woman whose family connections out-ranked his. Livia was a devoted wife who aided Augustus in political intrigues, but their otherwise happy relationship pro-duced no children. Yet Livia had two sons by a prior marriage, Tiberius and Drusus,* who became capable generals and servants of the Roman state. Nevertheless, Augustus made no secret of his intention that the descendants of Julia were to be his political heirs.

Like any aristocratic Roman father, Augustus treated his daughter as a brood mare to be married and bred for political profit. Julia was first married to Augustus' nephew Marcellus, whom the emperor promised to adopt if the marriage proved fruitful. However, the position of the Princeps was not im-

---

*Though Drusus died in 9 B.C., his children Germanicus and Livilla played important roles in the reign of Tiberius and his son Claudius eventually reached the imperial throne.

Augustus

Livia

pregnable, for he was dependent on the military skills of Marcus Agrippa who had fought all his battles. While he lacked polish and family background, Agrippa had helped to win the Augustan revolution and had no intention of being eclipsed by a youth whose only virtue was a familial bond with the Princeps. In 23 B.C. Augustus was gravely ill and worried by a recent conspiracy against his regime. Fearing that he was dying, the Princeps turned to Agrippa and gave him his signet ring as a symbol of authority. When the crisis had passed, Agrippa's position was strengthened, and Livia quickly married her son Tiberius to Agrippa's daughter Vipsania. When Marcellus conveniently died, Julia was left a widow but not for long. Though considerably older than Julia, Agrippa divorced his wife and married the daughter of Augustus, whose dynastic aims Agrippa could now support. To satisfy her father and her husband, the dutiful Julia produced five children—Gaius, Lucius, Julia the Younger, Agrippina the Elder, and Agrippa Postumus. In 18 B.C. Agrippa received permanent *imperium* and tribunician powers. The following year Augustus proudly adopted his grandsons Gaius and Lucius as his legal heirs, secure in the knowledge that their father would serve as regent during their minority. Outmaneuvered by Agrippa, Livia quietly bided her time. In 12 B.C. part of Augustus' plans were upset, for Agrippa died and Julia was again a widow.

For years, Livia had waited to capture the succession and now she had her opportunity. With the approval of Augustus, Livia forced her son Tiberius to divorce his wife and marry Julia. The new marriage proved to be a catastrophe, for Tiberius had been happy with Vipsania who had borne a son, Drusus. Already irritated by Augustus' preference for his grandsons, Tiberius was now forced to play the role of stepfather to Julia's boys who would inherit the throne which he had served so ably in the field and at Rome. The vivacious Julia was equally distressed by a forced marriage with the somber Tiberius, whom Livia had raised with old-fashioned strictness. In desperation, Julia sought escape in the hectic pleasures of high society and indulged in casual affairs with unworthy lovers. Livia was delighted, for Augustus had passed considerable legislation against adultery, and his own daughter was flagrantly guilty of mocking his laws. For the time being, Augustus ignored the open scandal, but Tiberius was humiliated by Julia's behavior. In 6 B.C. Tiberius retired from public life and sulked on the island of Rhodes, where he took up the study of astrology. At Rome, the court considered his career ended and old enemies openly suggested that the death of Tiberius would benefit the regime. To complete the tragedy, Augustus finally punished Julia for her indiscretions and imprisoned her on an island where she later died in lonely despair. The personal agonies of Julia and Tiberius meant nothing to the old Princeps, who was entranced with his maturing grandsons.

Reasonable men should never underestimate the irrational element of chance, which can upset the most careful plans of mice and men. In the last years of his life, chance factors wrought havoc with the hopes of Augustus. By 4 A.D. Gaius and Lucius had unexpectedly died, and their brother Agrippa Postumus was a delinquent youth whom the Princeps sentenced to an island prison. Deprived of the sons of Agrippa and Julia, the old despot could rely on no one but Tiberius, the bitter recluse who had left Rhodes and returned to Rome. Tiberius was now adopted as Augustus' heir and endowed with the tribunician power. After victories over barbarians and rebels in the Balkans, Tiberius received *imperium* and was ready to assume control of the state in the event of Augustus' death. However, Tiberius was forced to adopt his nephew Germanicus, who was married to Julia's daughter Agrippina. To further connect the two families, Tiberius' son Drusus married Livilla, the sister of Germanicus. As emperor, Tiberius would still be bound by the senile whims of Augustus who had kept the succession in his own blood line.

In the afternoon of August 19, 14 A.D., Augustus finally died. The historian Suetonius described the final hours of the Princeps:

On the day that he died, Augustus frequently inquired whether rumors of his illness were causing any popular disturbance. He called for a mirror and had his hair combed and his lower jaw, which had fallen from weakness, propped up. Presently he summoned a group of friends and asked: "Have I played my part in the farce of life creditably enough?" adding the theatrical tag: "If I have pleased you, kindly signify appreciation with a warm goodbye. . . ." Finally, he kissed his wife with: "Goodbye, Livia: never forget whose [wife] you have been!" and died almost at once. . . . The only sign that his wits were wandering, just before he died, was his sudden cry of terror: "Forty young men are carrying me off!" But even this may be read as a prophecy rather than a delusion, because forty Praetorians were to form the guard of honor that conveyed him to his lying-in-state. . . . He had given orders that "should anything happen" to his daughter Julia . . . her body must be excluded from the Mausoleum.[3]

As a statesman the old despot had played his role very creditably, but as a father he was a failure and had inflicted severe psychological injuries on the imperial family.

The new emperor was able, conscientious, and miserable. Always reserved, Tiberius was a gloomy middle-aged cynic for whom success had come too late. The taste of power was now bitter and he viewed the throne as a thankless burden. Tiberius had few illusions and little trust in humanity, for Augustus had spurned him for years until chance had removed the favored grandsons.* Courtiers who had sneered when Tiberius was out of favor were obsequious when his star rose again. Tiberius despised the court and the Senate and made no effort to hide his contempt. However, the emperor patiently presided over the Senate and listened to hours of idle rhetoric. To simplify the machinery of government, he entrusted consular elections to the senators who obediently ratified his candidates. With a wry smile, Tiberius deified his predecessor but refused honorary titles for himself. Fully aware of the responsibility of his office, the emperor was insistent on honest and efficient government in the provinces. He warned tax-hungry governors that they were sent to "shear the sheep but not flay them," and incompetent officials like Pontius Pilate dreaded the wrath of Tiberius. The keynote of his regime was economy, and the frugal Tiberius accumulated an enormous surplus in the treasury. Since he deplored the expenditure of public funds on entertainment, the people of Rome hated the stingy despot. However, except for the treason trials which marred his later years, the reign of Tiberius was a model administration and the emperor was a worthy successor to Augustus.

---

*Tiberius did not leave the fate of Agrippa Postumus to chance. Early in his reign, Tiberius executed Julia's surviving son as a possible contender for the throne. According to Tiberius, Augustus had left orders for the murder of the loutish young prince.

Despite his achievements as a ruler, Tiberius was an unhappy and lonely man. For decades, resentment had eroded his personality until the emperor was close to misanthropy. The few people whom Tiberius trusted sooner or later disappointed or betrayed him. His mother, the dowager empress Livia, was a domineering old woman who had hoped to control the state through him. However, Tiberius sent Livia into retirement and would not attend her funeral when she died. The emperor's son Drusus was a mediocrity, and his official heir Germanicus was a vain prince with an ambitious wife, Agrippina. The court seethed with intrigue and a dangerous faction formed around Agrippina, who was impatient for Germanicus to reach the throne. The emperor respected his astrologer Thrasyllus but loathed the other courtiers, whose smiles masked envy and hatred. Bored with social affairs, Tiberius preferred pedantic discussions with Thrasyllus but turned to the bottle whenever the conversation palled. As age and disappointment overtook him, the emperor became increasingly dependent on wine, but the administration of the empire never suffered from his indulgence in alcohol. Weary with power and isolated by suspicion, Tiberius had only one friend on whom he relied to share the burdens of state—the prefect Sejanus, who commanded the Praetorian guards.*

The Augustan era was an age of social mobility and many men had risen in status through faithful service to the Princeps. The old nobility was debilitated and many famous families had perished in the civil wars. The future lay with the minor gentry, or Equites, who had controlled the financial life of Rome during the Republic. Under the emperors, Equites increasingly dominated the civil service and earned noble status through promotion to consular rank. Most Equites were loyal public servants, but a few were ambitious schemers, like Lucius Aelius Sejanus. His father, Seius Strabo, was from Tuscany and served as Praetorian prefect in the last years of Augustus. To improve his social status, Strabo had married a lady from a powerful noble family, and their son Sejanus was later adopted into another noble clan, the

---

*Two Equites with the rank of prefect commanded the 9,000 Praetorian guards who protected the palace and the emperor. The senior Praetorian prefect held a position of great potential power, and occasionally there was only one prefect in charge of the guards.

Aelian family. Such adoptions were common practice among social climbers at Rome. While Strabo typified the revolutionary elite who rose with Augustus, Sejanus represented the second generation of Equites, who built on the achievements of their fathers. In his first official position, Sejanus served as an aide to a grandson of Augustus and may have met Tiberius while the future emperor was in self-imposed exile on Rhodes. Soon the able Sejanus became his father's colleague in the Praetorian guards. In 14 A.D. Tiberius appointed Strabo to a lucrative governorship in Egypt and promoted Sejanus to be the sole prefect of the Praetorians. Having won the confidence of Tiberius, Sejanus persuaded the emperor to move the guards to a permanent barracks on the outskirts of Rome. Since he held the life of the emperor in his hands, Sejanus was well aware of the political implications of his position as Praetorian prefect.

Like most successful politicians, the prefect gave an impression of great sincerity. Impressed by his ability and apparent loyalty, the lonely Tiberius trusted Sejanus implicitly and called him the "companion of my labors." A contemporary view of the Praetorian prefect was expressed by a retired colonel, Velleius Paterculus, who admired Tiberius and praised Sejanus without reservation:

Honor ever awaits the worthy; for the wicked, punishment is slow but sure. Fair play has now precedence over influence, and merit over ambition, for the best of emperors teaches his citizens to do right by doing it, and though he is greatest among us in authority, he is still greater in the example which he sets. It is but rarely that men of eminence have failed to employ great men to aid them in directing their fortune, as . . . the deified Augustus employed Marcus Agrippa and after him Statilius Taurus. In the case of these men, their lack of lineage was no obstacle to their elevation to successive consulships, triumphs, and numerous priesthoods. For great tasks require great helpers, and it is important to the state that those who are necessary to her service should be given prominence in rank, and that their usefulness should be fortified by official authority. With these examples before him, Tiberius Caesar has had and still has as his incomparable associate in all the burdens of the Principate Sejanus Aelius, son of a father who was among the foremost in the Equestrian order, but connected on his mother's side with old and illustrious families. . . . [Sejanus also] had brothers, cousins, and an uncle who had reached the consulship. He himself combined with loyalty to his master great capacity for labor and possessed a well-knit body to match the energy of his mind; stern but yet gay, cheerful but yet strict; busy, yet always seeming to be at leisure. He is one who claims no honors for himself and so acquires all honors, whose estimate of himself is always below the estimate of others, calm in expression and in his life, though his mind is sleeplessly alert.[4]

While typical of the new men who served the Principate, Sejanus unfortunately was not the paragon of virtue which he seemed to be in the uncritical judgment of Paterculus.

In reality, Sejanus had most of the unpleasant characteristics of Faulkner's scheming Flem Snopes. The historian Tacitus sneered that Sejanus was a "small town adulterer" as well as a prototype of the Praetorian kingmakers who often disrupted Roman politics. Though a few contemporaries were aware of his duplicity, the Praetorian prefect planned his political moves with consummate skill and carefully hid his ambitions from the aged and trusting Tiberius. As commander of the palace guards, Sejanus made every effort to win the personal loyalties of the Praetorians. He screened the selection of all officers and took care to address enlisted men by name. In the days of the Republic, Cicero had used similar tactics to win the loyalty of voters.

Not content with Tiberius' trust, Sejanus wanted absolute control over the emperor. The first obstacle was Germanicus, the nephew and adopted heir of Tiberius. On the German frontier, Germanicus had won fame in battles and his wife Agrippina impressed Roman troops with her courage during a mutiny. Sejanus persuaded the emperor that the growing popularity of Germanicus and Agrippina might prove a threat to Tiberius. When Germanicus died of fever in 19, rumor implicated Tiberius and Sejanus in his death, and Agrippina was convinced that her husband had been poisoned. With the death of Germanicus, Tiberius was free to show favor to his own son and began to groom Drusus for the succession. However, Sejanus resented Drusus' influence with Tiberius and often quarreled with the prince, who finally struck the prefect in anger. Intent on revenge, Sejanus seduced Drusus' wife Livilla, who had developed into a great beauty. Whatever reason drove her into Sejanus' arms, Livilla was only a tool for the prefect's far-reaching schemes. In

23 Tiberius suffered a great personal loss, the sudden death of his son Drusus, and turned again to Sejanus for comfort and support.

The old emperor showered Sejanus with honors, and statues of the prefect were erected in public places at Rome. In 25 a prominent historian, Cremutius Cordus, protested the excessive honors, but Sejanus easily engineered the death of his critic. Tacitus recounts the treason trial of Cordus in detail:

The following year began with the prosecution of Aulus Cremutius Cordus on a new and previously unheard-of charge: praise of Brutus in his *History* and the description of Cassius as the "last of the Romans." The prosecutors were dependents of Sejanus; that was fatal to the accused man. So was the grimness of Tiberius' face as he listened to the defence. This is how Cremutius, resigned to death, conducted it: "Senators, my words are blamed. My actions are not blameworthy. Nor were these words of mine aimed against the emperor or his parent to whom the law of treason applies. I am charged with praising Brutus and Cassius. Yet many have written of their deeds—always with respect. Livy, outstanding for objectivity as well as eloquence, praised Pompey so warmly that Augustus called him "the Pompeian." But their friendship did not suffer. And Livy never called Cassius and Brutus bandits and parricides—their fashionable designations today. He described them in language appropriate to distinguished men. . . . When Cicero praised Cato to the skies, the dictator Julius Caesar reacted by writing a speech against him—as in a lawsuit. Antony's letters, Brutus' speeches, contain scathing slanders against Augustus. The poems of . . . Bibaculus and Catullus—still read—are crammed with insults against the Caesars. Yet the divine Julius, the divine Augustus endured them and let them be. This could well be interpreted as wise policy and not merely forbearance. For things unnoticed are forgotten; resentment confers status upon them. I am not speaking of the Greeks. For they left license unpunished as well as freedom—or, at most, words were countered by words. But among us, too, there has always been complete uncensored liberty to speak about those whom death has placed beyond hatred or partiality. Cassius and Brutus are not in arms at Philippi now. I am not on the platform inciting the people to civil war. They died seventy years ago! They are known by their statues—even the conqueror did not remove them. And they have their place in the historian's pages. Posterity gives everyone his due honor. If I am condemned, people will remember me as well as Cassius and Brutus." Cremutius walked out of the Senate and starved himself to death. The Senate ordered his books to

be burned. . . . But they survived, first hidden and later republished.
This makes one deride the stupidity of people who believe that today's
authority can destroy tomorrow's memories.[5]

In this paraphrase of Cordus' speech, Tacitus ably expressed the
plight of all historians under the authoritarian Roman state.

Confident of his privileged position, Sejanus hoped to marry
Livilla, whose son Gemellus was Tiberius' only grandson and
would likely be his heir. When the prefect asked Tiberius for
approval, the emperor dryly replied that public opinion was not
yet ready for such an alliance. In 26 Tiberius also rejected
Agrippina's request to remarry, for he feared the marriage would
add strength to her faction. The aged Livia constantly criticized
the haughtiness and sharp tongue of Agrippina, and Sejanus'
agents trapped the princess into offending the emperor. Posing as
friends, they warned Agrippina that Tiberius planned to poison
her; accordingly, she refused to eat the food which he handed to
her at a banquet. The old despot interpreted her behavior as
proof that she was planning to poison him. Since the city of Rome
had always depressed him and court intrigues had become
unbearable, the emperor withdrew from the noisy capital, never
to return. While traveling in southern Italy, Tiberius was again
impressed by the loyalty of Sejanus. When the emperor's entou-
rage was dining in a scenic grotto, part of the roof collapsed and
the prefect shielded Tiberius from falling rocks by throwing himself over the ruler. Confident that Sejanus would guard his
interests at Rome, Tiberius retired to the Isle of Capri with a
small clique of intellectuals and astrologers. After 27, Sejanus
was the principal link between the emperor on Capri and the
Senate and court at Rome. Nevertheless, the wary Tiberius kept
a careful watch on events in the capital and received reports
from sources other than Sejanus.

At Rome, Sejanus devoted himself to the destruction of the
family of Germanicus. With his usual skill, the prefect played
Agrippina's two older sons against each other, and he seduced
their wives in order to learn the secrets of Agrippina's faction.
Since the armies were loyal to Tiberius, Agrippina did not dare to
appeal to the legions for support, for she was not inclined to the
desperate gambles of civil war. In 29 Livia died at the age of

Tiberius

Agrippina
the Elder

eighty-six, but Tiberius did not attend her funeral, where the principal oration was delivered by the eloquent Gaius "Caligula," the youngest son of Germanicus.* Though she had never liked Agrippina, the old dowager empress would not have tolerated harsh treatment of her granddaughter. With the death of Livia, Sejanus was free to attack Agrippina openly, and Tiberius was easily persuaded that she was guilty of treason. On the orders of the emperor, Sejanus imprisoned Agrippina and her two older sons as traitors. Only Gaius was left undisturbed until Sejanus could devise a trap for him. The prefect had every reason to be satisfied, for his statues were now placed in the legionary camps, and public prayers were offered for the continued good fortune of the emperor's indispensable aide. Covered with honors at Rome, Sejanus was surrounded by senators whose flattery hid subtle malice. Later, Gaius would remark that "the Senate had corrupted Sejanus," and many anecdotes suggest that his secret enemies deliberately praised the prefect and hoped that he would overplay his hand.

In 31 Sejanus was at the height of his career and shared the consulship with the absent Tiberius. Intoxicated with power, the prefect formed an elaborate plan to win the throne. Discarding his mistress Livilla, he extracted a promise from the emperor that he could marry her daughter Julia, who was Tiberius' granddaughter. As the husband of an imperial princess, Sejanus could then force the elderly Tiberius to adopt him as the official heir. However, the prefect's threats against Gaius brought about his downfall before the marriage or the coup could take place.† Sejanus had reckoned without Tiberius' sister-in-law, the wily old Antonia, who feared for the safety of her grandson Gaius. Unknown to Sejanus, Antonia sent her freedman Pallas to Capri with a report that the prefect planned to kill Gaius and wrest the succession from Gemellus. Convinced by Antonia's charges, the emperor removed Gaius to the safety of Capri and arranged a counterplot to outwit Sejanus. To gain time and throw the prefect off guard, Tiberius beguiled Sejanus with hints of another pro-

---

*As a child in his father's camp, Gaius had worn soldier's boots and was nicknamed "Little Boots" (Caligula) by the troops of Germanicus.

†For other versions of the fall of Sejanus, see Appendix One.

motion. Though he suspected that something was afoot, Sejanus tried to hide his anxiety from the Senate and the court. Finally, Tiberius' agent Sertorius Macro arrived from Capri with a letter for the Senate. He reassured the prefect that the letter contained an order to endow Sejanus with tribunician powers, but actually Macro bore a commission from Tiberius and secretly won over the Praetorian guards. On October 18, 31, the unsuspecting Sejanus presided over the Senate to hear a reading of the document which he expected would give him even greater authority. Slowly, Macro read the long letter which began with an appreciation of Sejanus' many services to the state, then gradually cooled in tone, and culminated in a flat accusation of treason against Sejanus and a plea that the Senate would take immediate action. His world collapsing about him, the former favorite sat dumbfounded, but the senators erupted with long-repressed hatred. Immediately, Sejanus was reviled, condemned as a traitor, and dragged to execution. Later, the city mob was given his corpse which they abused and threw into the Tiber. However, though the emperor had outwitted his crafty prefect, Sejanus dealt him a final blow. When the vindictive Senate ordered the execution of Sejanus' children, their mother* sent a bitter letter to Capri and committed suicide. Her letter informed Tiberius of the affair between the prefect and Livilla and their complicity in the death of Drusus who had died by poison at the hands of his unfaithful wife.   Contrary to Acton's dictum, power had not corrupted Sejanus but power had made him careless. The wily prefect had never been Tiberius' friend and had always played the old emperor for a fool.

In his memoirs, Tiberius offered the lame explanation that Sejanus had been destroyed because he had attacked the family of Germanicus. In reality, the emperor had little love for Agrippina or her family. Though he had rescued Gaius, Tiberius left Agrippina and her other sons to die in prison. His faithless daughter-in-law Livilla was placed under house arrest and soon starved herself to death. The morose emperor painfully resumed the burdens of government which once had been shared by the

---

*Earlier, Sejanus had divorced his wife Apicata when he had hoped to marry Livilla.

"companion of my labors." Formerly, the enemies of Sejanus had lived in fear but now the bitter Tiberius allowed the Senate to hound and punish the friends of Sejanus. However, the emperor often intervened to prevent the purge from turning into an unrestrained witch hunt. Tacitus reports the successful defense of a former supporter of Sejanus:

When everyone else was untruthfully disclaiming friendship with Sejanus ι . . . Marcus Terentius bravely accepted the imputation. "In my position," he observed to the Senate, "it might do me more good to deny the accusation than to admit it. And yet, whatever the results, I will confess that I was Sejanus' friend: I sought his friendship and was glad to secure it. I had seen him as joint-commander of the Guard with his father. Then I saw him conducting the civil as well as the military administration. His kinsmen, his relations by marriage, gained office. Sejanus' ill will meant danger and pleas for mercy. I give no examples. At my own peril only, I speak for all who took no part in his final plans. For we honored, not Sejanus of Vulsinii, but the member of the Claudian and Julian houses into which his marriage alliances had admitted him—your 'son-in-law,' Tiberius, your partner in the consulship, your representative in state affairs. It is not for us to comment on the man whom you elevate above others, or on your reasons. The gods have given you supreme control—to us is left the glory of obeying! Besides, we only see what is before our eyes: the man to whom you have given wealth, power, the greatest potentialities for good and evil—and nobody will deny that Sejanus had these. Research into the emperor's hidden thoughts and secret designs is forbidden, hazardous, and not necessarily informative. Think, senators, not of Sejanus' last day, but of the previous sixteen years. . . . We thought it grand even if Sejanus' ex-slaves and door-keepers knew us. You will ask if this defense is to be valid for all without discrimination. Certainly not. But draw a fair dividing line! Punish plots against the state and the emperor's life. But, as regards friendship and its obligations, if we sever them at the same time as you do, Tiberius, that should excuse us as it excuses you." This courageous utterance, publicly reflecting everyone's private thoughts, proved so effective that it earned Terentius' accusers, with their criminal records, banishment and execution.[6]

Because of his candor, Terentius was exonerated by Tiberius. His frank confession of careerism expressed the means whereby most men succeeded in politics at Rome or anywhere else.

To Roman moralists, the spectacular fall of Sejanus provided many sermons on the themes that Fortune is fickle and ambition digs its own grave. The poet Juvenal mocked the destruction of Sejanus' bronze statues:

Now the fires hiss hot—in the roar of bellows and furnace
Burns the head adored by the people. The mighty Sejanus
Makes a crackling sound, and out of that countenance, second,
Not so long ago, in the whole wide world, there are fashioned
Wine jars, frying pans, basins, and platters, and . . . pots.
Laurel your doors and lead the great chalked bull to Jove's altar!
Sejanus gets the hook, he is dragged along. What a picture!
Everybody is glad. "Believe me, I never could stand him.
What a puss he had! But what were the charges against him?
Who were the witnesses, the informant? How did they prove it?"
"Nothing like that at all: the only thing was a letter,
Rather wordy and long; it came from Capri." "That's all right, then.
That's all I wanted to know."
　　　　　And what are the people of [Rome]
Doing now? What they always do; they are following fortune,
Hating her victims, as always. Had [Fate] favored Sejanus,
Had the leader's old age been unexpectedly stricken,
This same mob would have hailed as Augustus the man now doomed.
　. . . "All right, let's go, in a hurry—
While he lies on the bank, let's give Caesar's foeman a few kicks."
"Yes, and be sure the slaves can see, so that all must admit it.
We don't want to be dragged to court at the end of a halter."
That was how they talked, at the time, about their Sejanus.
That was the way the crowd muttered and grumbled about him.

In the fall of Sejanus, the satirist found a more useful moral than the mere fickleness of the crowd:

So—would you like to have been Sejanus, popular, courted,
Having as much as he had, appointing men to high office,
Giving others command of the legions, renowned as protector
Of that Prince who's perched on the narrow ledges of Capri
With his Eastern seers and fortunetellers around him?
You would certainly like the spears, the horsemen, the cohorts,
The camp all your own. Why not? Even those with no craving for
　murder

Wish that they had the power. But what good would it be if it
   brought you
Risk in equal amount? Would you rather be robed like Sejanus,
Dragged along the streets like him, or would it be better
Taking charge of affairs in some little town like Fidenae,
Mayor of Gabii, or Inspector of Weights at Ulubrae?
So you acknowledge Sejanus did not know what to pray for,
Seeking excessive renown, excessive wealth, and preparing,
All the time, a tower whose stories soared to the heaven,
Whence he had farther to fall, a longer plunge to his ruin.[7]

Juvenal's cautionary verses echoed the sentiments of most Roman
politicians.

In imperial Rome competitive politics was dangerous and
the risks outweighed the profits. Civil service was far safer and
ultimately more rewarding. Many Equites served the state with
distinction and later entered the Senate and earned nobility by
elevation to the consulship. Under the emperors, organization
men prospered and mavericks perished. In the provinces and at
Rome practical men avoided political intrigue and left the
dangerous game to members of the imperial family. Though
savage power struggles took place in the palace, the armies held
aloof and civil servants were indifferent to the outcome. Unless
the ruler became psychopathic or was an extravagant spender,
the personality of the emperor was not as important as the
imperial system itself. The apparatus of Roman government was
a highly efficient machine even under Caligula or Nero. The
loyalty of the able men who performed the many tasks of government was reinforced by a common distaste for civil war and a
healthy awareness of the perils of ambition. The memory of
Sejanus was a constant reminder that the will to power can be
fatal to even the most cunning of men.

THREE

The Opportunist—Herod Agrippa

As the Roman empire expanded throughout the Mediterranean, many nations were left nominally free though dependent on Rome. Theoretically, these satellite kingdoms were allies and friends of the Roman state, but in practice, the kings were clients of Rome and their survival depended upon the good will of Roman officials. The client kings furnished taxes and troops in return for Roman protection and also spent large sums bribing important men at Rome. The most powerful client state, Egypt, remained independent until Cleopatra VII became involved in the civil war between Antony and Octavian. Cleopatra's neighbor and enemy, Herod the Great, was the most successful client king in the East. In the second century B.C. Palestine had been freed from Seleucid rule by the Hasmonean family, who exploited the prestige of the Maccabean revolt to create a petty oriental despotism in Judea. When Palestine came under Roman control in the first century B.C., the power behind the shaky Hasmonean throne was an Idumean Arab, Antipater, who sought the protection of Pompey. When Pompey abolished the Hasmonean monarchy, Antipater stayed in power but later shifted to Caesar, who made him governor of Judea. Despite the protests of Cleopatra, Antony favored Antipater's son Herod and made him king of Judea. The vigorous new monarch secured his throne by defeating Hasmonean pretenders and backed Antony in the civil war against Octavian. When Antony's cause collapsed, the crafty Herod offered his services to Augustus who respected the abilities of the ruthless Jewish king.

An able administrator and agile diplomat, Herod the Great made Judea into a powerful state. Wealthy and energetic, he built new cities and restored the Temple at Jerusalem. More Hellenistic than Jewish, Herod was popular with pagans and rich enough to subsidize the Olympic games. Conservative Jews were appalled by his indifference to the Torah and many were martyred for opposing Herod. Like Solomon, Herod married many times for political purposes and was plagued by a large and quarrelsome family. The palace seethed with intrigue, and the ruthless king did not hesitate to execute wives and sons when their loyalty was in doubt. Though unnecessarily cruel, Herod was not a royal ogre as he appears in Jewish and Christian tradition. A frequent visitor to Rome, the king took care to ingratiate his family with Augustus, and many Herodian princes were educated in the capital of the empire. Though defamed by pious Jews, Herod defended the cause of Judaism and convinced Augustus that the Jews of the empire were loyal supporters of Rome. Persuaded by Herod, the emperor confirmed the privileges which Caesar had granted to the Jews and excused them from participation in the imperial cult. The grateful Jews prayed to Yahweh for the success of Augustus and his descendants, and the Roman state paid for token sacrifices in the Temple. For Rome to keep its hands off the contributions which overseas Jews sent to the Temple was the most permanent achievement of Herodian diplomacy. Unfortunately for the Jews, few of Herod's descendants inherited his abilities or his iron will.

In 4 B.C. Herod the Great died, leaving a legacy of dissension to his large family. Though Herod's last will named his oldest son Archelaus as his successor, the king had chosen another son, Antipas, as heir in an earlier will. When riots broke out against the inept and unpopular Archelaus, Roman troops had to restore order in Palestine. Both Archelaus and Antipas rushed to Rome to lay their pleas at the feet of Augustus. The rival princes were followed by an embassy of Judean leaders who were disgusted with both Herodian and Hasmonean rule and wanted Palestine to be incorporated into the Roman province of Syria. However, the emperor felt obliged to keep Herod's family in power and divided the kingdom among three of his sons. While Archelaus received Judea, Galilee and a strip east of the Jordan went to Antipas, and their half-brother Philip was awarded territory in northern Palestine. Augustus gave Archelaus the title of ethnarch (ruler of the people) and promised him a crown if he could earn it. Antipas and Philip became tetrarchs (rulers of a fourth). The ablest of the sons, Philip, proved to be a competent ruler who quietly administered his territory until his death in 34 A.D. However, Archelaus and Antipas were hated despots who were also disliked because their mother was a Samaritan.

In a famous parable, Jesus alluded to the harsh character of Archelaus:

A man of noble birth went on a long journey abroad to be appointed king and then return. But first he called ten of his servants and gave them a pound each, saying, "Trade with this while I am away." His fellow citizens hated him, and they sent a delegation on his heels to say, "We do not want this man as our king." However, back he came as king and sent for the servants to whom he had given the money to see what profit each had made. The first came and said, "Your pound, sir, has made ten more." "Well done," he replied, "you are a good servant. You have shown yourself trustworthy in a very small matter, and you shall have charge of ten cities." The second came and said, "Your pound, sir, has made five more," and he also was told, "You too, take charge of five cities." The third came and said, "Here is your pound, sir, I kept it put away in a handkerchief. I was afraid of you because you are a hard man: you draw out what you never put in and reap what you did not sow." "You rascal!" he replied, "I will judge you by your own words. You knew, did you, that I am a hard man, that I draw out what I never put in and reap what I did not sow? Then why did you not put my money on deposit, and I could have claimed it with interest when I came back?" Turning to his attendants, he said, "Take the pound from him and give it to the man with ten." "But, sir," they replied, "he has ten already." "I tell you," he went on, "the man who has will always be given more; but the man who has not will forfeit even what he has. But as for those enemies of mine who did not want me for their king, bring them here and slaughter them in my presence."[1]

For a decade Archelaus vainly tried to impose his authority on Judea while his enemies kept Augustus well informed on the deteriorating situation. In 6 A.D. the worried ethnarch hurried to Rome to reassure the impatient Augustus. Irritated by Archelaus' excuses, the emperor deposed the ethnarch and exiled him to a small town in southern Gaul. Judea was converted into a Roman province and a memorable census was held to assess Rome's new property.

In Galilee, Antipas fared better. The tetrarch enjoyed the favor of Augustus and later cultivated the good will of Tiberius. Although Sejanus was reputed to be anti-Semitic, Tiberius was indifferent to Judaism until a noble Roman lady, who had been converted to the religion, was swindled by four Jewish confidence men. In 19 the outraged emperor expelled many Jews from the city of Rome and condemned 4,000 to conscript labor on Sardinia. However, Tiberius soon relented toward the Jews of Rome and did not interfere with the religious privileges of Jews throughout the empire. The emperor was often visited by Antipas, who honored Tiberius by naming his new capital on the Sea of Galilee, Tiberias. The tetrarch's cunning was well known, and Tiberius would have agreed with Jesus' quip that Antipas was "a fox." Unfortunately, Antipas did not display much wisdom when he fell in love with his cousin Herodias, the wife of his half-brother Herod-Philip.* When Herodias divorced Herod-Philip, Antipas put aside his own queen who fled to her father, the powerful Nabataean king of Petra. While conservative Jews complained that the marriage of Antipas and Herodias violated Mosaic law, the tetrarch's advisers worried over the international repercussions from Petra.

The Roman yoke weighed heavily on Judea, and the tiny province was filled with religious discontent. Though most overseas Jews saw Rome as a benefactor and protector, many Palestinian Jews resented Roman occupation and vented their opposition by bickering over religious subjects. In the cities of Palestine, Jews and pagans often clashed, and at Jerusalem Roman authority was flouted in the name of religious freedom. Sporadically, Messianic pretenders appeared as nationalism and religious frenzy were aggravated by Roman blunders. In 27 the troublesome province of Judea was subjected to the incompetent administration of Pontius Pilate, who tried to cow the Jews with brutality but was outwitted by them at every turn. At Jerusalem Pilate displayed legionary standards which were decorated with

---

*Herod-Philip was not the tetrarch Philip who was also a half-brother of Antipas.

human figures and worshiped by Roman troops. However, the Jews raised so much commotion that he had to remove the emblems from the holy city. Later, the governor placed ceremonial shields in Herod's old palace to honor Tiberius. Though the shields bore only inscriptions, the Jews protested the quasi-religious gesture, and Antipas joined in the furor to embarrass Pilate. When the Jewish leaders complained to Tiberius, the emperor ordered the shields to be removed. Emboldened by their success, the Jews accused Pilate of sacrilege because he had used Temple funds to improve the water supply at Jerusalem. When riots broke out in the city, the exasperated governor suppressed the disorders with excessive brutality. He also massacred fanatics from Galilee who were fomenting trouble in Judea. As the tetrarch of Galilee, Antipas sanctimoniously protested Pilate's use of force.

In his own domain, Antipas too was harassed by religious agitators. Galilee was disturbed by an unkempt desert prophet, John the Baptist, who threatened the social order and criticized Antipas and Herodias. The Gospel of Luke describes the behavior of John:

In the fifteenth year of the emperor Tiberius, when Pontius Pilate was governor of Judea, when Herod was prince of Galilee . . . the word of God came to John son of Zechariah in the wilderness. And he went all over the Jordan valley proclaiming a baptism in token of repentance for the forgiveness of sins. . . . Crowds of people came out to be baptized by him, and he said to them: "You vipers' brood! Who warned you to escape from the coming retribution? Then prove your repentance by the fruit it bears, and do not begin saying to yourselves, 'We have Abraham for our father.' I tell you that God can make children for Abraham out of these stones here. Already the ax is laid to the roots of the trees, and every tree that fails to produce good fruit is cut down and thrown on the fire." The people asked him, "Then what are we to do?" He replied, "The man with two shirts must share with him who has none, and anyone who has food must do the same." Among those who came to be baptized were tax-gatherers, and they said to him, "Master, what are we to do?" He told them, "Exact no more than the assessment." Soldiers on service also asked him, "And what of us?" To them he said, "No bullying; no blackmail; make do with your pay!" The people were on the tiptoe of expectation, all wondering about John, whether perhaps he was the Messiah, but he spoke out and said to them all, "I baptize you with water, but there is one to come who is mightier than I. . . ." In this and many other ways, he made his appeal to the people and announced the good news. But Prince Herod, when he was rebuked by him over the affair of his brother's wife Herodias and for his other misdeeds, crowned them all by shutting John up in prison.[2]

Even in prison the prophet awed the tetrarch, who was puzzled by his words and did not dare to kill him. However, the vengeful Herodias eventually tricked Antipas into ordering the execution of John.

The death of John weighed heavily on the conscience of the tetrarch. Hagridden by guilt, Antipas was soon terrified by rumors that John had returned from the dead as the miracle worker Jesus. The Gospel of Mark describes Antipas' concern over the new prophet:

Now King Herod heard of it, for the fame of Jesus had spread and people were saying, "John the Baptist has been raised to life, and that is why these miraculous powers are at work in him." Others said, "It is Elijah." Others again, "He is a prophet like one of the old prophets." But Herod, when he heard of it, said, "This is John whom I beheaded, raised from the dead." For this same Herod had sent and arrested John and put him in prison at the instance of his brother Philip's wife, Herodias, whom he had married. John had told Herod, "You have no right to your brother's wife." Thus Herodias nursed a grudge against him and would willingly have killed him, but she could not, for Herod went in awe of John, knowing him to be a good and holy man; so he kept him in custody. He liked to listen to him, although the listening left him greatly perplexed. Herodias found her opportunity when Herod on his birthday gave a banquet to his chief officials and commanders and the leading men of Galilee. Her daughter came in and danced and so delighted Herod and his guests that the king said to the girl, "Ask what you like and I will give it you." And he swore an oath to her: "Whatever you ask I will give you, up to half my kingdom." She went out and said to her mother, "What shall I ask for?" She replied, "The head of John the Baptist." The girl hastened back at once to the king with her request: "I want you to give me here and now, on a dish, the head of John the Baptist." The king was greatly distressed, but out of regard for his oath and for his guests he could not bring himself to refuse her. So the king sent a soldier of the guard with orders to bring John's head. The soldier went off and beheaded him in the prison, brought the head on a dish, and gave it to the girl, and she gave it to her mother.[3]

Though the story of Salome's dance may only be a romantic tale, the daughter of Herodias served Antipas by marrying Philip the tetrarch. The marriage brought the two Herodian rulers closer together.

Though he had seen the head of the Baptist on a platter, Antipas was haunted by the nagging fear that Jesus was the resurrected John. In his own court, the tetrarch was in constant contact with an admirer of the new prophet. Joanna, the wife of Antipas' steward, was a financial supporter of Jesus and often accompanied the prophet on his wanderings. By chance, Antipas was soon able to resolve his fears about Jesus. The tetrarch happened to be at Jerusalem when Jesus was denounced to Pilate for sedition. Though the prophet claimed to be King of the Jews, the Roman governor was not anxious to oblige the priests and Pharisees who had so often humiliated him, but Pilate could not risk another complaint to Rome. Learning that Jesus was a Galilean, the governor handed the prisoner over to Antipas. The Gospel of Luke depicts the tetrarch's treatment of the prophet:

When Herod saw Jesus he was greatly pleased. Having heard about him, he had long been wanting to see him and had been hoping to see some miracle performed by him. He questioned him at some length without getting any reply, but the chief priests and lawyers appeared and pressed the case against him vigorously. Then Herod and his troops treated him with contempt and ridicule and sent him back to Pilate dressed in a gorgeous robe. That same day, Herod and Pilate became friends; till then there had been a standing feud between them.[4]

Aware that Jesus was not politically subversive, Pilate tried to release the prophet and offered a scapegoat in the bandit Barabbas. However, the enemies of Jesus were determined on his death and the weak governor had the prisoner crucified as a traitor to Rome. The gesture earned Pilate little peace, and the harried governor sent troops against the followers of a Samaritan prophet in 36. The outraged Samaritans complained to the governor of Syria, Vitellius, who removed Pilate from office and sent him to Rome to face the wrath of Tiberius. The emperor died before Pilate arrived in the capital, but his successor Caligula was equally harsh on incompetents. The luckless Pilate was condemned to exile in Gaul, where he soon committed suicide.

At Jerusalem the tactful Vitellius conciliated the Jews by returning the vestments of the High Priest which Herod the Great had appropriated from the Temple. Earlier, Vitellius had negotiated a treaty with the Parthians with the aid of Antipas, who acted as interpreter and entertained the diplomats royally. The tetrarch soon needed Vitellius' assistance when the Nabataean king of Petra took revenge on Antipas, who had spurned his daughter to marry Herodias. The Arabs invaded the territory of Antipas, inflicted a crushing defeat on his troops, and retired with booty and glory. When the tetrarch begged Rome to make war on Petra, the emperor ordered Vitellius to take the field against the Nabataeans. Though he had little fondness for Antipas, the Roman commander assembled a large force, but the campaign was halted by unexpected news from Rome. While Vitellius and Antipas were at Jerusalem, reports arrived of the death of Tiberius and the accession of Caligula. On his own authority, Vitellius abandoned the war and withdrew into Syria, leaving Antipas angry and humiliated. Another Herodian prince, Herod Agrippa would soon play a major role in Palestinian politics.

Filled with improbable reversals of fortune, the career of Herod Agrippa had all the elements of cheap melodrama. However, the substance of his amazing story is corroborated by contemporary writers and well told by the Jewish historian Josephus, who relied on good Roman sources as well as the testimony of Herod Agrippa's children. Like Herod the Great, Herod Agrippa was a crafty opportunist who made the most of his luck. Like the emperor Tiberius, the Jewish prince tasted the dregs of failure and despair but finally emerged triumphant over all odds. Neither a saint nor a statesman, Herod Agrippa did well by the Jews, for he was a remarkable man and played a decisive role in the accession of the emperor Claudius. Though his luck was phenomenal, chance only dealt him the cards—Herod Agrippa knew how to play them.

If Antipas was an old fox, Herod Agrippa began as one of the little foxes who spoil the vines. Born in 10 B.C., Herod Agrippa was named after Marcus Agrippa, the right-hand man of Augustus. His mother Berenice had many friends at Rome and was particularly close to Germanicus' mother Antonia.* Agrippa's father Aristobulus was a son of Herod the Great but had been executed by the Judean despot. As a boy Agrippa was brought to Rome by his mother, whose patroness Antonia was also a widow and had borne a son in 10 B.C., Claudius. Both boys would one day wear crowns, but no one suspected it, least of all Claudius, who was shy and sickly. A lively and attractive youth, Agrippa grew up as a companion of Drusus, the son of Tiberius. While Berenice was alive, the young Jewish prince lived within his means, but after her death he entertained lavishly and scattered bribes among influential freedmen who had high posts at court. Though the frugal Tiberius disapproved of his extravagance, Agrippa considered the expenses a political investment which might win him a client kingdom in the East. The ambitious young Jew went deeper in debt, but his plans were upset in 23 when Sejanus poisoned Drusus. The old emperor could not bear to be reminded of Drusus, and Agrippa was no longer welcome at court. Hounded by creditors, Agrippa fled from Rome to Palestine, where he hid in the bleak desert of Idumea. Living in poverty in an old watchtower with his loyal wife Kypros, Agrippa was a failure at forty and seriously considered suicide.

Like Agrippa, Kypros was a descendant of Herod the Great, but she was made of sterner stuff than her husband and more than once would save his career. Rousing Agrippa from despair, Kypros wrote to his sister Herodias in Galilee. Her husband Antipas was not only Agrippa's brother-in-law but also his uncle, and the tetrarch took a malicious pleasure in rescuing Agrippa from destitution. Herodias' brother was given a minor post as market inspector at Tiberias. At Antipas' court, Agrippa was a poor relation, and the tetrarch enjoyed reminding him that he was dependent on charity. Unable to bear Antipas' sarcasm any longer, Agrippa fled to his old friend, the Roman governor of Syria who preceded Vitellius. However, Agrippa did not enjoy Roman

*The wife of Tiberius' brother Drusus, Antonia was the daughter of Mark Antony and Augustus' sister Octavia. Respected by Tiberius, Antonia later helped to topple Sejanus from power.

patronage for long, because he tried to peddle his influence with the governor and was asked to leave. In desperation, the adventurer decided to gamble on a trip to Rome, where he might recoup his fortunes. Again deep in debt, he scraped up travel expenses and escaped from Palestine barely ahead of his creditors. At Alexandria Agrippa tried to raise more funds but was considered a bad risk. However, Kypros persuaded a rich Jew to provide Agrippa with ready cash and a bank draft for Italy. While Kypros and their children returned to Palestine, Agrippa sailed on to Rome and an uncertain future.

Arriving in Italy, Agrippa found Tiberius in good humor and was invited to join the circle on Capri. However, reports soon arrived with details of Agrippa's debts and flight from the East, and the emperor forbade him to appear at court until he was solvent. Undaunted, the Jewish prince turned to his mother's old friend Antonia and borrowed the necessary funds. At last in Tiberius' favor, Agrippa managed to become the tutor of the emperor's grandson Gemellus, who was one of Tiberius' two heirs. The other heir was the adult son of Germanicus, Gaius "Caligula," whom Antonia had rescued from the clutches of Sejanus a few years earlier. Realizing that Caligula's prospects were brighter, Agrippa neglected Gemellus and paid court to the older prince. Borrowing again, the wily opportunist paid off his debts to Antonia and made costly presents to Caligula. In his eagerness to flatter the prince, Agrippa carelessly told him that he wished Tiberius were dead and Caligula on the throne. The unwise remark was overheard by a servant who was soon after accused of theft by Agrippa. Fearing that the imprisoned servant might betray his secret, Agrippa asked his patroness Antonia to persuade Tiberius to hold a quick trial. However, the emperor had already been informed of the servant's charges against Agrippa and delayed the hearing as long as possible. When the case was finally brought to trial, the thief blurted out that Agrippa was a traitor who had wished for the emperor's death. Rather amused by the whole affair, the sardonic Tiberius ordered the arrest of Agrippa, and the Jewish prince was led off to prison. Though Antonia bribed his jailers to treat him gently, Agrippa was kept in chains and pondered the malign fate which had brought him to such a plight after so much effort.

According to Josephus, one of Agrippa's fellow prisoners was a German chieftain who had prophetic gifts. During an exercise period Agrippa was strolling in the prison yard and idly leaned against a tree in which an owl was perched. Suddenly the German seer introduced himself to the melancholy prince and assured him in broken Latin that his fortunes would soon change and he would be free again. With a somber tone, the prophet added that the next time Agrippa would see the owl, he would die within five days. Unknown to Agrippa his deliverance was at hand, for Tiberius died in 37 and was succeeded by Caligula. The new emperor quickly freed his old friend and presented him with golden chains to commemorate his brief incarceration. Caligula also invested Agrippa with the title of king and the domains of the tetrarch Philip, who had died a few years before. Out of the depths, Agrippa had risen again to new heights.

The new emperor Caligula was twenty-five years old, tall, balding, and dissolute. As a child he had been epileptoid, and as an adult he suffered from chronic insomnia. Intelligent and eloquent, Caligula was an accomplished speaker and had delivered a fine oration at Livia's funeral. As emperor he restored the works of Cremutius Cordus and other books which had been removed from the state libraries by Augustus and Tiberius. However, Caligula was hasty and arbitrary and had Gemellus killed as a potential threat to his power. Inexperienced in government, the emperor spent money freely and soon squandered the treasury surplus which his stingy predecessor had accumulated. At the beginning of his reign Caligula was a popular ruler, but he suffered a nervous breakdown and became violent and dangerous. He had been raised in a hard school, for his mother was the scheming Agrippina the Elder and his father the vain Germanicus, whose mysterious death had become a family myth. Caligula's mother and older brothers had died in prison after Sejanus had maneuvered them into acts of treason. While he loved his sister Drusilla and deified her after death, Caligula was cursed with two other sisters, Julia and Agrippina the Younger, who plotted against him and were imprisoned after a major conspiracy had been uncovered. Plagued by constant intrigues, the emperor became morbidly suspicious.

Suspecting treachery everywhere, the emperor turned against

the senatorial class and revived the Sejanus affair. The files of Tiberius contained evidence against men who had pretended to support Agrippina the Elder but in reality were agents of Sejanus. Early in his reign Caligula promised that the documents would be burned, but he had saved them and now took vengeance on the false friends of his mother and anyone who had been close to Sejanus. Disgusted with the Senate, the emperor spoke of restoring consular elections to the people and taunted senators that he held their lives in his hands. Like Jonathan Swift, Caligula preferred animals to men and casually remarked that it would be an improvement if he made his horse a consul. Finally, the emperor succumbed to the ultimate effect of absolute power which permits men to become infants whose every wish is gratified. Without discipline or responsibility, an infantile ruler will respond to opposition with tantrums which can fill graveyards. Isolated by anger and fear, Caligula became a monstrous infant—omnipotent, sensual, and violent. Finally the wings of madness swept over him and Caligula insisted on being worshiped as a god. Though the imperial cult had already elevated the Roman rulers to superhuman status, only cynics should play at being gods. Like Alexander the Great, Caligula believed in his own divinity, and his whim placed Agrippa and the Jews in jeopardy.

En route to take possession of his kingdom in northern Palestine, Agrippa had stopped at Alexandria to show off his new grandeur in a city which had last seen him as a fleeing debtor. His timing was inopportune, for the metropolis was torn by religious strife between pagans and Jews. Alexandria had a huge Jewish population, and ethnic rivalries had troubled the city ever since the quarrels between Cleopatra and Herod the Great. While the Alexandrian Jews were loyal supporters of Rome, Egyptian nationalists resented Roman rule and relieved their frustrations in outbursts of anti-Semitism. When Agrippa staged an ostentatious parade through Alexandria, the Egyptians retaliated with a mock procession featuring a king of fools. The Jewish philosopher Philo described the episode:

There was a gentle madman called Carabas who . . . wandered through the streets day and night, stark naked regardless of the weather, and teased by idle children. . . . Now, the mob dragged this wretched creature to the public gymnasium and stood him on a platform where he could be seen by all. They made a crown of papyrus-leaf and put it on his head and threw a rug over his body as a robe. For a scepter, somebody gave him a piece of papyrus-stalk which had been picked up in the street. Thus, Carabas received the insignia of royalty and was decked out as a king. Like comic actors in a pantomime, some young men formed a mock bodyguard and stood about him with rods like pikes, and then other people approached him. While some pretended to do him homage, others played that they were laying a case before him, and others acted as though they had come to consult him on state affairs. The crowd stood around in a circle and shouted the strange cry, "Maran!" which is the Syriac word for "Lord." They knew that Agrippa was a Syrian by race and that his kingdom was a part of Syria.[5]

In many respects, the mocking of Carabas resembled the recent treatment of Jesus at Jerusalem.* Whatever religious significance the episode in Alexandria may have had, the Egyptians were primarily interested in displaying their contempt for Agrippa, who beat a hasty retreat from the troubled city. As disorders swept Alexandria, the Roman governor Flaccus permitted the nationalists to convert the Jewish quarter into a ghetto and conduct pogroms elsewhere in the city. Hoping to please Caligula, the Egyptians forcibly installed portraits of the emperor and other images in many synagogues. Meanwhile, Agrippa complained to Caligula about the troubles in Alexandria and the emperor ordered the removal from office and subsequent execution of Flaccus. In order to recover their lost privileges, the Jews of Alexandria sent an embassy headed by Philo to plead their case before Caligula. However, the erratic emperor kept the envoys cooling their heels in Italy.

After his humiliation in Alexandria, Agrippa found a family quarrel awaiting him in Palestine. His sister Herodias was furious that Agrippa was a king while her husband was still only a tetrarch. Although Antipas preferred to let well enough alone, Herodias was consumed with envy and dragged her husband to

---

*Both Romans and Jews abused Jesus as a mock king, but the Alexandrian Carabas was spared the violent fate which ended the "reign" of a king of fools in many areas.

Rome to beg the emperor for a crown. Unwittingly, she played into the hands of Agrippa, who sent Caligula a letter accusing Antipas of having been a friend of Sejanus and presently conspiring with the Parthians. Since Antipas had been stockpiling arms in his arsenals, the emperor suspected that at least the latter charge was true. Instead of receiving a promotion to kingship, the unhappy Antipas was hurried off to exile in Gaul. Since Herodias was Agrippa's sister, Caligula offered her freedom and permitted her to retain her riches. However, Herodias chose to exit from history with honor. Having ruined Antipas by her ambition, Herodias followed her aged husband into exile. With a fine sense of irony, Caligula bestowed the former domains of Antipas on his old friend Agrippa. To express his gratitude, Agrippa came to Rome, where his joy was soon turned to dismay by Caligula's latest whim.

When the emperor had proclaimed his divinity, the pagan residents of a coastal town in Palestine honored the new god with a small altar, which their Jewish neighbors quickly demolished. Learning of the insult, Caligula decided to meet the issue of Judaic privileges head on. Perhaps influenced by anti-Semitic advisers, the emperor ordered that a gold-plated statue of himself as Jupiter be placed in the Temple at Jerusalem. To the Jews, such a sacrilege would be the "abomination of desolation,"* which apocalyptic writers warned would take place in the days preceding the coming of the Messiah. The governor of Syria, Petronius, realized that the statue would unleash a religious war of vast proportions, and tried to dissuade the emperor. Since Caligula was adamant, Petronius delayed the completion of the statue and told the emperor that the artists needed more time. When Caligula had ordered the statue, Agrippa had been traveling to Rome and did not learn the news until the emperor casually told him that his image would soon stand in the Temple. Seeing his new kingdom swept away in a holy war, Agrippa fainted and was in a coma for two days. When he recovered, the king tried desperately to change the mind of the arbitrary emperor.

---

*In the second century B.C., the Seleucid king Antiochus IV had profaned the Temple with pagan altars and rites, the "abomination of desolation" of the Book of Daniel which was considered a prophetic work.

Posing as a pious Jew, Agrippa drafted a memorandum to his friend Caligula. The philosopher Philo of Alexandria has preserved the substance and tone of Agrippa's letter:

All people regard the customs of their own country as excellent, even if in reality they are not, because they judge them with feelings of affection rather than with their reason. I was born, as you know, a Jew. Jerusalem is my home where stands the holy Temple of the Most High God. My grandfathers and ancestors were kings. Most of them were appointed High Priests. . . . . Since my heritage is such a nation and city and Temple, I appeal to you on behalf of them all—on behalf of my nation . . . seeing that its attitude to all your family has been one of reverence and piety. . . . The Jews proclaim their reverence in the resolutions of their inmost souls rather than by word of mouth; they are people who do not merely *say* that they are Caesar's friends, but really *are* his friends. . . . I myself am one of the people who recognize that they have a lord and master but who are counted among his friends. In rank few are above me. In loyalty I am second to none—I will not go so far as to say that I stand first. Therefore, on the strength of my birth and the multitude of the kindnesses with which you have enriched me, I too might have made bold to ask for my native city, if not Roman citizenship, at least freedom or exemption from taxation. . . . Instead I make a very trifling request, a favor which it will cost you nothing to give, but which will be of greatest value for my city to receive. For what greater blessing could your subjects receive than the good will of their Princeps?

After recounting the favors which Augustus and Tiberius had extended toward Judaism and the Temple, Agrippa reminded Caligula of their own long friendship:

When you have granted me favors beyond my needs, my lord, do not take from me the necessities of life; and when you have brought me into the most brilliant light, do not cast me back afresh into the deepest darkness. But I relinquish those splendors; I do not object to returning to my former condition; I give up everything in exchange for one thing, the preservation of our native traditions unchanged. Otherwise, what would be my reputation among my fellow Jews or among all the gentiles? Of necessity I should be regarded as one of two things— either as a traitor to my people or as one who had forfeited your friendship. What greater evil could there be than these? For if I continue to be numbered among your friends, I shall have a reputation for treachery, unless my homeland is kept safe from all evil and the Temple is kept inviolate, since you great men protect the interests of your friends and of people who have taken refuge in the manifestations of your imperial power. If, however, any hostility lurks in your heart, do not imprison me, as Tiberius did, but destroy my anticipation of a second imprisonment by ordering me to be got rid of at once. For what good would it be to me to live, when my only hope of deliverance lay in your good will?[6]

Responding to Agrippa's frankness and their bond of friendship, Caligula relented and ordered Petronius to abandon the Temple project. However, according to Josephus, the emperor promised his friend Agrippa an unspecified favor at a banquet, and the king quickly asked Caligula not to place his statue in the Temple. Though entertaining, Josephus' story is too similar to the tale of the trick which Herodias played on Antipas, and Philo's account that Caligula was persuaded by Agrippa's letter is far more plausible. According to Philo, the erratic emperor again changed his mind and planned to personally install his image in the Temple. Though the death of Caligula soon solved the problem, the Jews would always remember that, whatever his motives, Agrippa had risked his life to save the Temple from violation.

In 41 Caligula was assassinated by a group of men whom he had driven from exasperation to blind hatred. Government officials had deplored his extravagant spending and senators had lived in fear of their lives. The suspicious emperor ordered the death of his middle-aged uncle Claudius, but one of the palace officials, the freedman Callistus, persuaded Caligula to spare Claudius. The powerful freedman had other plans for Claudius, who was Germanicus' brother and had unsuspected talents. With mixed motives, a group of Praetorian officers formed a conspiracy to murder Caligula; the plot was supported by Callistus and others who had far-reaching ambitions. Though the emperor had a personal bodyguard of German mercenaries, a Praetorian officer Chaerea managed to stab Caligula to death, while his fellow conspirators murdered the emperor's wife and brained their infant daughter against a wall. The killing of the child had no logical motive other than to clear the way for Claudius. In the hours following the assassination, Caligula's bodyguards rampaged through the city searching for his murderers. While the terrified Claudius

Claudius

hid in the palace, the Germans found and killed some of the conspirators. However, the Praetorian guards sent a detachment to
rescue Claudius and conveyed him to the safety of the Praetorian barracks.*

Meanwhile, the Senate was in turmoil over the selection of a
successor for Caligula. Not accustomed to making decisions of
such magnitude, a few senators spoke wildly of restoring the
Republic. The problem had already been settled by the Praetorians who hailed Claudius as emperor and gambled that the
legions would support their choice because he was the brother of
the popular Germanicus. Since Claudius needed the formal approval of the Senate, Herod Agrippa offered to serve as a neutral
negotiator between the proposed emperor and the senators. However, Claudius was the son of Agrippa's late patroness Antonia,
and the Herodian king secretly favored him in the haggling with
the Senate. While he assured the senators that the accession
of Claudius was both desirable and inevitable, Agrippa advised
Claudius to guarantee consular elections to the Senate. Pleased
by the gesture, the senators acclaimed Claudius as emperor. The

---

*The historical sources for these events are discussed in Appendix One.

adroit schemer, Herod Agrippa, had played the game of power politics at the highest level.

Like Agrippa, the new emperor Claudius was fifty years old and wise in the ways of the world. A sickly child, Claudius had been scorned by his grandmother Livia and was cruelly ridiculed by the court. Fond of books, Claudius had studied under Livy and became an authority on Etruscan and Carthaginian history. Aware of the fatal results of political failure, he had avoided palace intrigues and devoted himself to scholarship and wine. Playing the family fool, Claudius had seemed content with his books and bottles until fear of Caligula forced him to endorse the schemes of Callistus. As emperor, Claudius was an excellent ruler and sincerely interested in the administrative details of government. He was generous in granting Roman citizenship to provincials and promoted men from the provinces to high office. With regard to Alexandria, the emperor restored to the Jews their former privileges and warned both factions to refrain from further disorder. At Rome, the realistic Claudius carefully paid his political debts. The Praetorian guards received cash bonuses and Callistus was given a high administrative post. The emperor also rewarded the freedman Pallas, who had loyally served Antonia. To discourage future regicides, the emperor executed Chaerea, who had killed Caligula but had also opposed the elevation of Claudius. Toward his friend Agrippa, Claudius was particularly generous and enlarged Agrippa's kingdom to include Judea and the rest of the former domain of Herod the Great. Without war and by his wits alone, Agrippa was now as powerful a king as his ruthless grandfather had been.

In Palestine, Agrippa was enormously popular. Freed from direct Roman rule, the Jews idolized Agrippa for opposing Caligula's statue and restoring the Herodian kingdom. Aware of the tense religious situation in Palestine, Agrippa carefully displayed a new-found piety, resided at Jerusalem, and participated in religious ceremonies. To appease orthodox bigots, the king persecuted the followers of Jesus as heretics. While Peter narrowly escaped death at the hands of Agrippa, the king executed James, the brother of John. Like Herod the Great, Agrippa was a dedicated builder and began construction of the Third Wall at Jerusalem. The wall was not completed because Agrippa either ran out of funds or was afraid of the Roman governor of Syria, who had become suspicious over the new fortifications. To display his present success at the scene of a prior humiliation, Agrippa held a conference with neighboring client kings at Tiberias. However, the governor of Syria suspected that an alliance of buffer states was in the making, and he advised the visiting kings to return to their homes. The prudent monarchs promptly departed and left Agrippa frustrated and furious.

Although he ostentatiously played the role of King of the Jews, Agrippa was more at ease with his pagan subjects. He built extensively at the resort city of Beirut and provided its residents with elaborate shows and games. In one spectacular show, 1,400 gladiators died to amuse the Jewish king and his pagan subjects. Bored with the righteous sermonizing of priests and rabbis, Agrippa paid frequent visits to Caesarea, the former Roman capital of Palestine. There in 44, death came unexpectedly to the fifty-four-year-old Agrippa, who had appeared before his admirers dressed in a glittering cloth of silver. When the pagan crowds hailed him as a god, the Jewish king smiled good-naturedly and made no protest. Glancing up, he noticed an owl* perched on an awning and was immediately seized with abdominal pains. Convinced that the bird was a messenger of death, Agrippa languished in his palace at Caesarea and died on the fifth day. Both Christians and Jews attributed his sudden death to divine punishment for accepting worship as a god. Perhaps religious guilt contributed to Agrippa's rapid demise when the chance appearance of an owl recalled the chilling prophesy which the German seer had made years before.

The death of Herod Agrippa was a disaster for the Jews of Palestine. Since his son Agrippa II was only a child, an orderly transfer of power could not take place in the new kingdom. With the diplomatic Agrippa gone, the conflict between Jews and pagans erupted in bloody riots throughout Palestine. To restore order, the emperor Claudius made Palestine a Roman province again and gave Agrippa II a tiny state east of Galilee. For two decades frustrated Jewish nationalists would endure inept Roman governors, until the great revolt which ended in the sack of

*The bird of ill omen was the messenger (*angelos*) of Acts 12.23.

Jerusalem in 70 A.D. Had Herod Agrippa lived long enough to consolidate his makeshift kingdom and train his son for the exercise of power, Judea might have flourished as a loyal client state, and history would not have witnessed the suppression of the Jewish nation. Though he never achieved the stature of a statesman, Agrippa had kept the peace in Palestine, but death prevented him from making Israel a lasting state. However, Herod Agrippa was poorly equipped to be a Messiah, for the only role which he really knew was that of an agile schemer who triumphed over all obstacles with bluff and luck.

FOUR

The Missionary—Paul

Herod Agrippa was not the only Jew who sought the fulfillment of his hopes and ambitions at Rome. For years the Christian agitator Paul had dreamed of carrying his message to the capital of the world. Other missionaries had preceded him, and the Jews of Rome quarreled over the Messianic claims of Jesus until Claudius expelled the most violent disputants in 49. As the apostle to the gentiles, Paul felt that a unique destiny awaited him at Rome which would climax his years of struggle to adapt Christianity to the needs of the Roman world. Largely due to his efforts and against vigorous opposition from many apostles, a Jewish sect had been transformed into a universal church. Ironically, when at last he reached Rome, Paul arrived under guard and was "an ambassador in chains."

The spiritual odyssey of Paul reflected the contradiction in Judaism between narrow nationalism and religious universalism. Most pagans were repelled by circumcision and considered Judaic dietary laws ludicrous, and all gentiles were offended by the claim of Jews to be a chosen people. Since Jews were not required to participate in the imperial cult, their exceptional privileges brought much criticism from pagans. However, toleration of Judaism was an imperial policy of long standing, and Roman rule was generally supported by millions of Jews who lived outside of Palestine. In the Hellenistic era, many Jews had migrated to the great cities of the Mediterranean and adapted to the cosmopolitan atmosphere of urban life. The Jews of the Diaspora* were usually

*Originally the term "Diaspora" applied to the Jews who remained in Mesopotamia after the Babylonian Captivity, but by the first century A.D. the Diaspora had spread through the vast Roman empire.

less rigorous in religion than their brothers in Palestine, who clung to orthodox ways and nationalist dreams. Beyond the borders of the Roman empire, a large Jewish population dwelled in Mesopotamia under Parthian rule. In the eyes of many Jews, the Parthians were counterparts of the Persians of old, who had freed the Israelites from captivity in Babylon. Consequently, Parthian agents often played on Jewish sympathies to undermine Roman authority in the Near East. In the days of Herod the Great, the Parthians had briefly installed a Hasmonean pretender in Jerusalem, and many Jews believed that the Messiah would arrive with Parthian aid. The Roman government was well aware of the international repercussions which would result from religious interference in Palestine. As a result of Roman concern, Jews throughout the empire were exempted from the imperial cult.

While Jewish nationalism was a constant thorn in Roman flesh, the spiritual message of Judaism had a wide appeal among pagans. The beliefs and practices of Mosaic law were well known, and many Romans respected the substance of the Torah. Intellectuals approved of the notion of an incorporeal god of justice, and the ethics of the Decalogue seemed reasonable except for the sweeping damnation of polytheism. Jews applied the term "god-fearers" to gentiles who were sympathetic to Judaism but did not embrace the religion. Both Jesus and Peter had contacts with centurions "who worshiped God," and Nero's empress Poppaea was a "god-fearer." Since male proselytes had to submit to circumcision, few "god-fearing" men became Jews. However, a minority of rabbis argued that baptism alone should be sufficient for converts. In the kingdom of Adiabene near Armenia, a zealous Jew converted King Izates and did not require him to be circumcised. However, a more rigorous Jew soon persuaded Izates to observe the Mosaic law in its totality. The episode in Adiabene occurred about the same time that Paul was trying to convince James and Peter that circumcision should not be required of converts to Christianity.

Although much is known of Paul's activities and beliefs, many details in the life of the apostle are vague or controversial. The Acts of the Apostles is a propagandistic work and often contradicts the evidence in Paul's letters. Although the author of Acts obscured the fierce policy debates in the early Church, portions of the work (the famous "we" passages) were based on memoirs of a companion of Paul who witnessed many events in the apostle's career. Fortunately, the epistles of Paul provide a valuable check on the accuracy of Acts. Most modern scholars accept the authenticity of Paul's epistles to the Thessalonians, Corinthians, Galatians, Romans, and Philippians, and his letter to Philemon.* The epistle to the Ephesians is a later summary of Pauline views, and the letters to Titus and Timothy deal with problems of the second century. Despite editorial errors and interpolations, the Pauline epistles are a rare example of primary historical evidence in antiquity.

The man who became Paul was originally Saul of Tarsus, and proud of it: "I am a Jew, a Tarsian from Cilicia, a citizen of no mean city." In the Gospel accounts, Christianity had been born in the countryside, in dusty villages, and among working men. Jesus was a rustic carpenter and his first followers were fishermen and farmers; the prophet and his disciples were ill at ease in cities and highly critical of men of wealth and learning. However, Saul came from a different breed—he was a city man, a Diaspora Jew, whose urban speech was enriched with allusions to Greek games. Tarsus was a thriving cosmopolitan center, famed for its schools and lively politics. There Antony first met Cleopatra, and Athenodorus of Tarsus was a prominent intellectual at the court of Augustus. Saul often quoted tags of Greek poetry and did not neglect the writings of his compatriot, Aratus of Soli, who was also admired by Cicero. Following Jewish custom, Paul learned a trade, tent making, but did not practice it until his missionary days. According to Acts, Saul boasted that he was born a Roman citizen, a distinction which often saved him from ill treatment. As a hereditary Roman citizen, he must have come from a well-to-do Asian family. When he later broke with Judaism, Saul went by the name of Paul, which was probably his Roman name since birth.† On the other hand, Saul may have

---

*Among New Testament scholars, the authenticity of Colossians has been questioned, and some would reject Second Thessalonians.

†Provincials who received Roman citizenship adopted the name of the Roman who sponsored them. The patron of Saul's family was probably someone named Paulus.

received Roman citizenship and the name Paul from the governor of Cyprus, Sergius Paulus, whom he converted to Christianity. In any case, the Jewish name Saul was a handicap in Greek-speaking circles because "Saulos" meant "effeminate" in Greek. Among gentiles, the apostle would gain stature by using his Roman name Paul.

Like Herod Agrippa, Saul of Tarsus was a man of two worlds, Israel and Rome. However, the rigid personality of young Saul could not accommodate both Judaism and Greco-Roman culture, for he was a Pharisaic Jew: "Circumcised on my eighth day, Israelite by race, of the tribe of Benjamin, a Hebrew born and bred; in my attitude to the Law, a Pharisee; in pious zeal, a persecutor of the church; in legal rectitude, faultless."[1] Saul, who would later argue that faith was superior to works, was originally a scrupulous Pharisee of the type mocked by Jesus. Since Saul wished to become a scholar of the Law, his father sent him to Jerusalem to study with the great rabbi Gamaliel. Perhaps, Saul's father hoped that the righteous youth would mellow under the liberal influence of Gamaliel, who later opposed Agrippa's persecution of Christians. The famed Gamaliel was a follower of Hillel, who had summarized the Torah with an epigram: "Love your neighbor—all else is commentary." However, the young Pharisee rejected the liberalism of Gamaliel and brooded over apocalyptic visions of the wars and calamities which would herald the coming of the Messiah, the invincible Son of Man who had been described in the Book of Daniel and the Apocalypse of Enoch. In the wrath to come, most Jews would perish and only a remnant would inherit the new Israel. The Second Book of Esdras* warned:

The Most High made this world for the sake of many, but the world to come for the sake of few. . . . I will rejoice over the few who will be saved, because it is they who have made my glory to prevail more now, and through whom my name has now been honored. And I will not grieve over the great number of those who perish, for they are the ones who are now like vapor and counted as flame and smoke; they have burned and glowed and gone out.[2]

*A second century apocalypse, Second Esdras includes Christian passages but the core of the work preserves first century Jewish thought.

Like the Puritans of a later day, Saul fretted that he would not be
among the chosen elect.

For the young Pharisee, the armor of the Law was an in-
adequate protection against temptations to sin. To Saul, the Law
became a curse and an unbearable burden:

Except through law I should never have become acquainted with sin.
For example, I should never have known what it was to covet, if the
Law had not said, "Thou shalt not covet." Through that command-
ment, sin found its opportunity and produced in me all kinds of wrong
desires. In the absence of law, sin is a dead thing. There was a time
when, in the absence of law, I was fully alive; but when the com-
mandment came, sin sprang to life and I died.[3]

Until he was thirteen, a Jewish boy was not culpable before the
Law, but in the storms of adolescence Saul was personally
accountable to the Law.* Apparently the young man felt guilty
that he coveted women in defiance of the Law. In later life, Saul
confessed:

The Law is spiritual but I am not. I am unspiritual, the purchased
slave of sin. I do not even acknowledge my own actions as mine, for
what I do is not what I want to do, but what I detest. . . . It is no
longer I who performs the action, but sin that lodges in me. . . .
When I want to do the right, only the wrong is within my reach. In
my inmost self I delight in the Law of God, but I perceive that there
is in my bodily members a different law, fighting against the Law
that my reason approves and making me a prisoner under the law
that is in my members, the law of sin. Miserable creature that I am,
who is there to rescue me out of this body doomed to death?[4]

Hating the Law which caused his feelings of guilt, Saul was also
plagued by fear of supernatural creatures, the demonic princes
of the air who brought harm to men. To Saul, as to Jesus and
Luther, Satan was not a theological abstraction but a malignant
foe who was at war with mankind. The invisible demons pressed
about the tormented young Pharisee and jeered as he thrashed
frantically in the net of the Law.

*See the Mishnah, Sanhedrin 8:1; Niddah 5:5–6.

Saul soon found an outlet for his anguish and a scapegoat for his guilt, for Jesus had recently been crucified as a traitor to Rome. For Saul the execution of Jesus was fully justified because the Galilean prophet had claimed to be the Messiah and had spoken slightingly of the Law. Among the Diaspora Jews who resided in Jerusalem were a few followers of Jesus who were called Hellenists. The outspoken leader of the Hellenists was Stephen, who was soon stoned for his intemperate attacks on the Law and his insistence that Jesus was the Messiah. Feeding his crumbling faith with the blood of blasphemers, Saul willingly held the coats of the men who stoned Stephen, and helped to drag other Christians to prison. Apparently only the Hellenists were in danger, for James, Peter, and other Palestinian Jews who believed in both the Law and Jesus the Messiah weathered the storm. Enjoying his role as persecutor, Saul received authority from the High Priest to seek out other Christians in Syria. However, the absurdity of his role as a defender of the Law overwhelmed Saul on the road to Damascus.

The author of Acts describes the famous episode of Saul's conversion:

While he was still on the road and nearing Damascus, suddenly a light flashed from the sky all around him. He fell to the ground and heard a voice saying, "Saul, Saul, why do you persecute me?" "Tell me, Lord," he said, "who you are." The voice answered, "I am Jesus whom you are persecuting. But get up and go into the city, and you will be told what you have to do." Meanwhile, the men who were traveling with him stood speechless; they heard the voice but could see no one.* Saul got up from the ground, but when he opened his eyes he could not see; so they led him by the hand and brought him into Damascus. He was blind for three days and took no food or drink.[5]

In the city Saul was taken to a Christian who restored his sight by forgiving and baptizing the former enemy. However, the local Jews were angered by his change of heart and Saul had to flee

---

*However, in Acts 22:9, Paul claimed: "My companions saw the light but did not hear the voice."

from Damascus. True to Judaic tradition, the new Christian fled into the desert.

In the solitude of the Arabian wasteland, Saul underwent a spiritual moratorium, pondered his new values and beliefs, and emerged as Paul, the apostle to the gentiles. The humiliation and death of Jesus presented no problem, for the Biblical Deutero-Isaiah had depicted salvation through a scapegoat. Not only was the resurrection of Jesus attested by many of his followers, but Paul had experienced a personal visitation. In Paul's eyes, the risen Jesus had abrogated the laws of Moses and lifted the burden of the Law ʿrom the Jews and the cross of guilt from Saul of Tarsus. Identifying himself with the martyred Stephen, Paul embraced the position of the Hellenists and decided that he had been chosen to carry the message to the gentiles. In later life, the apostle recalled:

In the practice of our national religion, I was outstripping many of my Jewish contemporaries in my boundless devotion to the traditions of my ancestors. But then in his good pleasure God, who had set me apart from birth and called me through his grace, chose to reveal his Son to me and through me, in order that I might proclaim him among the gentiles. When that happened, without consulting any human being, without going up to Jerusalem to see those who were apostles before me, I went off at once to Arabia and afterwards returned to Damascus.[6]

Alone in the wilderness, Paul became convinced that the son of God had given him a unique mission to the pagan world.

The traumatic episode on the road to Damascus was not the only psychic experience in Paul's life. On at least one occasion he fell into a trance in the Temple at Jerusalem. Much later, Paul boasted to the Corinthians:

I know a Christian man who fourteen years ago (whether in the body or out of it, I do not know—God knows) was caught up as far as the third heaven. And I know that this same man (whether in the body or out of it, I do not know—God knows) was caught up into paradise and heard words so secret that human lips may not repeat them. About such a man as that, I am ready to boast, but I will not boast on my own account except of my weaknesses. If I should choose to boast, it would not be the boast of a fool, for I should be speaking the truth. But I refrain because I should not like anyone to form an estimate of me which goes beyond the evidence of his own eyes and ears. And so, to keep me from being unduly elated by the magnificence of such revelations, I was given a sharp pain in my body which came as Satan's messenger to bruise me; this was to save me from being unduly elated. Three times I begged the Lord to rid me of it, but his answer was: "My grace is all you need; power comes to its full strength in weakness."[7]

Among the many references to illness in his letters, Paul was thankful that the Galatians did not despise him or spit on him when he was afflicted. Since he added that the Galatians would have given him their eyes if they could, Paul apparently suffered from a repulsive illness which was followed by brief blindness. The trances, light flashes, falling, and traumatic aftereffects suggest that the apostle was epileptoid. Some epileptic attacks are followed by temporary blindness, and the peoples of antiquity loathed the disease and tried to ward off epilepsy by spitting at the sufferer.[*] If he had only ophthalmia or some other eye trouble, Paul would not have expected the Galatians to spit on him and been thankful when they did not. Obviously the apostle suffered from a more serious affliction.

Many great visionaries have been epileptoid, as were Muhammad, Pascal, and Dostoievski, and epilepsy did not incapacitate Caesar, Richelieu, or Napoleon. In personality, Dostoievski and Paul were similar, for the Russian's epilepsy was linked to neuroses which were rooted in hatred of his father and guilt over a murder. Like Paul, Dostoievski embraced the cult of the crucified Christ and preached submission to the emperor (the "little father" of Tsarist Russia). In *The Idiot*, the great novelist described the experience before an epileptic attack:

He always had one minute just before the epileptic fit (if it came on while he was awake), when suddenly in the midst of sadness, spiritual

[*]In his *Apologia* 44, the Roman writer Lucius Apuleius described the behavior of simple folk who spat on an epileptic boy. See also Pliny the Elder, *Natural History* 28:35.

darkness, and oppression, there seemed at moments a flash of light in his brain, and with extraordinary impetus all his vital forces suddenly began working at their highest tension. The sense of life, the consciousness of self, were multiplied ten times at these moments which passed like a flash of lightning. His mind and his heart were flooded with extraordinary light; all his uneasiness, all his doubts, all his anxieties were relieved at once; they were all merged in a lofty calm, full of serene, harmonious joy and hope. But these moments, these flashes, were only the prelude of that final second (it was never more than a second) with which the fit began. That second was, of course, unendurable. . . . Since at that second, that is at the very last conscious moment before the fit, he had time to say to himself clearly and consciously, "Yes, for this moment one might give one's whole life!" then without doubt that moment was really worth the whole of life. . . . "At that moment I seem somehow to understand the extraordinary saying that *there shall be no more time.* Probably . . . this is the very second which was not long enough for the water to be spilt out of Mahomet's pitcher, though the epileptic prophet had time to gaze at all the habitations of Allah."[8]

It was no disgrace for Paul to be one of those tortured thinkers whom Thomas Mann has called the "great invalids."

Whatever the nature of his affliction, Paul was convinced that God revealed truths to him, but his claims were not always accepted by other Christians. Many Hebrew prophets had criticized legalistic religion and insisted that the spirit had precedence over the letter of the Law. Though the sarcastic epigrams of Jesus were in the tradition of Amos and Isaiah, the words of the Galilean prophet had additional authority for Paul. Believing that Jesus was both the Messiah and the son of God, Paul saw a universal significance in his martyrdom. While the Messiah could only atone for the sins of Israel, the son of God had died for all men. By sacrificing his mortal body, Jesus had annulled the Law and outwitted the demons who controlled the cosmos. According to Paul, a new day of freedom had dawned on Calvary:

Christ bought us freedom from the curse of the Law by becoming for our sake an accursed thing, for scripture says, "Cursed is everyone who is hanged on a tree." And the purpose of it all was that the blessing of Abraham should in Jesus Christ be extended to the gen-

tiles, so that we might receive the promised Spirit through faith. . . .
Then what of the Law? . . . It was a temporary measure pending the
arrival of the "issue" to whom the promise was made. It was promul-
gated through angels, and there was an intermediary; but an intermediary is not needed for one party acting alone, and God is one. . . .
During our minority, we were slaves to the elemental spirits of the
universe, but when the term was completed, God sent his own son,
born of a woman, born under the Law, to purchase freedom for the
subjects of the Law, in order that we might attain the status of sons.[9]

Freed from the Law and the rule of demons, men should accept
the resurrection of the Messiah and prepare for his imminent
return, which Jesus had promised would take place within the
lifetime of his first followers.

After three years of spiritual reorientation in Arabia and
Syria, Paul visited Peter and James at Jerusalem and explained his
views to them. Understandably, the Christian leaders were wary
of a former enemy and suspected his claims of special revelations
from the risen Jesus. The apostles were not convinced that the
Law had been abolished by Jesus, and they may have feared
that Paul was an *agent provocateur*. In time Peter would be
converted to the position of the Hellenists, but James would
refuse to abandon Judaism. Although he had not accepted Jesus
as the Messiah until after the resurrection, James had great
authority in the Christian movement because he was the brother
of the dead prophet. After a polite visit with the two apostles,
Paul returned to Syria and Cilicia and eventually formed a
missionary partnership with the Hellenist Barnabas of Cyprus.
Preaching that Jesus had abrogated the Law, Paul did not
impose circumcision or dietary restrictions on pagan converts to
Christianity. For adults, circumcision was both painful and re-
pellent, and circumcised Christians were teased in the baths and
gymnasia of Greek cities. Most Christian missionary activity was
directed by Peter, who believed that pagan converts should
submit to circumcision and observe the dietary laws of Judaism.
However, the flexible Peter was often inconsistent with regard to
diet. Since many Christians had to shop in public markets,
where kosher foods were not available, a common feast between
Jewish and gentile Christians was often the scene of embarrass-
ment and occasionally of strife. When reports of Paul's liberal

policies reached Jerusalem, James sent Jewish Christians to infiltrate the congregation at Antioch and protest the new practices. In great indignation Paul and Barnabas hurried to Jerusalem to confer with the senior apostles.

In his epistle to the Galatians, Paul bitterly recalled his contacts with James and Peter:

Three years later [after the period of moratorium], I did go up to Jerusalem to get to know Cephas.* I stayed with him for a fortnight without seeing any other of the apostles except James the Lord's brother. What I write is plain truth; before God I am not lying. Next, I went to the regions of Syria and Cilicia and remained unknown by sight to Christ's congregations in Judea. They only heard it said, "Our former persecutor is preaching the good news of the faith which once he tried to destroy"; and they praised God for me. Next, fourteen years later, I went again to Jerusalem with Barnabas, taking Titus with us. I went up because it had been revealed by God that I should do so. I laid before them—but at a private interview with the men of repute—the gospel which I am accustomed to preach to the gentiles, to make sure that the race I had run and was running should not be run in vain. Yet, even my companion Titus, Greek though he is, was not compelled to be circumcised. That course was urged only as a concession to certain sham-Christians, interlopers who had stolen in to spy upon the liberty we enjoy in the fellowship of Christ Jesus. These men wanted to bring us into bondage, but not for one moment did I yield to their dictation. . . . But, as for the men of high reputation (not that their importance matters to me: God does not recognize these personal distinctions)—these men of repute, I say, did not prolong the consultation but on the contrary, acknowledged that I had been entrusted with the gospel for gentiles as surely as Peter had been entrusted with the gospel for Jews. For God, whose action made Peter an apostle to the Jews, also made me an apostle to the gentiles. Recognizing, then, the favor thus bestowed upon me, those reputed pillars of our society, James, Cephas, and John, accepted Barnabas and myself as partners and shook hands upon it, agreeing that we should go to the gentiles while they went to the Jews. All they asked was that we should keep their poor in mind, which was the very thing I made it my business to do.[10]

*According to Matthew 16:18, Jesus had given Simon bar-Jonah the Aramaic nickname Cephas ("Rock") which in Greek is Petros and Peter in English.

The collection of funds for the Christians at Jerusalem was Paul's trump card, for the Diaspora congregations were relatively well-to-do and James was dependent upon their support. In his policy struggles with James and Peter, Paul would often employ the crucial weapon of finance.

Although they had sanctioned Paul's liberalism, the senior apostles soon broke the gentlemen's agreement and forced Paul to challenge their authority:

When Cephas came to Antioch, I opposed him to his face because he was clearly in the wrong. For until certain persons came from James, he was taking his meals with gentile Christians, but when they came he drew back and began to hold aloof, because he was afraid of the advocates of circumcision. The other Jewish Christians showed the same lack of principle; even Barnabas was carried away and played false like the rest. But, when I saw that their conduct did not square with the truth of the gospel, I said to Cephas before the whole congregation: "If you, a Jew born and bred, live like a gentile and not like a Jew, how can you insist that gentiles must live like Jews?" . . . We know that no man is ever justified by doing what the Law demands, but only through faith in Christ Jesus. . . . No, if I start building up again a system which I have pulled down, then it is that I show myself up as a transgressor of the Law. . . . I will not nullify the grace of God; if righteousness comes by law, then Christ died for nothing.[11]

As the spokesman of a growing Hellenist majority, Paul won the day at Antioch and Christianity ceased to be a Jewish splinter group. However, ill will between the leading protagonists continued for years and many Christians clung dogmatically to Judaic practices. Paul's real opponent was not the equivocating Peter but the venerable James, whom the Jews would stone as a heretic in 62. Since the Christian community at Jerusalem was a petty caliphate, James was succeeded by Symeon, a cousin of Jesus. During the Jewish revolt against Rome, the Jerusalem Christians fled to Pella near the Jordan and became an obscure sect, the Ebionites.

After his triumph at Antioch, Paul had intensified his missionary activity and visited cities in Asia Minor, Macedonia, and Greece. Breaking with Barnabas, he sought the companionship of Timothy, Luke, and other gentiles. Unlike Peter and most of the apostles, Paul was unmarried and practiced a nervous continence. With allusions to Greek games, he defended his asceticism:

Every athlete goes into strict training. They do it to win a fading wreath; we, a wreath that never fades. For my part, I run with a clear goal before me; I am like a boxer who does not beat the air. I bruise my own body and make it know its master, for fear that after preaching to others I should find myself rejected.[12]

No longer shielded by the Law, the apostle mortified his rebellious flesh to tame the passions which still raged. However, Paul could not control his major weakness, pride. Since he supported himself while preaching the gospel, the apostle could not resist boasting that he did not live off charity. From hearsay, a second-century writer described Paul's physical appearance: "A man little of stature, thin-haired upon the head, crooked in the legs, of good state of body, with eyebrows joining and nose somewhat hooked, full of grace: for sometimes he appeared like a man, and sometimes he had the face of an angel."[13] The description seems plausible, and the apostle to the gentiles probably was a wiry little Jew whose face would light up with faith.

Jealous over his hard-won converts, Paul dominated congregations and resisted the incursions of rival Christian leaders:

More overworked than they, scourged more severely, more often imprisoned, many a time face to face with death. Five times the Jews have given me the thirty-nine strokes; three times I have been beaten with rods; once I was stoned; three times I have been shipwrecked, and for twenty-four hours I was adrift on the open sea. I have been constantly on the road; I have met dangers from rivers, dangers from robbers, dangers from my fellow-countrymen, dangers from foreigners, dangers in towns, dangers in the country, dangers at sea, dangers from false friends. I have toiled and drudged, I have often gone without sleep; hungry and thirsty, I have often gone fasting; and I have suffered from cold and exposure. . . . In no respect did I fall short of these superlative apostles, even if I am a nobody. The marks of a true apostle were there in the work I did among you, which called for such constant fortitude and was attended by signs, marvels, and miracles. Is there anything in which you were treated worse than the

other congregations—except this, that I never sponged upon you?
How unfair of me! I crave forgiveness.[14]

Though an effective polemist, Paul was a poor orator until a
subject would fire his enthusiasm. In working miracles, Paul did
not fall behind the other apostles, and many of the cures
attributed to him in Acts are plausible. However, magic was a
tricky tool for missionaries, for in Galatia admiring crowds hailed
Barnabas and Paul as the gods Zeus and Hermes.

The success of Christianity was not due to parlor tricks or
stupendous miracles, for the pagan world was well supplied with
magicians, fakirs, and saints. The missionaries won converts with
the good news that Jesus Christ had conquered death and would
soon return to judge the living and the dead. Though opposed to
a Judaic orientation for Christianity, Paul compromised on some
occasions, for he took Nazarite vows and even permitted the
circumcision of Timothy. A master salesman, Paul adapted his
message to his audience:

To Jews, I became like a Jew to win Jews; as they are subject to the
Law of Moses, I put myself under that Law to win them although I
am not myself subject to it. To win gentiles who are outside the Law,
I made myself like one of them, although I am not in truth outside
God's law, being under the law of Christ. To the weak, I became weak
to win the weak. Indeed, I have become everything in turn to men of
every sort, so that in one way or another I may save some. . . . Give
no offence to Jews or Greeks or to the church of God. For my part, I
always try to meet everyone half-way, regarding not my own good
but the good of the many, so that they may be saved.[15]

To win converts, the apostle even ate food which had been con-
secrated to pagan gods. The author of Acts emphasized the good
relationship which Paul enjoyed with Seneca's brother Gallio and
other Roman officials. Allowing for exaggerations in details,
the stories are not improbable, for Paul after all was a Roman
citizen.

While appealing to the poor, Christianity also attracted
world-weary and disenchanted men from all classes. At Athens,
Paul tried to impress a sophisticated audience with natural law
arguments, but the Greeks listened to his rhetoric with lofty

indifference. Elsewhere, he used paradoxes with success and won many converts with his clever nay-saying:

Where is your wise man now, your man of learning, or your subtle debater—limited, all of them, to this passing age? God has made the wisdom of this world look foolish. As God in his wisdom ordained, the world failed to find him by its wisdom, and he chose to save those who have faith by the folly of the gospel. Jews call for miracles, Greeks look for wisdom, but we proclaim Christ—yes, Christ nailed to the cross; and though this is a stumbling-block to Jews and folly to Greeks, yet to those who have heard his call, Jews and Greeks alike, he is the power of God and the wisdom of God. Divine folly is wiser than the wisdom of man, and divine weakness stronger than man's strength. My brothers, think what sort of people you are, whom God has called. Few of you are men of wisdom by any human standard; few are powerful or highly born. Yet, to shame the wise, God has chosen what the world counts folly, and to shame what is strong, God has chosen what the world counts weakness. He has chosen things low and contemptible, mere nothings, to overthrow the existing order.[16]

The nihilism in Christianity brought on a problem in church discipline. Abandoning old values, some converts felt free to indulge their desires, for they were sure that faith alone would save them from the wrath to come. Paul filled his epistles with denunciations of debauched and worldly Christians who had been unhinged by faith and reverted to old vices. The apostle warned Christians who thought that they were emancipated from moral law:

Make no mistake: no fornicator or idolater, none who are guilty either of adultery or of homosexual perversion, no thieves or grabbers or drunkards or slanderers or swindlers, will possess the kingdom of God. Such were some of you. But you have been through the purifying waters; you have been dedicated to God.[17]

Eventually, the evolution of the episcopal system solved problems in discipline, for the bishops kept a watchful eye on Christian backsliders.

Sometimes piety, rather than sensuality, aroused Paul's anger. Christian congregations welcomed rival apostles and strange prophets whose views caused dissent. Christian doctrines were still flexible and religious practices varied from city to city. In general, early Christians held communal suppers which had a sacramental aspect. Eating a savior god was common pagan practice, and Paul insisted that Christians partake of the body and blood of Jesus, in the guise of bread and wine. The rite was more appealing to gentiles than to Jews but was viewed by all Christians with awe. Paul warned the Corinthians that men who took communion in a sinful state of mind would sicken and die. The other major Christian rite, baptism, also had magical properties and zealous Christians often baptized dead relatives and friends. The church at Corinth was particularly lively and held exciting services with ecstatic prophets and raving communicants who babbled in "strange tongues." Impatient with religious hysteria, Paul scolded the Corinthians:

The man who falls into ecstatic utterance should pray for the ability to interpret. If I use such language in my prayer, the Spirit in me prays but my intellect lies fallow. What then? I will pray as I am inspired to pray, but I will also pray intelligently. I will sing hymns as I am inspired to sing, but I will sing intelligently too. . . . I am more gifted in ecstatic utterance than any of you, but in the congregation I would rather speak five intelligible words for the benefit of others as well as myself, than thousands of words in the language of ecstasy. Do not be childish, my friends. Be as innocent of evil as babes, but at least be grown-up in your thinking. . . . If the whole congregation is assembled and all are using the "strange tongues" of ecstasy, and some uninstructed persons or unbelievers should enter, will they not think you are mad?[18]

Paul was also displeased that women were permitted to address the congregation at Corinth. "If there is something they want to know," he growled, "they can ask their own husbands at home."[19] In his hometown of Tarsus, many women wore veils, and none were allowed to intrude into male society.

The antics of the lunatic fringe and the misbehavior of some Christians reflected the hysterical atmosphere of the church in the first century, when the second coming of Jesus was expected at any moment. Paul too was confident that the Day of the Lord would soon be upon them: "At the sound of the archangel's voice and God's trumpet-call, the Lord himself will descend from heaven; first the Christian dead will rise, then we who are left alive shall join them, caught up in clouds to meet the Lord in the air."[20] Naturally, the apocalyptic event would also feature the slaughter of sinners, the humiliation of kings, and the overthrow of demonic powers. However, certain episodes borrowed from the Book of Daniel would precede the return of Jesus, as Paul reminded the Thessalonians:

I beg you, do not suddenly lose your heads or alarm yourselves, whether at some oracular utterance or pronouncement or some letter purporting to come from us, alleging that the Day of the Lord is already here. . . . That day cannot come before the final rebellion against God, when wickedness will be revealed in human form, the man doomed to perdition. He is the Enemy. He rises in his pride against every god, so called, every object of men's worship, and even takes his seat in the Temple of God claiming to be a god himself. . . . You must now be aware of the restraining hand which ensures that he shall be revealed only at the proper time. For already the secret power of wickedness is at work, secret only for the present until the Restrainer disappears from the scene. And then he will be revealed, that wicked man whom the Lord Jesus will destroy with the breath of his mouth and annihilate by the radiance of his coming.[21]

Caligula had almost enacted the role of the wicked Enemy but his plans had fallen through. The identity of the Restrainer is not clear, but Paul felt that some rash ruler would soon profane the Temple and bring on the Day of the Lord.

The early epistles of Paul—Thessalonians I and II, Galatians, First Corinthians, and Second Corinthians, chapters 10–13—are characterized by an imperious pride and impatience with opposition which are less evident in his later letters. Apparently, the change reflected a physical and spiritual crisis which he experienced at Ephesus.* In the document which forms the first nine chapters of Second Corinthians, the apostle confessed:

We should like you to know, dear friends, how serious was the trouble that came upon us in the province of Asia. The burden of it was far too heavy for us to bear, so heavy that we even despaired of life. Indeed, we felt in our hearts that we had received a death sentence.

*On the psychological break in Second Corinthians, see Appendix One.

This was meant to teach us not to place reliance on ourselves, but on God who raises the dead.[22]

While he was seriously ill, Paul's authority was challenged at Corinth and also at Ephesus where he refers to "fighting with wild beasts." The episode is obscure, but Ephesus was a stronghold of Apollos of Alexandria, who was originally a disciple of John the Baptist. Perhaps Paul despaired during his illness and lost face with the Ephesians. However, the apostle was probably most disturbed by the thought that he might die without having witnessed the return of Jesus or accomplished the conversion of the gentiles. With his pride punctured, the apostle became a saint:

Though our outward humanity is in decay, yet day by day we are inwardly renewed. Our troubles are slight and short-lived, and their outcome an eternal glory which outweighs them far. Meanwhile our eyes are fixed, not on the things that are seen, but on the things that are unseen. . . . With us therefore, worldly standards have ceased to count in our estimate of any man; even if once they counted in our understanding of Christ, they do so now no longer.[23]

Softened by humility, Paul became a more attractive human being.

Before his final return to Palestine, Paul wrote an epistle to the congregation at Rome and enjoined all Christians to adjust to pagan society and submit willingly to secular authority. While not abandoning his belief in Christians as a predestined elect, Paul reconciled himself to his Jewish background and insisted that Israel too would be saved following the conversion of the gentiles. The apostle also mellowed toward pagans who were ignorant of the gospel but obeyed the injunctions of natural law —Christ would judge them fairly on the Day of the Lord. With high hopes, Paul assured the Roman Christians that he would soon visit them in person and go on to Spain, carrying the gospel to the limits of the known world. Before his trip to Rome, Paul delivered funds to the Christians at Jerusalem, but some Asian Jews accused him of a capital offense, bringing gentiles into the precincts of the Temple. In physical danger from his accusers, the apostle was rescued by a Roman officer and held in protective custody. Brought before the Sanhedrin, Paul won Pharisaic support by claiming to be a Pharisee whose only offense was belief in the resurrection of the dead. Since the Sadducees denied immortality, the Sanhedrin dissolved in a rowdy dispute between the two rival religious factions. However, a group of Jewish fanatics had sworn to assassinate Paul, and his Roman captors sent him to the protection of the governor Felix at Caesarea. A brother of the powerful freedman Pallas, Felix had governed Palestine since 52 and married Drusilla, a daughter of Herod Agrippa. Though badgered by Paul's enemies, Felix delayed the trial of the apostle, for he hoped to extort a bribe from the prisoner. In 60 Felix was replaced as governor by Festus, who sought to placate the Jews by bringing Paul to trial. However, the apostle insisted on his rights as a Roman citizen and demanded a hearing before the emperor. He received the expected reply from Festus: "You have appealed to Caesar, and to Caesar you shall go."

Before his departure for Rome, the controversial prisoner was shown off by Festus to two prominent guests, Agrippa II and his sister Berenice. At an interview with the Herodian king and princess, Paul rose to the occasion and embroidered the story of his conversion on the road to Damascus by having the voice quote Euripides: "Saul, Saul, why do you persecute me? It is hard for you, this kicking against the goad." Presumably, Paul hoped that his educated audience would remember that the god Dionysus spoke the line in Euripides' "Bacchae" to rebuke King Pentheus who was unwittingly persecuting a deity. According to Acts, Festus became impatient with Paul's rhetoric but Agrippa was favorably impressed by the apostle. After a hectic sea voyage and a shipwreck on Malta, Paul finally reached Rome in chains. Since his crime meant little outside of Palestine, Paul was permitted to live in private lodgings under police surveillance. Acts ends with the abrupt remark: "He stayed there two full years at his own expense, with a welcome for all who came to him, proclaiming the kingdom of God and teaching the facts about the Lord Jesus Christ quite openly and without hindrance."[24] According to Christian tradition, Paul was beheaded by Nero.

It is strange that the author of the Acts of the Apostles did not record the martyrdom of Paul, for the Christian historian composed his work under the Flavian emperors who succeeded Nero and had no objections to horror tales about his injustice and cruelty. Perhaps the apostle never received a trial but died with the throng of anonymous Christians during Nero's brief persecution in 64. At any rate, Paul was "in prison" when he wrote to the Philippians. For years he had expected success as an evangelist in Rome and his epistle mentions Christians in the imperial establishment. However, the same letter reveals his weariness and despair over the factional strife which isolated him from the Roman congregation. Backed only by the loyal Timothy, Paul complained that the Christians "stir up fresh trouble for me as I lie in prison. . . . There is no one else here who sees things as I do and takes a genuine interest in your concerns; they are all bent on their own ends, not on the cause of Christ Jesus."[25] Old, exhausted, and disappointed, Paul begged the distant Philippians to remain loyal to his teaching:

Show yourselves guileless and above reproach, faultless children of God in a warped and crooked generation, in which you shine like stars in a dark world and proffer the word of life. Thus, you will be my pride on the Day of Christ, proof that I did not run my race in vain or work in vain.[26]

This is the tragic spectacle which the author of Acts discreetly hides—the old lion at bay, surrounded by yelping hounds. Probably Nero's executioner put an end to Paul's agony.

Whatever one may think of Paul's beliefs, the apostle was a great man who towered over the vacillating Peter and the obdurate James. Adamant on principles, Paul was willing to compromise with men. An able organizer, he knew the arts of persuasion and inspiration which hold groups together after the glow of conversion has subsided. Blinded by pride and ambition, the apostle often confused the good of the cause with his own success, but he provided the driving dedication and energy which humbler men lacked. Though he was not the first Hellenist in the Christian fold, Paul carried out the Hellenist program and transformed a Jewish heresy into a universal church. The older apostles may have known Jesus better, but later Christians have seen Christ largely through Paul's eyes. The words of Paul to the Corinthians may serve as his epitaph:

In the end, [Jesus] appeared even to me, though this birth of mine was monstrous, for I had persecuted the church of God and am therefore inferior to all other apostles—indeed not fit to be called an apostle. However, by God's grace I am what I am, nor has his grace been given to me in vain. On the contrary, in my labors I have outdone them all—not I, indeed, but the grace of God working with me. But, what matter, I or they?[27]

He had come a long way since that fateful trip to Damascus.

FIVE

The Courtier—Seneca

By chance, Paul's arrival in Rome coincided with Seneca's fall from power. A Spanish intellectual, Seneca had ruled the Roman world as Nero's prime minister. The Spanish courtier was also an effective essayist and an eloquent proponent of Stoic philosophy. Though Seneca was a pagan agnostic, his highly moralistic writings had a wide appeal for Christians, and Tertullian referred fondly to "our Seneca." In late antiquity, Christians venerated fourteen letters which supposedly had been exchanged between Paul and Seneca. Though a clumsy forgery, the correspondence misled Jerome in the fourth century to list Seneca among the great men of Christianity. With such high recommendations, the writings of the Roman Stoic were popular in the Middle Ages, when handbooks of aphorisms were called "Seneks." In "The Monk's Tale," Chaucer expressed a common view of the Roman philosopher:

> This Seneca, of which that I devyse,
> By-cause Nero hadde of him swich drede
> For he fro vyces wolde him ay chastyse
> Discreetly as by worde and nat by dede;—
> "Sir," wolde he seyn, "an emperour moot nede
> Be vertuous and hate tirannye"—
> For which he in a bath made him to blede
> On bothe his armes, til he moste dye.[1]

In the Renaissance, Montaigne relished Seneca and Elizabethan playwrights imitated his grisly dramas. Voltaire, Boswell, and Emerson had high opinions of Seneca, and his words are often quoted today. Few men have said wise things so well as Seneca, but T. S. Eliot warns: "Between the idea and the reality, between the motion and the act, falls the Shadow." Worldly-wise and self-serving, Seneca the man mocked Seneca the moralist.

Highly critical of conventional religion, Seneca struck a modern note when he disparaged "this ignoble crowd of gods which the superstition of ages has amassed." He scorned gross myths and orgiastic cults and mocked the Roman state religion, but the Stoic also insisted on compliance with the law and dutifully attended religious ceremonies. Seneca rationalized his behavior on the pragmatic grounds that a wise man should feign respect without belief. While admiring Seneca's attacks on superstition, the Christian philosopher Augustine of Hippo accused the Stoic of hypocrisy:

Though philosophy had freed his mind, he was still an exalted senator of the Roman people and worshiped what he condemned, did what he criticized, and adored what he despised. . . . He was an actor, not on the stage, but in the temples. Such conduct should be condemned, particularly because he played his role so successfully that people thought he was acting sincerely.[2]

Augustine might have added that Seneca did not pretend piety in order to spare the simple faith of the masses. The Stoic courtier was not motivated by a concern for pious believers, but by the personal profit which resulted from participation in the state cult.

As a philosopher, Seneca was an attractive exponent of Stoicism. While too many Stoics were stiff-necked and self-righteous, Roman Stoicism was flexible and eclectic. For Stoics, the world was controlled by Divine Providence, the ways of which were often hidden to man but were considered to be good and just. Not a sparrow fell without divine approval, and men were expected to faithfully execute the roles to which Providence had assigned them. In practice, the doctrines of duty and submission were endorsements of the established order—hence the popularity of Stoicism at Rome. Though moralists sensed a danger in fatalistic approval of the status quo, redress was left to Providence which was responsible when rulers abused their authority. According to Seneca, awareness of sin was a sinner's worst punishment. Though he often criticized contemporary luxury, the Spanish Stoic conceded that young people were more moral in his era than in the Rome of Cicero and Caesar. Respectful toward rival philosophies, Seneca admired the saintly Epicurus whose views were anathema to most Stoics. Like many Romans, Seneca loathed the senseless brutality and bloodshed of the gladiatorial games. He had a high regard for women and praised conjugal fidelity, but the philosopher had difficulty following his own precept.

In Roman society slavery was a running sore which no one was willing to cauterize. However, responsible Romans treated their slaves with consideration and criticized cruel owners who abused bondmen. In the Senate and salons of Rome, severity and liberality toward slaves were hotly debated. It is to his credit that Seneca was on the side of sanity:

I am glad to learn, through those who come from you, that you live on friendly terms with your slaves. This befits a sensible and well-educated man like yourself. "They are slaves," people declare. Nay, rather they are men. "Slaves!" No, comrades. "Slaves!" No, they are unpretentious friends. "Slaves!" No, they are our fellow-slaves, if one reflects that Fortune has equal rights over slaves and free men alike. That is why I smile at those who think it degrading for a man to dine with his slave. . . . The result of it all is that these slaves, who may not talk in their master's presence, talk about their master. But the slaves of former days, who were permitted to converse not only in their master's presence but actually with him, whose mouths were not stitched up tight, were ready to bare their necks for their master, to bring upon their own heads any danger that threatened him; they spoke at the feast but kept silence during torture. Finally, the saying, in allusion to this same high-handed treatment, becomes current: "As many enemies as you have slaves." They are not enemies when we acquire them; we make them enemies.[3]

In vivid detail, Seneca described the indignities which slaves suffered in some homes:

When we recline at a banquet, one slave mops up the disgorged food, another crouches beneath the table and gathers up the left-overs of the tipsy guests. Another carves the priceless game birds; with unerring strokes and skilled hand, he cuts choice morsels along the breast or the rump. Hapless fellow, to live only for the purpose of cutting fat capons correctly. . . . Another, who serves the wine, must dress like a woman and wrestle with his advancing years; he cannot get away from his boyhood; he is dragged back to it; and though he has already acquired a soldier's figure, he is kept beardless by having his hair smoothed away or plucked out by the roots, and he must remain awake throughout the night, dividing his time between his master's drunkenness and his lust; in the chamber he must be a man, at the feast a boy. Another, whose duty it is to put a valuation on the guests, must stick to his task, poor fellow, and watch to see whose flattery and whose immodesty, whether of appetite or of language, is to get them an invitation for tomorrow.[4]

While few Roman owners were as dissolute, most masters did not acknowledge the essential bond of humanity between themselves and their slaves. Yet, freedmen, who had once been chattel, could rise to great heights in Roman society.

The syndrome of slavery contained glaring contradictions which were obvious to all Romans but disturbing to only a few. Like Shakespeare's Shylock—"Hath not a Jew eyes? . . . When you prick us, do we not bleed?"—Seneca protested against the false distinctions which society made between men:

Kindly remember that he whom you call your slave sprang from the same stock, is smiled upon by the same skies, and on equal terms with yourself, breathes, lives, and dies. It is just as possible for you to see in him a free-born man as for him to see in you a slave. . . . Despise, then, if you dare, those to whose estate you may at any time descend, even when you are despising them. I do not wish to involve myself in too large a question and to discuss the treatment of slaves, towards whom we Romans are excessively haughty, cruel, and insulting. But this is the kernel of my advice: Treat your inferiors as you would be treated by your betters. And as often as you reflect how much power you have over a slave, remember that your master has just as much power over you. "But I have no master," you say. You are still young; perhaps you will have one. Do you not know at what age Hecuba entered captivity, or Croesus, or the mother of Darius, or Plato, or Diogenes?[5]

From bitter experience, Seneca knew that free men were often slaves in reality, particularly when they served a despot.

Behind his reflections on slavery lay Seneca's deep belief in the brotherhood of man and the overriding importance of the human mind:

Let us grasp the idea that there are two commonwealths—the one, a vast and truly common state, which embraces alike gods and men, in which we look neither to this corner of earth nor to that but measure the bounds of our citizenship by the path of the sun; the other, the one to which we have been assigned by the accident of birth. This will be the commonwealth of the Athenians or of the Carthaginians or of any other city that belongs, not to all, but to some particular race of men. Some yield service to both commonwealths at the same time—to the greater and to the lesser—some only to the lesser, some only to the greater. This greater commonwealth we are able to serve even in leisure—nay, I am inclined to think, even better in leisure—so that we may inquire what virtue is, and whether it is one or many; whether it is nature or art that makes men good; whether this world, which embraces seas and lands and the things that are contained in the sea and land, is a solitary creation or whether God has strewn about many systems of the same sort; . . . what God is—whether he idly gazes upon his handiwork or directs it; whether he encompasses it without, or pervades the whole of it; whether the world is eternal or is to be counted among the things that perish and are born only for a time. And what service does he who ponders these things render unto God? He keeps the mighty works of God from being without a witness![6]

Centuries later, the Christian philosopher Augustine would be impressed by Seneca's dichotomy between the all-important City of God and the trivial City of Man.

As a participant in the human comedy, Seneca found it difficult to maintain an Olympian attitude. According to the Roman Stoic, the happy life consists of "peace of mind and lasting tranquillity." Since these qualities are rarely found in slums and garrets, Seneca advised sages to seek the favor of kings and profit from their bounty. In Seneca's eyes, worldly possessions were not a handicap for philosophers but a positive aid to virtue:

The wise man does not deem himself undeserving of any of the gifts of Fortune. He does not love riches, but he would rather have them; he does not admit them to his heart but to his house, and he does not reject the riches he has, but he keeps them and wishes them to supply ampler material for exercising his virtue. Who, however, can doubt that the wise man finds in riches, rather than in poverty, this ampler material for displaying his powers, since in poverty there is room for only one kind of virtue—not to be bowed down and crushed by it— while in riches, moderation and liberality and diligence and orderliness and grandeur all have a wide field?[7]

In practice, Seneca found it impossible to push a camel through the eye of a needle. He constantly whined that worldly friends led him astray and that social pressures made him observe a luxurious standard of living. Above all, the philosopher discovered that worldly success came at a high price in compromise and duplicity.

The life of Seneca was more than a moral parable, for his rise to power reflected the increasing importance of provincials at Rome. Seneca came from the province of Spain, which earlier had furnished Rome with the same commodity the Americas would one day supply to Spain—silver. Unlike the later Spanish kingdom, the Roman empire had an enlightened attitude toward talented Creoles, and many Spaniards found fame and success at Rome. In the first century A.D. Spain produced a galaxy of distinguished literary men, the two Senecas, the rhetorician Quintilian, the poet Lucan, and the epigrammatist Martial. The political abilities of provincials could not be denied, and the emperor Claudius was particularly anxious to broaden the base of the Roman ruling class. The emperor himself had been born at Lyons and admitted Gallic aristocrats into the Senate. His speech in defense of this policy had been preserved in a bronze inscription, but Tacitus' version of Claudius' wordy address is more readable:

The experience of my own ancestors, notably of my family's Sabine founder Clausus who was simultaneously made a Roman citizen and a patrician, encouraged me to adopt the same national policy by bringing excellence to Rome from whatever source. . . . After the enfranchisement of Italy across the Po, our next step was to make citizens of the finest provincials too; we added them to our ex-soldiers in settlements throughout the world and by their means reinvigorated the exhausted empire. This helped to stabilize peace within the frontiers and successful relations with foreign powers. Is it regretted that the Cornelii Balbi immigrated from Spain and other equally distinguished men from southern Gaul? Their descendants are with us, and they love Rome as much as we do. What proved fatal to Sparta and Athens, for all their military strength, was their segregation of conquered subjects as aliens. . . . The admission to office of the sons of ex-slaves is not the novelty it is alleged to be. In early times it happened frequently. "The Senonian Gauls fought against us," it is objected. But did not Italians, Vulsci and Aequi, as well? "The Gauls captured Rome," you say. But we also lost battles to our neighbors— we gave hostages to the Etruscans, we went beneath the Samnites' yoke. Actually, a review of all these wars shows that the Gallic war took the shortest time of all—since then, peace and loyalty have reigned unbroken. Now that they have assimilated our customs and culture and married into our families, let them bring in their gold and wealth rather than keep it to themselves. Senators, however ancient any institution seems, it was once new. First, plebeians joined patricians in office. Next, the Latins were added. Then came men from other Italian peoples. The innovation now proposed will, in its turn, one day be old. What we seek to justify by precedents today will itself become a precedent.[8]

As a student of history, Claudius invoked the evidence of the past. As a politician, he added the incentive that provincial leaders would bring wealth as well as ability to Rome. The future proved the wisdom of his views.

Though not the first provincial to prosper at Rome, Lucius Annaeus Seneca rose higher than most in the world of politics. Born at Cordova in 4 B.C., he was one of three sons of Seneca the rhetorician. An old-fashioned man, the elder Seneca disapproved of his wife educating herself and complained when his sons, Lucius, Gallio, and Mela, took up the study of philosophy. Their father knew that Lucius and Gallio were ambitious and would go far, but he preferred Mela, who became a financial magnate and influenced politics behind the scenes. Mela's son Lucan would be a successful poet and write a melodramatic epic on the Civil Wars. As a child, Lucius Seneca was raised by his aunt in Rome. Throughout his life he suffered from a variety of ailments, including asthma which he described as "practicing how to die." Sickly and scrawny, young Seneca once contemplated suicide but decided that the shock would be too great for his father. Plagued with a delicate stomach, Seneca criticized people who ate foods which he could not enjoy—shellfish, mushrooms, and rich sauces. Briefly attracted to Pythagoreanism, he became a vegetarian, but when his father protested that only subversive cranks abstained from meat, Seneca gave up his diet. Tormented by claustrophobia and other morbid fears, Seneca was highly neurotic and prone to hypochondria. Like Augustus, he was a chronic invalid who lived to a ripe old age. Grumbling about his poor health, Seneca would be seventy years old when Nero forced him to commit suicide.

At Rome, Seneca had begun his career as an orator and held his first political office under Tiberius in 33. However, the emperor Caligula disliked Seneca and sneered that his speeches were only "copy-book exercises" and "sand without lime." According to gossip, the tyrant planned to execute Seneca, but a court lady persuaded Caligula that the orator would soon die of consumption. Giving up oratory as too dangerous, Seneca devoted himself to writing essays and tragedies. Filled with descriptions of horror and agony, his dramas would later inspire the Elizabethan Tragedy of Blood. However, unlike "The Duchess of Malfi" and "Titus Andronicus," the plays of Seneca were designed for recitation only and were not performed on a stage. In 41, under the emperor Claudius, a real tragedy befell Seneca. To advance his career, the Spaniard became too friendly with Claudius' nieces, Julia and Agrippina the Younger, who enjoyed the emperor's favor.* However, Claudius' beautiful wife Messallina was jealous of Julia and soon arranged her downfall and death. The fall of Julia was disastrous for Seneca, who was exiled to Corsica on a charge of adultery with the princess.

On the dismal island of Corsica, Seneca spent eight years in boredom and despair. To console his mother Helvia, the philosopher wrote brave sentiments:

How little it is that we have lost! Wherever we betake ourselves, two things that are most admirable will go with us—universal Nature and our own virtue. Believe me, this was the intention of the great creator of the universe, whoever he may be, whether an all-powerful God, or

---

*Earlier the princesses had plotted against their brother Caligula and had been imprisoned for treason, but Claudius released them and was especially fond of Julia.

incorporeal Reason contriving vast works, or divine Spirit pervading all things from the smallest to the greatest with uniform energy, or Fate and an unalterable sequence of causes clinging one to the other —this, I say, was his intention, that only the most worthless of our possessions should fall under the control of another. All that is best for a man lies beyond the power of other men, who can neither give it nor take it away. This firmament, than which Nature has created naught greater and more beautiful, and the most glorious part of it, the human mind that surveys and wonders at the firmament, are our own everlasting possessions, destined to remain with us so long as we ourselves shall remain. Eager, therefore, and erect, let us hasten with dauntless step wherever circumstance directs, let us traverse any lands whatsoever. Inside the world there can be found no place of exile, for nothing that is inside the world is foreign to mankind.[9]

Despite his noble words, Seneca found exile unendurable and wrote cringing appeals to Claudius' freedman Polybius, lauding the merits of the emperor and his henchmen. Nevertheless, his pleas for mercy went unheeded and Seneca found himself a middle-aged failure expecting to die in exile.

Unknown to Seneca, events in Rome would soon bring about a change in his fortune. Though she had borne Claudius a son, Britannicus, and a daughter, Octavia, Messallina was often unfaithful to the emperor. Exasperated by her flagrant behavior, Claudius was persuaded by his administrative assistant Narcissus to order the execution of Messallina. Though Narcissus had another candidate to replace Messallina, the finance minister Pallas backed Agrippina the Younger, who was Claudius' niece. Unlike Messallina, Agrippina was not a stunning beauty, but she captivated Claudius and became his empress in 49. A calculating and ambitious woman, she had only one passion, the pursuit of power. The historian Tacitus has drawn a skillful portrait of Agrippina:

From this moment the country was transformed. Complete obedience was accorded to a woman—and not a woman like Messallina who toyed with national affairs to satisfy her appetites. This was a rigorous, almost masculine despotism. In public, Agrippina was austere and often arrogant. Her private life was chaste—unless power was to be gained. Her passion to acquire money was unbounded. She wanted it as a stepping-stone to supremacy.[10]

Agrippina
the Younger

The new empress planned that Claudius would be succeeded by
her son Nero, whose dead father Ahenobarbus had been an
incompetent brute from an illustrious family.* Remembering her
old friend Seneca, Agrippina brought the philosopher back from
exile and appointed him Nero's tutor. Though he gave the boy an
excellent education, Seneca still found time for court intrigue.
By 52 his brother Gallio was a governor in Greece and on one
occasion listened with indifference to a complaint against Paul.

Though Claudius was fond of his son Britannicus, Agrippina
persuaded the emperor to adopt Nero as his heir. To insure
harmony in the imperial family, Nero was married to his step-
sister Octavia. The empress gained further strength when her
friend, Sextus Afranius Burrus, became Praetorian prefect. A
battle-scarred officer from Gaul, Burrus won the respect of the
Praetorian guards and had many friends in the army high
command. When Claudius tired of his wife's nagging demands
and began to favor Britannicus, Agrippina formed a cabal with

*Through both Ahenobarbus and Agrippina, Nero was descended from
Mark Antony and Octavia, the sister of Augustus. Agrippina also had the
blood of the divine Augustus.

Seneca and Burrus to remove the emperor.* Agrippina served
Claudius a dish of poisoned mushrooms, but the emperor vomited
the potion and had to be dispatched with an enema of deadly
colocynth. Nero easily succeeded to the throne, and Rome was
in the hands of Agrippina and her clique. Though the new
regime deified Claudius, Seneca wrote a vicious lampoon on the
late emperor, who had exiled him to Corsica. Disparaging
Claudius' achievements and mocking his apotheosis through
colocynth, Seneca's *Apocolocyntosis* showed that the Stoic philosopher could be petty and vengeful.

In 54 the Roman throne was held by a polite, handsome
adolescent who had blond hair and blue eyes. Trained by
Seneca to appreciate Greek literature, Nero had a good voice and
was fond of the theater. Though he was only seventeen years
old, the new ruler could rely on his shrewd mother, his wise
tutor, and the loyal prefect of the Praetorians. Seneca composed
Nero's inaugural address, which promised a reign of moderation
and clemency on the Augustan model. When Burrus presented
him with his first order of execution, the young emperor sighed
that he wished he had never learned how to write. However, his
mother was not so squeamish. On the grounds that he had
plundered the treasury, Agrippina deposed her old enemy
Narcissus and demanded his death. All of Claudius' freedmen
had enriched themselves at public expense, but the emperor had
ignored their graft because the efficiency of his aides had more
than compensated for their peculations. Not satisfied with the
death of Narcissus, Agrippina planned to purge others at the
court. But the dowager empress ran into unexpected opposition
from Seneca and Burrus, as Tacitus reports:

These two men, with a unanimity rare among partners in power, were,
by different methods, equally influential. Burrus' influence lay in
soldierly efficiency and seriousness of character, Seneca's in amiable
high principles and his tuition of Nero in public speaking. They col-
laborated in controlling the emperor's perilous adolescence; their
policy was to direct his deviations from virtue into licensed indul-
gences. Against Agrippina's violence inflamed by all the passions of
ill-gotten tyranny, they united.[11]

*For Seneca's complicity in the plot, see Appendix One.

At first, Agrippina had the support of Pallas, but the wily freedman soon realized that power had shifted to the opposition.
Having amassed a huge fortune, Pallas retired to private life and
escaped the fierce struggle in the palace. To keep Nero dis-
tracted, Seneca provided the young emperor with a beautiful
slave girl, Acte, who could not hope to be more than a mistress.
Delighted with Acte, Nero ignored his wife Octavia, whose
humiliation was ridiculed by the court. Thwarted at every turn,
Agrippina raged at Seneca and Burrus and tried to play Britannicus against Nero. In her fury, she threatened to appeal to the
Praetorian guards: "Let them listen to Germanicus' daughter
pitted against the men who claim to rule the whole human race—
the cripple Burrus with his maimed hand, and Seneca the
deportee with the professorial voice!"[12] In 55 Nero had Britannicus poisoned and hinted that his mother would suffer the same
fate if she did not retire from politics.

Though Nero had shown a capacity for violence, Seneca and
Burrus believed that they could still control the young emperor.
While they managed the government, Nero spent his time with
Acte, composed poetry, and sang in the theater. Old-fashioned
Romans disapproved of actors, but Nero yearned for acclaim and
his performances amused the mob. Under Seneca's administration, the empire ran smoothly and considerable profits went into
the pocket of the Spanish prime minister. Though his writings
deplored avarice and high interest rates, Seneca had a flair for
finance as did his brother Mela. Like most Roman officials, the
prime minister peddled political influence and dabbled in various
enterprises. Near Rome, he purchased vineyards at high prices
and sold them at a profit. "What branch of learning," a critic
snorted, "what philosophical school, won Seneca 300,000,000
sesterces during four years of imperial friendship? In Rome, he
entices into his snares the childless and their legacies. His huge
rates of interest suck Italy and the provinces dry."[13] According to
his enemies, Seneca forced loans on British tribes and brought on
a rebellion when he called in the debts. In 58 Nero considered
abolishing indirect taxes, for Seneca had managed the imperial
budget with great skill. Though the tax reform did not take place,
the Roman empire was never run so well as during the first five
years of Nero's reign. At least, such was the verdict of the

Spanish emperor Trajan on the period when the Spaniard Seneca dominated Nero.*

For his political ideal, Seneca looked back to the time of Augustus and praised Marcus Agrippa as "the only man who rose to fame and power in the civil wars and really succeeded as a statesman. Agrippa used to say that he had learned a lot from the proverb, 'Harmony expands small things and discord shrinks great ones.' "[14] Unfortunately, Seneca lacked Agrippa's strength of character and could not cope with Nero's outbursts of violence. Seneca's personal formula for political success was compliance and duplicity:

Reflect on the things which goad man into destroying man; you will find that they are hope, envy, hatred, fear, and contempt. Now, of all these, contempt is the least harmful, so much so that many have skulked behind it as a sort of cure. When a man despises you, he works you injury, to be sure, but he passes on; and no one persistently or of set purpose does hurt to a person whom he despises. . . . You can avoid the envious hopes of the wicked so long as you have nothing which can stir the evil desires of others, and so long as you possess nothing remarkable. . . . You will escape envy if you do not force yourself upon the public view, if you do not boast your possessions, if you understand how to enjoy things privately. Hatred comes either from running foul of others: and this can be avoided by never provoking anyone; or else it is uncalled for: and common sense will keep you safe from it. Yet, it has been dangerous to many; some people have been hated without having had an enemy. As to not being feared, a moderate fortune and an easy disposition will guarantee you that; men should know that you are the sort of person who can be offended without danger, and your reconciliation should be easy and sure. Moreover, it is as troublesome to be feared at home as abroad; it is as bad to be feared by a slave as by a gentleman. . . . Contempt remains to be discussed. He who has made this quality an adjunct of his own personality, who is despised because he wishes to be despised and not because he *must* be despised, has the measure of contempt under his control. Any inconveniences in this respect can be dispelled by honorable occupations and by friendships with men who have influence with an influential person; with these men it will profit you to

---

*Perhaps Trajan only meant to praise Nero's building activity at Rome. The remark is quoted by Sextus Aurelius Victor, *de Caesaribus* 5:2.

Nero

engage but not to entangle yourself, lest the cure may cost you more than the risk. Nothing, however, will help you so much as keeping still—talking very little with others and as much as may be with yourself.[15]

Such sentiments befitted a Uriah Heep but proved fatal in Nero's prime minister.

To keep pace with the young emperor, Seneca had to be both agile and wary. When Nero fell in love with the haughty and beautiful Poppaea Sabina, Seneca suggested that her husband Otho would be happier as governor of Lusitania. The emperor agreed and Otho departed for his distant post, leaving Poppaea behind in Rome. Nero's running quarrel with his mother was not resolved as amiably, for Agrippina now posed as the champion of his neglected wife Octavia. Despite the efforts of Seneca and Burrus to restrain him, the emperor had Agrippina murdered in 59. Though her death was no loss to Rome, Nero was guilty of matricide. To soothe public opinion, Seneca composed a defense of the crime which Nero delivered before the Senate. However, Seneca was criticized in many quarters as an apologist for murder. After Agrippina's death, her guilt-ridden son sought

distraction in dissolute amusements, but the extent of his misbehavior was exaggerated by salacious gossip. Physically, the
dissipated ruler became fat and flabby. Though he indulged in
private orgies, Nero still bored the court with his musical
recitals, and more than one politician ruined his career by falling
asleep while the emperor was performing. The major flaw in
Nero was a growing taste for blood, which Seneca had failed to
curb. The emperor readily purged senators whose loyalty was
in doubt. In 62 the stalwart Burrus died, supposedly poisoned by
Nero, and was succeeded as Praetorian prefect by the vicious
Ofonius Tigellinus, who encouraged the emperor to more crimes.
Without Burrus, Seneca was defenseless and isolated. Claiming
that illness and old age incapacitated him from further service to
the state, Seneca presented most of his wealth to Nero and retired
to private life. The emperor politely accepted Seneca's resigna-
tion and took up more pressing matters, the divorce and murder
of Octavia and a quick marriage to Poppaea. After the great fire
of 64, Nero rebuilt the burned areas of Rome with wide streets,
stone buildings, and mandatory cisterns for fire-fighting. However,
his cruel treatment of the Christians, whom he blamed for the
fire, offended public opinion in the capital.

In retirement, Seneca returned to intellectual pursuits and
wrote a moralistic handbook on natural history. On scientific
matters, Seneca was often inaccurate, for he relied on research
assistants who were not always competent. Like many moderns,
he believed in scientific progress: "The people of the coming
generation will know much that we do not know; much is
reserved for ages which will have forgotten our names. The
world is a tiny thing, except that it contains questions enough
for all the world."[16] Fretting in retirement, Seneca could not
overcome his desire to meddle in politics:

Although people may often have thought that I sought seclusion
because I was disgusted with politics and regretted my hapless and
thankless position, yet, in the retreat to which apprehension and
weariness have driven me, my ambition sometimes develops afresh.
For it is not because my ambition was rooted out that it has abated,
but because it was wearied or perhaps even put out of temper by the
failure of its plans.[17]

Fearing that the erratic Nero might poison him, Seneca confined his diet to fresh fruit and spring water.

By 65 Nero's purges of suspected senators had spread fear among the Roman aristocracy. A makeshift conspiracy was formed to replace Nero with an incompetent noble, C. Calpurnius Piso, but the plot was betrayed and the emperor executed everyone suspected of complicity. Apparently, Seneca had given moral support to the Piso clique, for Nero ordered his former tutor to commit suicide. True to form, Seneca posed before his friends as a Roman Socrates and told them to remember his splendid life of virtue. The historian Tacitus dismissed the public scene as humbug and described Seneca's final hours with vivid reality:

Seneca embraced his wife and, with a tenderness very different from his philosophical imperturbability, entreated her to moderate and set a term to her grief and take just consolation in her bereavement from contemplating his well-spent life. Nevertheless, she insisted on dying with him and demanded the executioner's stroke. Seneca did not oppose her brave decision. Indeed, loving her wholeheartedly, he was reluctant to leave her for ill treatment. "Solace in life was what I commended to you," he said. "But you prefer death and glory. I will not grudge your setting so fine an example. We can die with equal fortitude. But yours will be the nobler end." Then, each with one incision of the blade, he and his wife cut their arms. But Seneca's aged body, lean from austere living, released the blood too slowly. So he also severed the veins in his ankles and behind his knees. Exhausted by severe pain, he was afraid of weakening his wife's endurance by betraying his agony—or of losing his own self-possession at the sight of her sufferings. So he asked her to go into another bedroom. But even in his last moments, his eloquence remained. Summoning secretaries, he dictated a dissertation. . . .

However, his brave wife Paulina was not allowed to share death with her martyred husband:

Nero did not dislike Paulina personally. In order, therefore, to avoid increasing his ill repute for cruelty, he ordered her suicide to be averted. So, on instructions from the soldiers, slaves and ex-slaves bandaged her arms and stopped the bleeding. She may have been unconscious. . . . She lived on for a few years, honorably loyal to her husband's memory, with pallid features and limbs which showed how

much vital blood she had lost. Meanwhile, Seneca's death was slow
and lingering. Poison, such as was formerly used to execute state
criminals at Athens, had long been prepared; and Seneca now entreated his well-tried doctor, who was also an old friend, to supply it.
But when it came, Seneca drank it without effect. For his limbs were
already cold and numbed against the poison's action. Finally he was
placed in a bath of warm water. He sprinkled a little of it on the
attendant slaves, commenting that this was his libation to Jupiter.
Then he was carried into a vapor-bath where he suffocated. His cre-
mation was without ceremony, in accordance with his own instructions
about his death—written at the height of his wealth and power.[18]

After a life of sham and compromise, Seneca died well. However,
his nephew Lucan, who too had been involved in the Piso affair,
met death with dishonor, for he denounced his innocent mother
in hopes of winning Nero's pardon. Lucan's father Mela had
avoided active politics but also perished in the Piso debacle, and
even Gallio was dragged down in the purges. After years of
success and wealth, the Seneca brothers died by violence far from
Spain.

Except for its sensational aspects, Seneca's career was representative of a major development in Roman history, the prominence of provincials in the intellectual and political life of the
capital. However, the personal life of Seneca was a moral tragedy
of noble words mocked by ignoble deeds. While Stoics were often
prigs, they were not supposed to be scheming opportunists, as
was Seneca. Nietzsche called him the "toreador of virtue," and
Seneca received similar criticism in his own lifetime. With his
usual frankness, Seneca anticipated the charges which posterity
would level against him:

If, therefore, any of those who bark against philosophy, should ask
the usual thing: "Why then do you talk so much more bravely than you
live? Why do you speak humbly in the presence of a superior and
deem money a necessary equipment, and why are you moved by a
loss, and why do you shed tears on hearing of the death of your wife
or a friend, and why do you have regard for your reputation and let
slander affect you? Why do you till broader acres than your natural need
requires? Why do your dinners not conform to your own teaching?
Why do you have such elegant furniture? Why is the wine that is
drunk at your table older than you are yourself? Why this show of an

aviary? Why do you plant trees that will supply nothing but shade? Why does your wife wear in her ears the revenue of a rich house? Why are your young slaves dressed in costly stuffs? Why is it an art to attend at your table and instead of the plate being set out carelessly and as you please, why is there expertness of service, and why to carve your meat is there a professional?" Add, too, if you like: "Why do you have domains across the sea? Why more than you have seen? And shame to you!—you are either so careless that you do not know your handful of slaves by sight, or so pampered that you have more than your memory can recall to your knowledge!" Later I shall outdo your reproaches and bestow on myself more blame than you think of; for the moment I shall make this reply: "I am not a wise man, nor—to feed your malevolence!—shall I ever be. And so require not from me that I should be equal to the best, but that I should be better than the wicked. It is enough for me if every day I reduce the number of my vices, and blame my mistakes.[19]

Unfortunately, Seneca's apology was incomplete and lame.

The Spanish Stoic cannot be blamed for turning out a bad pupil in Nero, for Socrates failed with Alcibiades and Aristotle had questionable success with Alexander. However, Seneca set Nero an excellent example of duplicity and self-interest and encouraged the vices of the young ruler in order to keep power in his own hands. To advance his career, Seneca had committed adultery with Julia and condoned the murder of Claudius. It was an easy step to pander to Nero and justify the death of Agrippina. An attentive pupil, Nero became an intellectual dabbler and a completely immoral man. Compromise was the least of Seneca's sins, and many of his deeds were motivated solely by a blind will to power. Since few moral problems are simple choices between right and wrong, the moral flexibility of Seneca was preferable to the doctrinaire fanaticism of a Calvin or a Robespierre. Nevertheless, a man cannot put on and take off morality as he would a coat. A Christian contemporary of Seneca realized that words without works are hollow: "So with faith; if it does not lead to action, it is in itself a lifeless thing."[20] Centuries earlier, Socrates had demonstrated that morality was not a matter of eloquent words but of difficult actions.

SIX

The Jew—Josephus

IN 61 a young Jewish priest, Josephus, visited Nero's Rome on a diplomatic mission. On some obscure charge, a group of Jewish clergy had been sent by the governor of Palestine to be tried by the emperor at Rome. Josephus hoped to intercede on behalf of the prisoners who tried to observe a Mosaic diet and were subsisting on fruits and nuts. Though shipwrecked like Paul on his way to Rome, Josephus eventually reached the capital and contacted a Jewish actor who had excellent connections in the palace. Through the actor, the young clergyman met the empress Poppaea, who was sympathetic to Judaism. Won over by Josephus' pleas, Poppaea persuaded Nero to release the priests. Enriched with gifts from the empress, Josephus returned to Palestine, where a major revolt had broken out. Forced to choose between Rome and the rebels, Josephus vacillated and served briefly with the rebels but finally supported the Romans. Uncomfortable in postwar Palestine, Josephus returned to Rome and began a distinguished career as a historian. To many modern Jews, Josephus was a renegade, and historians of other faiths often criticize his flexible character. However, the Jewish priest was a complex man in a troubled time.

Born in Palestine in 37, Josephus was the son of a wealthy priest. Through his mother he was descended from the royal Hasmoneans and could anticipate a profitable career in the clergy. In later life Josephus boasted that he had been a precocious student who astounded his elders—at any rate, he was bright and well-read. In adolescence he experienced the religious stirring which excites many sensitive children and often leads to hasty conversions. Josephus could choose between three major

Jewish sects, the Sadducees, Pharisees, and Essenes. Conservative in politics and religion, the Sadducees rejected such newfangled notions as angels and immortality. Their rivals, the Pharisees, believed in an afterlife and rigorous observance of both the Law and tradition. The smallest sect, the Essenes, were extreme Pharisees who practiced ascetic communism in desert monasteries. Though priests tended to be Sadducees, Josephus investigated each of the sects and became a disciple of a hermit who lived in the wilderness, dressed in bark, and ate roots and berries. Tiring of asceticism at the age of nineteen, Josephus returned to the comforts of the priesthood but embraced the doctrines of the Pharisees. Though Jesus mocked their excessive literalism, the Pharisees encouraged education and permitted considerable latitude in thought—the liberal rabbis Hillel and Gamaliel were Pharisees. According to Josephus, the Sadducees were haughty and quarrelsome, but the Pharisees bickered less and were more respected by the public. Since the aristocracy favored the priestly Sadducees and the masses supported the Pharisees, the behavior of the two religious factions often reflected class attitudes. Both priest and Pharisee, young Josephus was a Whig in a Tory profession.

In the time of Josephus, Palestine was in turmoil. When Herod Agrippa died in 44, his realm reverted to provincial status and his son Agrippa II received a tiny domain in the north of Palestine. Jewish nationalists were deeply disappointed that Judea had ceased to be a client kingdom, and the return of Roman tax collectors brought complaints from all quarters. The Jewish poor saw the Romans as money-grubbing alien oppressors, a nation of Shylocks, whose overthrow would somehow solve all economic problems.* Since the wealthy classes in Judea supported Rome as the protector of property and order, popular hatred of landowners and merchants fed the flames of nationalist agitation against Roman rule. Despite bitter memories of Hasmonean and Herodian despotism, Jewish nationalism had considerable appeal, and self-appointed Messiahs periodically disrupted public

---

*Similar images have been used by European and American politicians to inflame urban masses and rural poor against a remote and sinister money power supposedly made up of Jewish bankers.

order in Palestine. However, Diaspora Jews were generally indifferent to Messianic pretenders, and the Palestinian rebels would receive little support from Jewish communities overseas. In Palestine nationalist agitators exploited popular resentment against Roman governors who tried to maintain order in the unruly province. Most governors of Judea were incompetent, some were brutal, and none were successful—least of all Philo's nephew Tiberius Alexander, who was an apostate from Judaism. Religion always adds a dangerous dimension to politics, for religious sanctions are invoked to explain political actions and excuse indiscriminate plunderings. In Judea extreme nationalists became terrorists and justified the murder of their rivals as the execution of collaborators. Like the Ku Klux Klan, the Jewish terrorists claimed to defend God and virtue, hated all foreigners, and insisted that an oppressive government had driven them to violence. Most Sadducees and many Pharisees opposed the nationalists, and all moderates deplored the acts of the terrorists.

As a priest and a property owner, Josephus had no objection to Roman rule, and he loathed the terrorists:

When the countryside had been cleared of bandits, another type sprang up in Jerusalem, known as *sicarii* ["knife-men"]. These in broad daylight and in the middle of the city committed numerous murders. Their favorite trick was to mingle with festival crowds, concealing under their garments small daggers with which they stabbed their opponents. When their victims fell, the assassins melted into the indignant crowd and through their plausibility entirely defied detection. First to have his throat cut by them was Jonathan the High Priest, and after him many were murdered every day. More terrible than the crimes themselves was the fear they aroused, every man as in war hourly expecting death. They watched at a distance for their enemies, and not even when their friends came near, did they trust them. Yet, in spite of their suspicions and precautions, they were done to death; such was the suddenness of the conspirators' attack and their skill in avoiding detection.[1]

Frustrated factions frequently turn to violence and degrade the idealistic slogans which they invoke to justify murder and mutilation. Even against Tsarist or Nazi oppression, the motives of resistance fighters were a mixture of noble ideals and personal drives. In the national revolutions of the twentieth century, violence has often been employed for elusive aims. Albert Camus warned the Muslim terrorists in Algeria:

If it is true that in history, at least, values—whether those of the nation or those of humanity—do not survive unless they have been fought for, the fight is not enough to justify them. The fight itself must rather be justified and elucidated by those values. When fighting for your truth, you must take care not to kill it with the very arms you are using to defend it.[2]

Regardless of high-sounding sanctions, terror too often ceases to be a means and becomes an end in itself.

In Josephus' Palestine, religion was a burning issue and hopelessly entangled in politics:

There was formed another group of scoundrels, in act less criminal but in intention more evil, who did as much damage as the murderers to the well-being of the city. Cheats and deceivers claiming inspiration, they schemed to bring about revolutionary changes by inducing the mob to act as if possessed, and by leading them out into the wild country on the pretence that there God would show them signs of approaching freedom. Thereupon, Felix, regarding this as the first stage of revolt, sent cavalry and heavy infantry who cut the mob to pieces. [The governor Felix used the same severity against the followers of an Egyptian prophet.]. . . When this fever too had died down, another festering sore appeared in the body politic. The religious frauds and bandit chiefs joined forces and drove numbers to revolt, inciting them to strike a blow for freedom and threatening with death those who submitted to Roman rule; men who willingly chose slavery would be forcibly freed. Then splitting up into groups, they ranged over the countryside, plundering the houses of the well-to-do, killing the occupants, and setting fire to the villages, till their raging madness penetrated every corner of Judea. Day by day, the fighting blazed more fiercely.[3]

As a spokesman for the propertied classes, Josephus denied any sincerity on the part of the rebels. However, the rationale of the Judean rebels was the same blend of social protest and bigotry which has sparked pogroms of Jews in Christendom for the last 1,500 years.

In 66 the governor of Judea was the headstrong Florus, who could not cope with the degenerating situation. In the person of Florus, obstinate Roman brutality clashed head on with inflexible Jewish fanaticism. The venal governor plundered the province and encouraged pagans to attack Jews. Unlike Florus, the governor of Syria Gallus was a reasonable man and tried in vain to restrain his colleague in Judea. Even Tacitus, who disliked Jews, admitted that Florus' regime was unendurable. A quarrel between Jews and pagans at Caesarea gave the governor an excuse to move troops into Jerusalem, where he extorted funds from the Temple treasury. When an irreverent mob ridiculed him, the angry Florus ignored the apologies of Jewish leaders and ordered his troops to pillage and kill in Jerusalem. Crowning the atrocities, he crucified some prominent Jews who held Roman citizenship. By chance, Queen Berenice was in the city and vainly begged Florus to spare the people of Jerusalem. When the populace began to resist his troops, Florus evacuated the city and retreated to Caesarea. Agrippa II, who often acted as an intermediary between the Jews and Rome, hurried to Jerusalem and together with Berenice tried to calm the crowds. Realizing that the rioting was turning into a revolt, Agrippa advised the Jews that Florus would be removed as soon as the emperor learned of his misdeeds. However, Agrippa warned, if the Jews continued to resist, the Romans would surely crush them.

The substance of Agrippa's cautionary speech at Jerusalem has been preserved by Josephus:

Look at the far-flung empire of Rome and contrast your own impotence. Why, our forces have been worsted even by our neighbors again and again, while their arms have triumphed over the whole world! And even the world is not big enough to satisfy them. Euphrates is not far enough to the east, or Danube to the north, or Libya and the desert beyond to the south, or Cadiz to the west; but beyond the ocean, they have sought a new world, carrying their arms as far as Britain, that land of mystery. Why not face facts? Are you richer than the Gauls, stronger than the Germans, cleverer than the Greeks, more numerous than all the nations of the world? What gives you confidence to defy the power of Rome?[4]

The Herodian king also warned that the Parthians and the Arabs
would not come to the aid of the Jews:

So there is no refuge left except to make God your ally. But he too is
ranged on the Roman side, for without his help so vast an empire
could never have been built up. Think too how difficult it would be,
even if you were fighting feeble opponents, to preserve the purity of
your religion, and how you will be forced to transgress the very laws
which furnish your chief hope of making God your ally, and so will
alienate him. If you observe the custom of the Sabbath with its complete cessation of activity, you will promptly be crushed, as were your
ancestors by Pompey who was most active in pressing the siege on
the days when the besieged were passive. But, if in the war you
transgress your ancestral Law, I don't see what you have left to fight
for, since your one desire is that none of your ancestral customs should
be broken. . . . It is wise, while the vessel is still in harbor, to foresee
the approaching storm and not to sail out into the middle of the hur-
ricane to sure destruction. For those on whom disaster falls out of the
blue are at least entitled to pity, but a man who plunges into destruction with his eyes open earns only contempt. Possibly, some of you
suppose that you are making war in accordance with agreed rules, and
that when the Romans have won, they will be kind to you and will
not think of making you an example to other nations by burning down
your holy city and destroying your entire race. I tell you, not even if
you survive will you find a place of refuge, since every people recog-
nizes the lordship of Rome or fears that it will have to do so. Again,
the danger threatens not only ourselves here but also those who live
in other cities, for there is not a region in the world without its Jewish
colony. All these, if you go to war, will be massacred by your opponents, and through the folly of a few men, every city will run with
Jewish blood.[5]

Unconvinced by Agrippa's speech, the nationalists retained control of Jerusalem and declared their independence by halting the
sacrifices for the emperor in the Temple. As Agrippa and Berenice
withdrew from the insurgent city, news came in of Jewish attacks
on gentiles and pagan massacres of Jews in Syria and Egypt.

Sure that Judea had gone made, Josephus took refuge in the
Temple with the chief priests and leading Pharisees. The worried
Jewish leaders awaited a relief column from the governor of Syria,
but Gallus was unexpectedly defeated and the Jewish revolt

gathered momentum from its first victory. The ruling class now had to choose between the insurgents and Rome, and many prominent Jews abandoned their property to the rebels and fled to the protection of Agrippa. While some stayed in Judea and tried to remain neutral, other Jewish leaders hoped to reduce plundering and violence by accepting positions of authority with the rebel government. Hoping to keep the revolt within bounds, Josephus joined the insurgents and expected that Rome would soon solve his dilemma. When the Sanhedrin sent him to assume control of Galilee, Josephus found his authority challenged by the local partisan leaders. Suspected by extremists and distrusted by moderates, the wily priest tried to win the confidence of the insurgents and was dragged deeper into the rebel cause. Putting aside his earlier misgivings, Josephus emerged as a minor rebel general, but he also made enemies among the Galilean partisans, who would have long memories.

Early in 67 the situation in Galilee shifted against the rebels, for Nero had appointed Vespasian to put down the Jewish revolt. A middle-aged general, T. Flavius Vespasianus had served with distinction under Claudius, and his career had been backed by the freedman Narcissus. Though Agrippina disliked Vespasian, Nero employed the old soldier until he tactlessly fell asleep during one of the emperor's recitals. The outbreak of the war in Judea revived the fortunes of Vespasian, who was an able and careful commander. His strategy was simple and effective—the rebels were to be driven from the countryside and herded into Jerusalem, where congestion and famine would force a quick surrender of the city. When Vespasian routed the rebel bands from Galilee, Josephus and his men were besieged in the fortress of Jotapata. By July the Romans took the stronghold, but Josephus and forty soldiers held out in a cave. A Jewish officer who had gone over to the Romans tried to persuade the men in the cave to surrender. Josephus needed little persuading, for he was convinced that their situation was untenable:

The memory came to him of those dreams in the night by which God had forewarned him both of the calamities coming to the Jews and of the fortunes of the Roman emperors. Moreover, in the matter of interpreting dreams, he was capable of divining the meaning of equivocal utterances of the Deity. He was familiar with the prophecies of Holy Scripture, being a priest himself and the descendant of priests. At this very moment, he was inspired to understand them, and seizing on the terrifying images of his recent dreams, he sent up a secret prayer to God: "Inasmuch as it pleaseth Thee to visit Thy wrath on the Jewish people whom Thou didst create, and all prosperity hath passed to the Romans, and because Thou didst choose my spirit to make known the things to come, I yield myself willingly to the Romans that I may live, but I solemnly declare that I go, not as a traitor, but as Thy servant."[6]

Apparently, the companions of Josephus were not prone to anxiety dreams, for they had no intention of surrendering and threatened to kill Josephus on the spot.

Faced with death in the crowded cave, the crafty priest saved himself with characteristic ruse:

In this predicament, his resourcefulness did not fail him. Putting his trust in divine protection, he staked his life on one last throw. "You have chosen to die," he exclaimed, "well then, let's draw lots and kill each other in turn. Whoever draws the first lot shall be dispatched by number two, and so on down the whole line as luck decides. In this way, no one will die by his own hand—it would be unfair when the rest were gone if one man changed his mind and saved his life." The audience swallowed the bait, and getting his way Josephus drew lots with the rest. Without hesitation, each man in turn offered his throat for the next man to cut in the belief that a moment later his commander would die too. Life was sweet but not so sweet as death if Josephus died with them! But Josephus—shall we put it down to divine providence or just to luck?—was left with one other man. He did not relish the thought either of being condemned by the lot or, if he was left till last, of staining his hand with the blood of a fellow Jew. So he used persuasion, they made a pact, and both remained alive.[7]

While many men have had to accept an unpleasant reality and surrender in war, Josephus' convenient lots have raised many an eyebrow. However, the patriarch Jacob had been a trickster, and his son Joseph the Dreamer was a shrewd opportunist who prospered in the service of a foreign prince. Perhaps Josephus saw himself as another Joseph.

Though a prisoner of war, Josephus' luck held. He knew that the Romans had heard Messianic prophecies that a world ruler

would begin his reign in Palestine, and in his dreams Josephus had
seen Vespasian in that role. Dragged before the Roman commander, the wily priest played his trump card and hailed Vespasian
as emperor. Later, Josephus recalled: "At the time, Vespasian
seemed unwilling to take these suggestions seriously, assuming that
Josephus was lying to save his skin. But, gradually he became
convinced, for God was already awakening in him imperial
ambitions."[8] Though still a prisoner, Josephus was treated leni-
ently and was allowed to marry a fellow captive, but the woman
soon left him. Meanwhile, events at Rome were about to confirm
Josephus' lucky prophecy. Suspecting a conspiracy among the
military, Nero had ordered a number of prominent generals to
commit suicide. During the emperor's purge of the senatorial
class, the armies had held aloof, but the legionary officers would
not tolerate an attack on their own leaders. In Gaul the governor
Vindex rose against Nero and was quickly suppressed, but the
governor of Spain, Galba, was more successful. Faced with the
threat of civil war, the Praetorian guards refused to fight for
Nero and declared for Galba, who was accepted by the Senate
as emperor. In June 68, the Senate deposed Nero and sentenced
him to death by torture. Fleeing to escape capture, the former
emperor despaired and killed himself, moaning, "What an artist
dies in me!" The devoted Acte buried Nero's body in his family
tomb. In January 69—the Year of the Four Emperors—the elderly
Galba occupied Rome but was soon slain and replaced by Otho,
the former husband of Poppaea. In April the emperor Otho committed suicide after being defeated by the army of a mutinous
general, Vitellius. An obese glutton, Vitellius made an unim-
pressive emperor. Unwilling to recognize Vitellius as ruler, the
legions in the East hailed their commander Vespasian as emperor.
Another Roman army in the Balkans declared for Vespasian, and
the days of Vitellius were numbered.

Now a prophet with honor, Josephus enjoyed the favor of
Vespasian and accompanied him to Egypt, where the emperor
seized the strategic province which supplied much of the grain
for the city of Rome. In Alexandria the Jewish priest married
again but soon returned to Palestine. While Vespasian held Egypt,
his military supporters in the Balkans marched on Rome to
unseat Vitellius. Within the capital, Vespasian's brother tried to

rally the masses to the Flavian cause, but Vitellius suppressed the uprising and Vespasian's son Domitian barely escaped with his life. During the disorders the great temple of Jupiter on the Capitol went up in flames. When the Flavian armies stormed the city late in 69, the wretched Vitellius was captured and tortured to death. In 70 the triumphant Vespasian arrived at Rome and began a memorable reign. In Gaul, the Druids had hailed the burning of the Capitol as an omen and proclaimed a holy war against Rome, but the Gallic revolt was quickly crushed. At Jerusalem, the Jewish rebels were also encouraged by news of the destruction of the Capitol, but their hopes proved as vain as the dreams of the Druids.

In Judea Josephus had joined the staff of Vespasian's son Titus, who was completing the siege of Jerusalem. The Roman forces were augmented by Jewish loyalists, and Titus' second-in-command was the ex-Jew Tiberius Alexander. Agrippa and Berenice were frequent visitors in the Roman camp, and Josephus often rode around the walls of Jerusalem, pleading with the defenders to surrender the city. Within Jerusalem the rebels had split into three fanatic factions which slaughtered each other without mercy and desecrated the Temple with bloodshed. The city had become a deathtrap where famine, disease, and occasional acts of cannibalism added to the horrors of the siege. Nevertheless, the defenders were confident of divine aid and refused to surrender Jerusalem. In the final stage of the siege, some Jews swallowed coins and fled from the doomed city but were killed by Arab troopers, who then disemboweled all refugees in hopes of finding money. To intimidate the rebels Titus ordered the crucifixion of prisoners who had been captured from raiding parties which ventured beyond the walls. Soon the city was surrounded by a forest of crosses on which hung the rotting corpses of captive rebels.

By summer of the year 70 the Romans had penetrated the walls of Jerusalem and slowly fought their way from house to house. The center of rebel resistance was at the Temple, where hysterical crowds expected a momentary miracle. In Hebrew legend, angelic aid had once saved Jerusalem from the Assyrian Sennacherib. Now, in the death throes of the Jewish nation, fanatics looked for armies of angels to descend from the sky and

smite the heathen. However, the hosts of heaven never arrived
and the Temple was stormed in August. In the chaos Roman
soldiers hurled firebrands into the sanctuary of the Temple,
although Titus wanted to spare the building and loot its treasures.
With graphic details, Josephus described the fall of the Temple:

As the legions charged in, neither persuasion nor threat could check
their impetuosity; passion alone was in command. Crowded together
round the entrances, many were trampled by their friends, many fell
among the still hot and smoking ruins of the colonnades and died as
miserably as the defeated. As they neared the sanctuary, they pretended not even to hear Caesar's commands and urged the men in
front to throw in more firebrands. The partisans were no longer in a
position to help; everywhere was slaughter and flight. Most of the
victims were peaceful citizens, weak and unarmed, butchered wherever
they were caught. Round the altar, the heap of corpses grew higher
and higher, while down the sanctuary steps poured a river of blood
and the bodies of those killed at the top slithered to the bottom. The
soldiers were like men possessed and there was no holding them, nor
was there any arguing with the fire. . . . While the sanctuary was
burning, looting went on right and left, and all who were caught
were put to the sword. There was no pity for age, no regard for rank;
little children and old men; laymen and priests alike were butchered;
every class was held in the iron embrace of war, whether they defended themselves or cried for mercy. Through the roar of the
flames as they swept relentlessly on, could be heard the groans of
the falling. Such were the height of the hill and the vastness of the
blazing edifice that the entire city seemed to be on fire, while as for
the noise, nothing could be imagined more shattering or more hor-
rifying. There was the war-cry of the Roman legions as they converged;
the yells of the partisans encircled with fire and sword; the panic
flight into the arms of the enemy of the people cut off above; their
shrieks as the end approached. The cries from the hill were answered
from the crowded streets; and now many who were wasted with
hunger and beyond speech, when they saw the sanctuary in flames,
found strength to moan and wail. Back from Peraea and the mountains
round about came the echo in a thunderous bass.[9]

Because a mad prophet had promised deliverance in the Temple,
many civilians died needlessly there in the flames. The Romans
carried off captured leaders to be executed at Rome, and

Vespasian

thousands of rebels would later die in gladiatorial games to honor the victors. As late as 73 a handful of *sicarii* held out at the fortress of Masada and committed suicide when faced with surrender. As a result of the revolt, much of Jerusalem was destroyed and the once prosperous province of Palestine was devastated.

The effects of the Jewish rebellion were far-reaching and traumatic for Judaism. With the loss of the Temple, the Sadducees disappeared from history and the Pharisees became the spiritual leaders of Jewry. Since the Torah had to replace the Temple as the focal point of Judaism, the content of the scriptures became a matter of extreme concern. At the rabbinical academy at Jamnia (Jabneh), scholars established the definitive canon of the Old Testament and discarded much Hellenistic Jewish literature as apocryphal. The revolt in Judea had done serious harm to the Jews of the Diaspora, whose loyalty was now questioned by the Romans. Since most pagans had only a vague knowledge of Judaic beliefs, Josephus set himself the task of explaining the Jews and their history to a suspicious pagan world. The Jewish historian was able to accomplish his aim because Vespasian was his patron.

The Flavian emperor Vespasian was a practical man with a deep sense of responsibility to his subjects. In his long career Vespasian had experienced personal defeats and financial reverses, and his sons had known poverty in their childhood. A middle-class Italian, the emperor favored Equites and provincials and encouraged the internationalization of the ruling class. Because of Nero's extravagance and the damages of the recent civil war, Vespasian took over an insolvent state, but through thrift and rigorous taxation soon built up a sizable treasury surplus. The Temple tax, which Jews had once sent to Jerusalem, now went into the imperial treasury. Despite his frugality, Vespasian rebuilt the Capitoline temple of Jupiter and began the construction of the Colosseum, which provided work for the urban poor at Rome. The realistic emperor scoffed at his pretentious predecessors and retained a lively sense of humor. When Titus complained that a tax on urinals was undignified, his father waved a coin under the prince's nose and assured him that money had no odor. Though he firmly put down conspiracies, Vespasian overlooked most criticism from the Senate. However, the irascible senator Helvidius Priscus pushed the emperor too far and was sentenced to death. A widower for years, Vespasian kept a concubine and did not remarry, for fear of causing dynastic strife. His sons, Titus and Domitian, were adults and the emperor insisted that the throne now belonged to the Flavian family— "The future will be my sons or anarchy." The older brother Titus was groomed as the imperial heir and assumed command of the Praetorian guards. During the war in Judea, Berenice had become Titus' mistress, although she was ten years his senior. When he returned to Rome to celebrate his eastern triumph, Titus brought along Berenice, her brother Agrippa, and Josephus. Though the Romans had given him an estate in Palestine, the priest was afraid to live in his homeland, exposed to the vengeance of irreconcilable rebels.

As a permanent resident of the capital, Josephus received Roman citizenship and a pension from Vespasian. Adopting the name Flavius Josephus, he frequented the court in the company of Agrippa. When Berenice offended the Roman public with her haughty behavior, gossips whispered that the Jewish princess was another Cleopatra, and Titus reluctantly sent her back to

Palestine. Secure in Vespasian's esteem, Josephus survived a libelous charge that he was involved in a Jewish disorder in Libya. The emperor displayed his confidence in the priest by adding to Josephus' properties in Judea. Less happy in his domestic life, Josephus divorced his second wife but kept custody of their son and soon married a rich Jewess from Crete. His third wife bore him two sons, one of whom was named after Agrippa. In postwar Palestine, Josephus had composed an Aramaic account of the Jewish revolt for the benefit of Semitic readers in Syria, the Arab buffer states, and the Parthian realm. As Flavian propaganda, the book displayed the Romans in the best light and depicted the Jewish rebels as desperate fanatics. At Rome Josephus revised his history of the Jewish war in a Greek edition aimed at pagan readers in the Roman empire. The historian added valuable material from the military memoirs of Vespasian and Titus and used literary assistants to polish his shaky Greek. As a Jewish apologist, Josephus now presented the Judean revolt as a national tragedy, the work of misguided zealots who brought a great people to ruin. Though he denied that the rebels had divine sanction, Josephus insisted on the heroism of the Jewish resistance fighters and emphasized the moral grandeur of his ancestral religion.

In his introduction to the *Jewish War,* Josephus explained the significance of the struggle:

The war of the Jews against the Romans was the greatest of our time; greater too, perhaps, than any recorded struggle whether between cities or nations. Yet, persons with no first-hand knowledge, accepting baseless and inconsistent stories on hearsay, have written garbled accounts of it; while those of eyewitnesses have been falsified either to flatter the Romans or to vilify the Jews, eulogy or abuse being substituted for factual record. . . . When it occurred, Rome herself was in a most unsettled state. Jewish revolutionaries took advantage of the general disturbance; they had vast resources of men and money; and so widespread was the ferment that some were filled with hope of gain, others with fear of loss, by the state of affairs in the East; for the Jews expected all their Mesopotamian brethren to join their insurrection. From another side, Roman supremacy was being challenged by the Gauls on their borders, and the Celts were restive —in fact, after Nero's death disorder reigned everywhere. Presented with this opportunity, many aspired to the imperial throne, while the soldiery were eager for a transference of power as a means of enriching themselves. . . . Were the Greeks and those Romans who took no part in it to remain ignorant of the facts, deluded with flattery or fiction? Yet, the writers I have in mind claim to be writing history, though beside getting all their facts wrong, they seem to me to miss their target altogether. For they wish to establish the greatness of the Romans while all the time disparaging and deriding the actions of the Jews. But I do not see how men can prove themselves great by overcoming feeble opponents! Again, they are not impressed by the length of the war, the vastness of the Roman forces which endured such hardships, and the genius of their commanders, whose strenuous endeavors before Jerusalem will bring them little glory if the difficulties they overcame are belittled. However, it is not my intention to counter the champions of the Romans by exaggerating the heroism of my own countrymen; I will state the facts accurately and impartially. At the same time, the language in which I record the events will reflect my own feelings and emotions, for I must permit myself to bewail my country's tragedy. She was destroyed by internal dissensions, and the Romans who so unwillingly set fire to the Temple were brought in by the Jews' self-appointed rulers, as Titus Caesar, the Temple's destroyer, has testified. For throughout the war, he pitied the common people who were helpless against the partisans; and over and over again, he delayed the capture of the city and prolonged the siege in the hope that the ringleaders would submit. . . . The misfortunes of all other races since the beginning of history, compared to those of the Jews, seem small; and for our misfortunes we have only ourselves to blame.[10]

While his history was pro-Flavian, Josephus' condemnation of the rebels followed the established theme of Hebrew historiography —political catastrophes were the result of Israel's straying from righteousness. Josephus also drew a glorified picture of himself as a rebel general, for he did not wish to reveal the equivocal role which he had actually played in Galilee. As a writer, he had the usual faults of a historian in antiquity—rhetorical descriptions, exaggerated statistics, and occasional inconsistencies. Awed by Roman victory, Josephus was in good company, for the great Hellenistic historian Polybius had also been a frank admirer of the invincible Romans.

In 79 the aged Vespasian died of fever. In his last moments he struggled to his feet to die standing, as emperors should. His son Titus succeeded him but ruled only briefly. Though he opened the Colosseum with elaborate games, the reign of Titus was marred by fires and plague at Rome and the destruction of Pompeii by the eruption of Mount Vesuvius. In 81 Titus died and was succeeded by his brother Domitian, who proved to be an able and effective administrator. Though Domitian later became harsh and oppressive, Josephus did not lose favor at court:

The treatment which I received from the emperors continued unaltered. On Vespasian's decease, Titus who succeeded to the empire showed the same esteem for me as did his father and never credited the accusations to which I was constantly subjected. Domitian succeeded Titus and added to my honors. He punished my Jewish accusers and for a similar offense, gave orders for the chastisement of a slave, a eunuch and my son's tutor. He also exempted my property in Judea from taxation—a mark of the highest honor to the privileged individual. Moreover, Domitia, Caesar's wife, never ceased conferring favors upon me. Such are the events of my whole life; from them, let others judge as they will of my character.[11]

With the aid of the Flavian emperors and other patrons,* Josephus continued his prolific writing career.

In his second major work Josephus summarized the history of Israel for pagan readers. Appearing in 94, his *Jewish Antiquities* was written to impress gentiles with the long history and moral grandeur of Judaism. Like modern popularizers, Josephus played down the miraculous element in the scriptures and relied on secular historians, Strabo and Nicolaus of Damascus, for material not found in the Old Testament. The Whiston translation of the *Jewish Antiquities* was once kept in many American homes next to the Bible, because an inept Christian forger had inserted a statement into the Greek text that Jesus was the Messiah and had risen from the dead.† However, the third-century Christian

---

*Josephus dedicated some of his later works to Epaphroditus, "a devoted lover of truth." The identity of this literary patron is unknown, for the powerful freedman Epaphroditus at Domitian's court was executed years before the appearance of these works.

†Similar additions in the Slavonic text of the *Jewish War* are even clumsier forgeries.

scholar Origen denied that the Jewish historian had ever held such beliefs. Josephus was quite aware that Christians existed, for he mentioned with disapproval the stoning of James. Though adding nothing to our knowledge of Christianity, Josephus filled in vital gaps in Roman history. Agrippa II informed him of the relations between Herod Agrippa and Claudius, and Vespasian's mistress Caenis had been Antonia's secretary and could recall the events which led to the fall of Sejanus. With these and other valuable contacts, Josephus became a major source for Roman history in the first century A.D.

Outliving Domitian, Josephus was still active at Rome in the early second century. Shortly after the death of Agrippa in 100 an old enemy from Galilee wrote a book in which he accused Josephus of complicity in the Jewish revolt. The historian responded with an autobiographical sketch which was largely a defense of his actions in Galilee. In his frank autobiography Josephus described his military career in less heroic terms than he had used in the *Jewish War*. The indignant old priest also cited Titus' endorsement of his historical work and quoted two of the sixty-two letters in which Agrippa had praised him. Josephus added the autobiography to the second Greek edition of the *Jewish Antiquities* which he had revised to treat Herod the Great more critically than he had done when his friend Agrippa II was alive. In his final work Josephus wrote a valuable essay against the Egyptian Apion, who had composed anti-Semitic tracts in the time of Caligula. With ease and zest the Jewish historian refuted Apion and other writers who misrepresented Jewish history.* According to Apion, Antiochus IV Epiphanes had rescued a prisoner whom the Jews were fattening for a ritual sacrifice:

The practice was repeated annually at a fixed season. They would kidnap a Greek foreigner, fatten him up for a year, and then convey him to a wood where they slew him, sacrificed his body with their

---

*In a digression, Josephus pointed out that the Greeks had no history before 500 B.C. and that even the greatest Hellenic historians were careless and contradictory. His perceptive comment on the late date of the Homeric poems prompted Friedrich Wolf to reopen the Homeric question in modern times.

customary ritual, partook of his flesh, and, while immolating the Greek, swore an oath of hostility to the Greeks.[12]

Josephus dryly asked why the Seleucid king did not parade the anonymous Greek, whom he had rescued, about his realm and stir up public opinion against the cannibalistic Jews. Despite Josephus' refutation, the myth of ritual murder by Jews would be revived many times and immortalized by Chaucer in "The Prioress' Tale."

At the conclusion of the essay against Apion, Josephus asked his readers to consider the Jewish laws:

A glance at them showed that they teach not impiety, but the most genuine piety; that they invite men not to hate their fellows, but to share their possessions; that they are the foes of injustice and scrupulous for justice, banish sloth and extravagance, and teach men to be self-dependent and to work with a will; that they deter them from war for the sake of conquest, but render them valiant defenders of the laws themselves; inexorable in punishment, not to be duped by studied words, always supported by actions. For actions are our invariable testimonials, plainer than any documents. I would therefore boldly maintain that we have introduced to the rest of the world a very large number of very beautiful ideas. What greater beauty than inviolable piety? What higher justice than obedience to the laws? What more beneficial than to be in harmony with one another, to be a prey neither to disunion in adversity, nor to arrogance and faction in prosperity; in war to despise death, in peace to devote oneself to crafts or agriculture; and to be convinced that everything in the whole universe is under the eye and direction of God?[13]

While not a Zionist, Josephus was also not a renegade, and his reasoned arguments did much to achieve understanding for Judaism in a suspicious pagan society.

After his death a statue of Josephus was erected at Rome. The Jews paid him no honors, but the historian deserved better of his countrymen, for his view of the revolt of 66–70 was clearly in Jewish tradition. While the riots against Florus were legitimate protests against oppression, the insurrection against Rome—the protector of Judaism—was quite another matter. Since the rebels invoked a religious sanction for their actions, Josephus felt that their defeat proved that God was not impressed by their claims.

Denouncing the factional warfare which polluted the Temple, the priest Josephus assumed the tone of an Old Testament prophet:

Unhappy city, what have you suffered from the Romans to compare with this? They entered your gates to purge with fire the filthiness within you. You were no longer the place of God. You could not continue, now that you were the burial-place of your own sons and had turned the Temple into a common grave for those who had slain each other. Even now you might be restored to life, if only you would make atonement to God who destroyed you![14]

This passage was not a turncoat's cant but the sincere opinion of a religious man. Despite his many frailties, Josephus was similar to the prophet Jeremiah who centuries earlier had suffered physical abuse and public opprobrium for opposing a revolt to free Jerusalem from the Babylonians. Like Josephus, Jeremiah had counseled submission to alien rule and clashed with rival prophets who were proven wrong by the outcome of events. Also like Josephus, Jeremiah was granted special favors by a grateful foreign power after Jerusalem had been sacked and the Temple lay in ruins. Though not a man of heroic character, Josephus was a sincere Jew and a major historian.

THE ROMAN EMPIRE
117 A.D.

SEVEN

The Wizard—Apollonius of Tyana

Ultimately, all roads in the empire led to Rome, and some were traveled by saints who were anxious to set the world right. Such a man was Apollonius of Tyana, who hoped to reform paganism but would be remembered chiefly as a wizard. In the Roman world there were always a few men who heard a "different drummer" and deserted society to seek their own salvations. On streetcorners at Rome ragged Cynic preachers damned conformity and called for a wholesale return to nature. Only slightly less anarchic were the Stoic individualists who even in the Senate harassed the emperors and praised the ideal of a Republic. The philosophic critics of Nero and Domitian were silenced by exile, prison, or death, and even the tolerant Vespasian banished abusive philosophers from the capital. However, men like Apollonius and Paul did not wish to alter the social order—they wanted to kindle a spiritual rebirth and bring humanity closer to God. While Paul preached a new gospel and denounced established creeds, Apollonius tried to reform the many cults of paganism and purify religious life in the empire. Both as a man and later as a myth, the pagan prophet reflected the religious anxieties of the imperial era.

Like the great Hebrew prophets, Apollonius insisted that morality was paramount in religion. For centuries pagan philosophers had agreed on the importance of virtue apart from obedience to the civil laws of Greece and Rome. Since the philosophers did not agree on the definition of virtue, personal morality usually required a religious sanction. According to the Hellenistic rationalist Polybius, the state employed religion for police purposes when it taught the masses that the gods would punish even hidden sins. While philosophers hoped that men would do good without fear of divine reprisals, the established religions used fears of the afterlife as an incentive to virtue. In the Hellenistic age most Jews adopted the idea that men were punished or rewarded in the afterlife, and many pagans believed in a vague Hades. Like Christianity, the pagan mystery cults relied heavily on the horrors of Hell and exclusive salvation for the initiated. However, most nations of antiquity did not enforce religious beliefs, and only token participation was required by the state cults. Views of the afterlife varied from individual to individual, and the notion of immortality was savagely ridiculed by Epicurus and Lucretius. According to Seneca, not even children really believed in the bogies of the afterlife. While there was no certainty that Hell awaited sinners, there was a general consensus among pagans that all men should observe traditional piety and practice the conventional virtues.

In the shrine of the Lydian goddess Agdistis, an inscription testifies to a high standard of pagan morality:

Let men and women, slave and free, when coming into this shrine swear by all the gods that they will not deliberately plan any evil guile or baneful poison against any man or woman; that they will neither know nor use harmful spells; that they will neither turn to nor recommend to others nor have a hand in love-charms, abortives, contraceptives, or doing robbery or murder; that they will steal nothing but will be well-disposed to this house. . . . A man is not to have relations with the wife of another, whether a free woman or a married slave, or with a boy or with a virgin, or to counsel this to another. . . . These commands were set up by the rule of Agdistis, the most holy guardian and mistress of this shrine. May she put good intentions in men and women, free and slave alike, that they may abide by what is here inscribed. . . . O Savior Zeus, hear our words and give us a good requital, health, deliverance, peace, safety on land and sea.[1]

In everyday life the majority of pagans were as moral as most Christians, but commonplace morality did not satisfy saints who required perfection. The prophet Apollonius insisted that piety was not just compliance with ritual. In his eyes piety must include the highest standard in morality because only the pure in heart were acceptable to the gods.

Most details of the life of Apollonius have been obscured by pious legends. However, his birthplace, Tyana in rural Cappadocia, was significant in the religious development of the prophet. Like Tarsus, Tyana was a Hellenized city in Asia Minor, but while Tarsus was a cosmopolitan seaport, Tyana was a sleepy town in the back country. Though the kings of Cappadocia had modernized Tyana in the second century B.C., the city was an ancient settlement which had been called "Tuwanuwa" in Hittite times. In the Near East, religious traditions were tenacious, and the natives of Tyana regarded the Greek deity Apollo as the Anatolian sun god who was the divine protector of justice on earth. During centuries of Persian rule, Zarathustrian concepts of strict morality and religious purity had spread through the area, and in the Roman era, local Magi still celebrated bloodless sacrifices to Ahuramazda and Mithra. The veneer of Hellenism was thin on Tyana and on Apollonius as well, for the prophet was greatly influenced by the religious traditions of his homeland. Two centuries before Apollonius, the rebel leader Aristonicus of Pergamum had rallied peasant worshipers to a revolutionary City of the Sun, but his movement was crushed by the legions of Rome. In the first century A.D., Apollonius of Tyana tried to transform the Roman world into a spiritual City of the Sun.

Like the life of Jesus, the career of Apollonius is a frustrating topic for historians because the sources are late and suspect. The only surviving biography of Apollonius was composed by Philostratus of Lemnos in the early third century. Although he used good sources, Philostratus produced a work which was filled with contradictions, rhetorical padding, and extraneous digressions. Nevertheless, any account of Apollonius must rest on Philostratus' narrative, which is trustworthy if used with great caution. According to the biographer, the prophet was born into a wealthy family at Tyana late in the reign of Augustus. Though legend suggested that the god Proteus might have been his father, Apollonius did not claim divine parentage. At the age of fourteen Apollonius was sent to Tarsus to complete his education, but the boy was uncomfortable in the sophisticated city and moved to nearby Aegae. There his philosophy professor was worldly and superficial, but the eager student was excited by ideas and underwent an adolescent conversion. At the age of sixteen Apollonius decided to model his life after the saintly Pythagoras. While the scientific and mathematical aspects of Pythagoreanism had little attraction for him, the young convert was inspired by the asceticism and mysticism of the half-legendary philosopher of the past. With youthful zeal, Apollonius renounced meat, wine, and haircuts, went barefoot, and dressed only in linen. Residing in a temple of Asclepius, the god of medicine, Apollonius warned the priests not to be impressed by gifts of gold and jewels, because the intent of a donor was more important than the value of his donation. Like his hero Pythagoras and the Magi of Cappadocia, Apollonius opposed the religious sacrifice of animals, and throughout his life he tried to stamp out the practice. Since the ritual slaughter of a cow, sheep, or pig was followed by a public feast in the temple, the masses did not appreciate Apollonius' position, but they always respected his sincerity.

Like most successful prophets, Apollonius was both an idealist and a poseur. With great care he cultivated the personal traits of a charismatic leader and always spoke with downcast eyes, as if his words were inspired. He also practiced celibacy and even observed a Pythagorean vow of silence for a few years. During a famine at Aspendus, Apollonius calmed an irate mob and prevented an attack on grain hoarders. When he ordered the monopolists to share their grain with the people, the frightened businessmen readily complied. Though he rarely discussed social problems, Apollonius observed that men would do well to practice the communism of sparrows. His admirers claimed that the prophet knew all languages and had been taught by Arabs the secret of conversing with birds. Throughout his life, Apollonius was credited with performing miracles, casting out demons, and curing the blind and lame. However, the prophet often suggested a natural cause for his miracles and attributed most of his famed foresight to astrology and common sense. Yet on some occasions he claimed divine inspiration. Though apocryphal epistles in Greek were later circulated in his name, Apollonius preferred to write on religion and astrology in his own Cappadocian language. Ill at ease with sophisticated audiences, he usually spoke in short, pithy epigrams which had great effect on simple folk. The prophet was fond of the fables of Aesop and recommended a simple prayer—"May the gods grant me what I deserve." As a devotee of the sun, Apollonius felt that the best time for prayer was at sunrise. Shocked by the public baths at Antioch, he delivered a puritanical tirade against bathing in hot water. To justify his opposition to blood sacrifices the prophet taught the transmigration of souls and the common brotherhood of all living beings. As a moralist, Apollonius insisted that "it is not enough to abstain from doing evil—one must actively do good." In contrast to the negativistic ethics of Stoicism and Epicureanism, Apollonius' advocacy of an active moral life was in the Socratic tradition.

According to Philostratus, Apollonius made a pilgrimage to India to visit the sages of the East. To the Greeks and Romans India was a mysterious land of lamas and gurus who guarded ancient wisdom and secret lore. During his Indian campaign Alexander the Great had met a Hindu holy man who returned to Persia with the king and burned himself to death. In the reign of Augustus, the historian Nicolaus of Damascus met three Indian envoys at Antioch who were on their way to present gifts to the ruler of the world.* In their party was a fakir who later immolated himself at Athens. Awed by reports of similar episodes, Apollonius succumbed to the spell of the East and wished to commune with the wise men of India. In Assyria the prophet met Damis of Nineveh, who became his disciple and served as his interpreter in Parthia—apparently, Apollonius' gift of tongues did not include a command of Persian. The devoted Damis later wrote a valuable memoir of his life with Apollonius. Unfortunately, Philostratus embellished the travels of Apollonius with improbable episodes and irrelevant geographical descriptions which he cribbed from standard Greek accounts of India. Though Philostratus claimed that his hero saw the Ganges and conversed with Brahmans, Apollonius probably only reached the Punjab and understood little of what the Indians said. Supposedly, the prophet returned by sea, much inspired by his encounters with the sages of the East. Regardless of unlikely details, Apollonius'

---

*The three Indian emissaries are probably the basis for the Three Wise Men in the Jesus story.

trip to India was not impossible, for Pliny the Elder met ambassadors from Ceylon at the court of Nero.

Back in Asia Minor, Apollonius toured the cities of Ionia, where he preached against blood sacrifice and encouraged sun worship. At Smyrna he offered advice on municipal politics:

If you want your city to be truly well-ordered, you must permit a mixture of party spirit with civic harmony, and this can be done without upsetting the safety of the city. . . . May your community never know the factionalism which makes men take up weapons and stone each other, for our children must be brought up properly and we must respect the laws. We also need citizens who can both speak and behave well, [and we welcome] mutual rivalry between them with respect to the common good. If one man can give better advice than another, or be a better magistrate, or serve more ably as an ambassador or an official . . . the community will profit from the competition. . . . It is better when each man does what he understands best and what he can do best. Then, the city will enjoy peace with pride as one man is admired for influence with the people, another for wisdom, another for generous donations to public projects, another for gentleness, another for severe and inflexible treatment of criminals, and another because his reputation is above suspicion.[2]

The counsel of Apollonius expressed the apolitical tone of life in Greek cities under the Roman yoke.

At Ephesus the prophet revealed that he had not yet shed the cruder aspects of his religious heritage. Since the Ionian city was ravaged by plague, the populace of Ephesus asked the miracle-worker for aid:

Apollonius summoned the Ephesians and said: "Fear not, for this day I will deliver you from the plague." Then, he led the whole population to the theater where the statue of the Averting God now stands. There, he spied what seemed to be an old beggar who was blinking his eyes as if he were blind. Dirty and destitute, the wretch was dressed in rags and was clutching a bag with a crust of bread in it. Apollonius stationed the Ephesians around the beggar and said: "Gather all the stones you can and throw them at this enemy of the gods." His words puzzled the Ephesians who were shocked at the idea of murdering a poor stranger, and the beggar was now crying and begging for mercy. Nevertheless, Apollonius was unmoved and urged the Ephesians to

attack him before he could escape. As soon as a few stones began to
fly, the beggar stopped blinking and glared at them with fire in his
eyes. At once the Ephesians realized that he was a demon, and they
stoned him until the rocks formed a great heap over him. After a
while, Apollonius told them to lift away the stones and see the terrible
beast whom they had slain. When they uncovered the corpse, the
body of the beggar had disappeared, and in its place was a Molossian
hound as big as a lion. Before their very eyes lay the demon, smashed
by the stones and drooling foam as mad dogs do.[3]

The pestilence soon abated, and the prophet explained that the
slain beggar had actually been a plague demon. In the Ionian
cities the human scapegoat was an institution of long standing,
but the lynching of the old beggar was instigated by Apollonius,
whose attitude toward supposed demons was similar to the
Biblical injunction: "You shall not allow a witch to live." Like
his neighbor Paul, the prophet from Tyana believed that the
world was infested with demons.

Visiting Greece, Apollonius was more successful at Athens
than Paul had been, for the university students left their studies
and sports to welcome the famous visitor from Tyana. True to
form, the prophet criticized the frivolity and easy living of the
Athenians and condemned them for adopting gladiatorial games
in imitation of their Roman masters. For some years Apollonius
had been followed about by a group of young disciples, who
were unnerved when they heard that the prophet now intended
to go to Rome. Fearing that he would perish at the hands of
Nero, the timid disciples deserted Apollonius, but the dreaded
encounter between the saint and the tyrant did not take place.
In 66 the Asian prophet arrived in the capital and supposedly
received a sympathetic hearing from the consul Gaius Telesinus,
who asked Apollonius:

"What is your wisdom?" Apollonius said, "I am inspired to teach men
how to pray and sacrifice to the gods." [The consul smiled]: "But, my
dear philosopher, who does not know that already?" The prophet
replied, "Many men do not and if a few do, they will profit from
hearing a wise man confirm their beliefs." [Telesinus asked]: "What
do you pray for when you approach the altars?" Apollonius answered:
"I personally pray that justice will prevail, that the laws will be

observed, that wise men will continue to be poor, and that other men will make money honestly." "But," said the consul, "since you ask for so much, do you think that you will get it?" "Yes, by Zeus," Apollonius replied, "for I squeeze all my petitions into a single prayer. When I go before the altars, this is how I pray: Oh gods, bestow on me whatever is fitting. If I am worthy, I will obtain more than I have asked for; but if the gods consider me wicked, they will send me the opposite of what I asked. If my faults bring me punishment, I shall not blame the gods."[4]

While this conversation is not historically factual, Telesinus would have been favorably impressed by the prophet. Apollonius always insisted that worshipers should bring a clear conscience into the temples and not be afraid to ask for their just rewards.

At Rome Apollonius did not meddle in politics, but the Praetorian prefect Tigellinus suspected that the prophet lacked enthusiasm for Nero's regime. According to Philostratus, the prefect interviewed Apollonius and asked him:

"Why do you not fear Nero?" "Because," replied Apollonius, "the same gods, who make him appear formidable, allow me to feel no fear." The prefect asked, "But what do you think about Nero?" Apollonius answered: "Much better than you do. You think it is proper for him to sing, but I think it is better when he keeps silent." Tigellinus was puzzled and said: "You may go, but you must pay a bond for your continued good behavior." Apollonius answered: "Who can give a bond for a body that no one can bind?" His words struck Tigellinus as inspired and superhuman. Not wishing to contend with a god, the prefect said: "You can go wherever you want, for your power is beyond my control."[5]

If Tigellinus had actually met Apollonius, the brutal prefect would not have been so gentle with the haughty prophet. While in the capital, Apollonius saved a girl from premature burial when he noticed her faint breath in the chill air. As a result of this episode, he was credited with raising the dead.

Though he had not raised any controversies at Rome, Apollonius went on to Spain where he criticized Nero as an effeminate despot who disgraced his office with luxurious living and needless cruelty. According to Philostratus, the prophet encouraged the generals in the West to rebel against Nero, but the episode is unlikely. In 69 Apollonius appeared in Alexandria and sought an interview with Vespasian. Because of Josephus, the new emperor respected prophets and granted Apollonius an audience. However, the Cappadocian immediately clashed with the famous philosopher Euphrates who attended Vespasian and considered Apollonius a religious crank. A quick-witted Syrian intellectual who was respected by both Epictetus and Pliny the Younger, Euphrates quarreled with Apollonius and ridiculed his pretensions. Later the conversation turned to politics and Euphrates suggested that Vespasian might restore the Republic, but Apollonius expressed a view which was closer to the emperor's heart:

Personally I have no interest in constitutions because my life is governed by the gods. Nevertheless, I would not want to see the human flock perish for want of a shepherd who is both just and moderate. When a democracy is led by a man who is outstanding in virtue, that government is really an autocracy. Likewise, the rule of a single man can be considered popular government if the monarch is truly concerned with the welfare of all.[6]

Apollonius advised Vespasian to avoid political purges and be equally just to the rich and the poor. He also warned the emperor not to promise his sons the succession until they had earned it. Men of action rarely listen to sermons on political theory,* and Vespasian did not need advice from Apollonius. Whatever happened at Alexandria, Apollonius and Euphrates became bitter enemies, and the philosopher later wrote pamphlets against the prophet. After his encounter with Vespasian, Apollonius withdrew to more compatible surroundings and visited the hermits of Egypt and Ethiopia before returning to Asia Minor.

Late in the reign of Domitian, the prophet gave moral support to the faction which wished to replace the emperor with an elderly senator, Nerva. The suspicious Domitian ordered that Apollonius be brought to Rome and tried on charges of wizardry,

---

*Philostratus' friend, the historian Dio Cassius, invented a similar discussion between the aides of Augustus, with Agrippa defending the Republic and Maecenas recommending autocracy. Centuries earlier, Herodotus had set the pattern with an unlikely debate on political science among the Persian nobles who supported the coup of Darius the Great.

human sacrifice, and accepting divine honors. In prison the prophet awed his fellow captives when he slipped off his chains and replaced them to show that he could escape if he wished. Brought to trial before the emperor, Apollonius indignantly denied the false charges and demanded that his accusers produce witnesses of the alleged crimes. Impressed by his defense, Domitian ordered the acquittal of the prophet and wished to speak with him in private, but "Apollonius vanished from the court." Though the details were exaggerated by Philostratus, the imprisonment and trial of Apollonius are not improbable. According to the historian Eusebius, Domitian also tried the grand-nephews of Jesus and listened politely as they explained their beliefs. Satisfied that the Christians were simple yokels, the emperor released them unharmed.

In 96, on the very day that Domitian was assassinated at Rome, Apollonius interrupted a sermon at Ephesus and told his astonished audience that the emperor had just been murdered. Since the two cities were hundreds of miles apart, the prophet must have known the date of the assassination in advance. Earlier in Germany, a legionary soldier, Proculus, had foretold the date of Domitian's death and was in prison at Rome when the assassins struck. Apparently, both Proculus and Apollonius were privy to a widespread plot against Domitian,* whose successor, Nerva, offered Apollonius a position in the government. However, the aged prophet was in poor health and had to decline the honor. A year or two later, Apollonius died at Ephesus, but his followers insisted that the gods had spirited him away from a temple in Crete. At Tyana his disciples saw apparitions of the late prophet, and cults of Apollonius sprang up throughout Asia Minor.

While the prophet of Tyana lived in the first century, his biographer Philostratus wrote in the third century and expressed the values of a much different era. In the early third century Rome was controlled by the Severan dynasty, which was founded by the harsh militarist Septimius Severus. His empress Julia Domna was a proud Syrian beauty, and his sons Caracalla and Geta were headstrong and cruel. When Severus died in 211,

---

*On the involvement of Apollonius in the conspiracy, see Appendix One.

Caracalla became emperor and murdered his brother Geta. In 217 Caracalla was assassinated, and after a year the throne passed to a grandson of Julia Domna's sister. The new emperor was an effeminate Syrian youth who was a priest of the sun god Elagabalus and took the name of his deity. After a brief and bizarre reign, Elagabalus was succeeded as emperor by his prim cousin Severus Alexander, who was the last of the Severan rulers. During the reign of Caracalla, descendants of Damis of Nineveh had presented Julia Domna with a copy of Damis' book on Apollonius. A devotee of the sun god, the dowager empress was greatly impressed by the life of the pagan saint but not by Damis' literary style. In order that the life of Apollonius might reach a wider audience, she commissioned Philostratus to rewrite Damis' simple memoir in a more elegant form. In the Severan era, miracle tales were avidly read by all classes, and Julia Domna hoped that a biography of Apollonius would add prestige to the cult of the Syrian sun god. However, the old empress did not live to read Philostratus' life of Apollonius, which was completed in the reign of Severus Alexander and reflected the ideals of that broad-minded ruler.

To compose a biography of Apollonius, Philostratus relied on many sources, but the core of his work was Damis' memoir. In addition to Damis, he used a book by Maximus of Aegae, who described Apollonius' student years. Philostratus collected pious legends from various cities where the prophet had worked miracles or instituted ritual reforms. He also examined the hostile tracts of Euphrates and a book by a certain Moeragenes, who had depicted Apollonius as a sinister wizard. Possibly, Philostratus was familiar with the Gospel of Luke and the Acts of the Apostles, for he embellished many episodes in the life of Apollonius with details which recall the adventures of Jesus and Paul. While the parallels with Christianity may be only coincidental, Philostratus revised Damis' account with a free hand and portrayed Apollonius as an Asian Greek and a zealous defender of Hellenic culture. However, Philostratus was a careless writer and his biography contains much evidence that Apollonius was more Cappadocian than Greek. In antiquity writers often discussed contemporary politics in the guise of recounting history, and Philostratus tailored his portrayal of Domitian to fit Caracalla and used Nero to attack Elagabalus. Apollonius' advice that Vespasian should be cautious in giving power to his sons Titus and Domitian, was really a criticism of Septimius Severus who had indulged his sons Caracalla and Geta. Since the emperor Severus Alexander considered his predecessors tyrants, Philostratus could safely make oblique attacks on Septimius Severus, Caracalla, and Elagabalus. Though Apollonius' interviews with Telesinus and Tigellinus are unlikely, the opposition of the prophet to Domitian is probable in view of the Proculus episode and Apollonius' friendship with Nerva.

If Philostratus is such an erratic source, what can one believe about Apollonius? Some modern critics suspect that Philostratus composed a pious hoax to please Julia Domna, and a few feel that he wrote a pagan parody of the Gospels. Nevertheless, most historians accept the substance of Philostratus' account as valid. By historiographical standards Apollonius of Tyana was as real as Jesus, whose historicity is accepted by all modern scholars regardless of inaccuracies in the Gospels. Long before Philostratus, the cult of Apollonius was popular in the East, and the prophet was mocked by the second-century satirist, Lucian. The emperor Hadrian was interested in the apocryphal letters of Apollonius, and Caracalla built a shrine to the prophet years before Philostratus' book appeared. The historian Dio Cassius described Apollonius' "vision" of Domitian's death, and the emperor Severus Alexander set up a statue of Apollonius beside images of Orpheus, Abraham, and Jesus in his private chapel. Both Dio Cassius and the emperor were learned friends of Philostratus and would not be taken in by a piece of recent fiction. A few years earlier, the grotesque emperor Elagabalus had discredited the cult of the god Elagabalus, and Severus Alexander now hoped that Philostratus' biography of Apollonius would help to rehabilitate the Syrian solar deity.

While the masses thought of Apollonius as a wizard and accorded him semidivine honors, intellectuals viewed the famous prophet as an exponent of solar henotheism—the concept that the sun was the ranking deity in the pantheon—which the emperor Elagabalus had tried to impose on the Roman empire. In time a Roman governor in the East, Hierocles, realized that Philostratus' book could be used against the Christians and became the first pagan writer to compare Jesus unfavorably with Apollonius. Throughout the third century, the cult of the Cappadocian prophet continued to grow. In 271 the emperor Aurelian claimed that a vision of Apollonius prevented him from destroying the city of Tyana which had risen against Rome. Soon after the episode at Tyana, Aurelian defeated his enemy Zenobia of Palmyra and attributed the victory to the intervention of the god Elagabalus. The triumphant emperor changed the deity's name to Sol Invictus, the Unconquerable Sun, and made the Syrian god the supreme divinity of the Roman empire. Later, Sol Invictus was the family god of the emperor Constantius Chlorus, whose son Constantine claimed that the solar deity paid him personal visits in Gaul. In 312 Constantine had a dream of another divinity, Jesus, and became a patron of Christianity. His court historian, Bishop Eusebius of Caesarea, wrote a blistering polemic against Hierocles and attacked Philostratus in the process. With erudition, common sense, and humor, Eusebius subjected the biography of Apollonius to higher criticism and discredited the inconsistencies and miraculous elements in Philostratus' book. According to Eusebius, the real Apollonius was a pagan sage who had many worthy ideas but was distorted into a wizard by gullible contemporaries and the naive piety of posterity. Most modern historians agree with Eusebius' evaluation of the prophet of Tyana.

While Apollonius represented the better aspects of paganism, the worst elements were personified by the oraclemonger Alexander of Abonoteichos, who once studied under a disciple of Apollonius. With great relish, the essayist Lucian of Samosata described Alexander's career as a religious humbug. A sardonic foe of religion and fraud, Lucian was the H. L. Mencken of the second century. He had seen Alexander in operation and wrote a devastating exposé of the false prophet who was born in the small town of Abonoteichos in Paphlagonia on the southern coast of the Black Sea. Alexander was glib, wily, and handsome— "some of his hair was his own, and his toupee was such a perfect match that most people didn't realize he was wearing one." In his youth Alexander had traveled about Greek Asia and picked up a knowledge of medicine and the arts of swindling. At Pella in Macedonia he bought a large tame snake and returned to

Abonoteichos to set himself up in business as an oracle. His methods were imaginative, well planned, and superbly executed. Before appearing in public, Alexander planted in the temple of Apollo engraved brass plates which announced the imminent epiphany of the healing god Asclepius, whose common form was a serpent. As soon as the plates were discovered, the charlatan showed himself in a splendid costume:

Having staged this dramatic come-back into his home-town, he still further increased his reputation by pretending to be insane and occasionally foaming at the mouth. This was quite easily done by chewing the root of a herb called soap-wort, which is used in the dyeing trade, but it seemed to them a fearful manifestation of divinity. Another piece of equipment that he'd already prepared for their benefit was a semi-human snake-head made of linen. It was painted to look quite lifelike with a mouth that could be made to open and shut by means of horse-hairs, and a forked black tongue sticking out which was similarly operated. And then, of course, there was the snake from Pella which had been kept at his house for some time, waiting for its cue to appear and take part in the performance—or rather, to play the lead. . . . He went off one night to the place where they'd been digging the foundations of the new temple. A certain amount of water had collected on the site—I suppose it had seeped up out of the ground, or it may have been rainwater. In it he deposited a goose-egg, the contents of which had been emptied out and replaced by a newly-hatched snake. He tucked it away under the mud and went back home. Next morning, he leapt into the market-place stark naked except for a loin cloth—needless to say, a gold one. . . . He climbed on to a high altar and did a bit of tub-thumping, congratulating the town on the fact that it would soon see the god in bodily form. Everyone present—and by this time practically the whole population, irrespective of age or sex, had come rushing to the spot—everyone was struck with awe and knelt down and prayed. Alexander then uttered some unintelligible sounds which might have been either Hebrew or Phoenician, thus impressing his audience even more—for they had no idea what he was saying, except that it included frequent references to Apollo and Asclepius. He then ran off at full speed to the site of the new temple. He made straight for the excavations which contained the prearranged source of the oracle, stepped into the water, and sang a loud hymn to Asclepius and Apollo. . . . Next he asked for a bowl which was duly produced, plunged it below the surface, and promptly fished out, along with a good deal of muddy water, the egg in which the deity was enclosed. He'd stuck the two halves of the shell together with a mixture of wax and white lead. Taking the egg into his hands, he solemnly intoned the words: "Asclepius is here!" Everyone was watching intently to see what would happen next, for the mere discovery of the egg had already caused a big sensation. But when he broke the shell and dropped the baby snake into the palm of his hand, so that people could see it moving about and wriggling round his fingers, they immediately let out a yell and started celebrating the advent of the god, congratulating one another on their good fortune and gabbling off prayers for health, wealth, and happiness. Alexander then dashed off home again, taking with him the new-born Asclepius.

The miraculous birth of Asclepius was only a prelude to a swindle of grand proportions:

Alexander stayed at home for a few days after that, rightly anticipating that when the story got round, vast numbers of Paphlagonians would come flocking in from all directions. At last, when the town was absolutely packed with mental defectives who resembled *homo sapiens* only in their appearance and were otherwise indistinguishable from sheep, he gave a reception in a small room of his house. Having got himself up to look quite divine, he seated himself on a couch with Asclepius of Pella in his lap. This snake was, as I said, a very large and beautiful specimen, and he wound it round his neck with its tail hanging down. There was so much of it, that part of it overflowed his lap and trailed along the ground. The only bit that he didn't show them was its head. This he kept well up his sleeve—for the snake didn't mind what you did to it—and poked out the linen head from behind his beard, as though it belonged to the body that they could see. Well, you can just imagine what it was like. There was this tiny room with a surging mass of excited people outside it, all in a highly impressionable state and expecting something fantastic. In they came, and there was this huge snake instead of the tiny creature that they'd seen a few days before. Naturally, it seemed like a miracle, especially as the snake looked so tame and had an almost human face. The next moment, they were being hustled toward the exit by the queue of people behind them, before they'd got a chance to examine anything closely.[7]

Having convinced the yokels that Asclepius now resided in their city, Alexander was ready to make a profit.

When the problems of life seem too pressing, men consult the occult arts and cling desperately to any apparent demonstration of prophetic powers while ignoring all failures or equivocations by an oracle. The major step in establishing a successful oracle is to win confidence, and Alexander did not leave this to chance:

He told each client to write his question on a piece of paper, fold it up, and seal it with wax or clay or something like that. He then took the pieces of paper into the Holy of Holies . . . and told an assistant prophet-cum-receptionist to call up the inquirers one by one. After consulting the god, he would hand each paper back, still sealed, but with the god's answer written inside it, immediately below the question. . . . Of course, he'd merely thought up various methods of removing the seals, so that he could read the questions, write down appropriate answers, seal the papers up again and hand them back to their astonished owners. . . . Method No. 1 was to melt the wax underneath the seal with a red-hot needle, and take it off like that. Then, when he'd read and answered the question, he used the same needle to warm the underside of the wax and simply stuck it on again. Another method was to use stuff called collyrium which is made out of Bruttian pitch, bitumen, powdered quartz, wax, and resin. Having mixed this compound, he applied it hot to the seal, which he'd previously smeared with grease, and thus took an impression of it. As soon as the collyrium had set, he just opened the paper in the normal way and read it, after which he replaced the wax, stamped it with the collyrium cast, which was now as hard as a rock, and left it looking exactly the same as before. And here's a third method. He made a waxlike substance by adding chalk to the glue used for book-binding. While it was still pliable, he applied it to the seal and immediately took it off again—for it set very quickly. . . . He was then able to duplicate the original seal. . . . In deciding what answers to give, he relied upon common sense, combined with a certain amount of imagination and guesswork. Sometimes his responses were rather obscure and ambiguous, and sometimes they were down-right unintelligible—which he considered in line with the best traditions of his trade. He encouraged or discouraged people's plans, according to what seemed wisest in the circumstances. He also gave advice on diet and medical treatment, for . . . he knew quite a lot about medicine. His favorite prescription was a Cytmis—which was a name he'd invented for a sort of pick-me-up concocted out of goat-fat. But legacies and all forms of good fortune or success he invariably postponed to a later date, adding a note to the effect that "all such

things will come in my own good time, when my prophet Alexander
has made intercession for you." . . . He knocked up an annual income
of seven or eight thousand, for his clients were so insatiable that they
consulted him ten to fifteen times a year. However, it wasn't all clear
profit and he couldn't accumulate any capital, as he had a large
number of employees—attendants, detectives, script-writers, librarians,
copying-clerks, seal-experts, and interpreters—who had to be paid
appropriate salaries. He now started sending out foreign representatives to advertise the oracle and tell people how good he was at
predicting the future, locating runaway slaves, detecting burglars,
discovering buried treasure, and in some cases resurrecting the dead.
The result was a mad rush of new customers. Gifts and offerings came
pouring in, and the holy prophet doubled his fees.[8]

With ample publicity and judicious advertising, the oracle at
Abonoteichos was a great success. However, opposition from
skeptics and cynics made Alexander seek protection in bigotry:

At this point, the more intelligent members of the community began to
turn against him. . . . The movement was led by the Epicureans who
were fairly numerous, and in the big towns information started leaking
out about his various theatrical devices. To scare them off, he produced
an oracle declaring that Pontus was full of atheists and Christians,
who had most wickedly blasphemed against him and must be stoned
and driven out of the land if his people wished to find favor in his
sight.[9]

In addition to denouncing Christians, Alexander constantly
disparaged Épicureans and publicly burned a copy of the works
of Epicurus.

Soon, the fame of the oracle spread to Rome, where Alexander
had a staunch champion in a retired official, Rutilianus, who was
a religious enthusiast and addicted to occultism. Through Rutilianus, members of the imperial court began to consult the oracle
at Abonoteichos. The crafty Alexander refused to answer
inquiries involving politics but saved the letters and blackmailed
the writers. The wily prophet was now an international figure:

Once Alexander started doing business in Italy, he got even bigger
ideas. He sent missionaries all over the Roman empire, warning every
town to look out for plagues, earthquakes, and conflagrations and

offering to protect them against such disasters. During the great epidemic [in the reign of Marcus Aurelius], he sent each country a copy of the following oracle . . . "Phoebus, lord of unshorn tresses, will not let the plague come nigh thee." Soon you could see these words scribbled on front doors everywhere, as a form of immunization. In most cases, it had precisely the opposite effect, for as it happened, the first households to go down were the ones with these inscriptions. I don't mean to suggest that the words had anything to do with it— doubtless it was pure coincidence. Or perhaps, their faith in the oracle made people careless about taking other precautions. . . . He stationed a large number of private detectives in Rome to report what his clients were like, what questions they were going to ask, and what they particularly wanted, so that he could work out his answers in advance. To whip up trade in Italy, [and at home] he also established a three-day festival, complete with torchlight services and initiation ceremonies. On the first day, as at Athens, there was a proclamation: "If any atheist, Christian, or Epicurean has come to spy upon our sacred mysteries, let him begone! But let all true believers be made holy before the god!" This was immediately followed by an expulsion ceremony. Alexander led off with the words: "Out with all Christians!" to which the congregation made the response: "Out with all Epicureans!"[10]

Although he was a cynical fraud, Alexander became in practice a staunch defender of religion and a vigorous foe of godlessness.

Religion is always the breeding ground of saints and the last refuge of scoundrels. Like Francis of Assisi and Elmer Gantry, Apollonius and Alexander were two sides of the same coin. Their successful careers were built on the hopes and fears of average men who felt helpless in an indifferent universe. Both the reformer and the charlatan set religious revivals in motion, and Alexander's injunction to "stone the atheists and the Christians" had a grim precedent in Apollonius' misguided attack on the "plague demon" at Ephesus. Though he could not persuade the Romans to give up animal sacrifices, Apollonius of Tyana encouraged a new religious orientation with the solar cult which eventually trans- formed Elagabalus into Sol Invictus. Ironically, even the prophet himself became an object of worship in some cities. The enormous appeal, which Apollonius had for both his contemporaries and posterity, is proof that the tides of faith ran strong in the Roman world.

EIGHT

The Gentleman—Pliny the Younger

In his *History of the Decline and Fall of the Roman Empire,* the British scholar Edward Gibbon depicted the second century A.D. as a Golden Age:

> If a man were called to fix the period in the history of the world, during which the condition of the human race was most happy and prosperous, he would without hesitation name that which elapsed from the death of Domitian to the accession of Commodus. The vast extent of the Roman empire was governed by absolute power under the guidance of virtue and wisdom. The armies were restrained by the firm but gentle hand of four successive emperors whose characters and authority commanded involuntary respect. The forms of the civil administration were carefully preserved by Nerva, Trajan, Hadrian, and the Antonines, who delighted in the image of liberty and were pleased with considering themselves as the accountable ministers of the laws. Such princes deserved the honor of restoring the Republic had the Romans of their days been capable of enjoying a rational freedom.[1]

Though Gibbon's judgment was warped by his Tory bias, the second century was an era of stable and efficient government, general prosperity, and internal security for the Roman world. The absence of political freedom and economic equity did not disturb Gibbon or his Roman heroes who preferred to ignore the unpleasantness which tarnished the Golden Age. The letters of Pliny the Younger reveal the mentality of the men who prospered in the new era.

A successful lawyer and civil servant, Pliny had good manners, safe virtues, and no vices—in short, he was a gentleman.

140

His faults were mainly those of omission—he was not a hero and did not wish to be a martyr. Likewise, his virtue was largely the absence of bad traits, for Pliny lacked the greed and ambition of Sejanus and Seneca and the self-righteousness of Paul and Josephus. Unlike Herod Agrippa, Pliny considered political intrigues too risky, and he could not take religion as seriously as Apollonius did. The times called for talent without distinction and rewarded conscientious mediocrity. Neither saint nor sinner, Pliny the Younger was an honest and amiable man and a representative Roman of the upper classes.

Like Vergil and Livy, Gaius Plinius Caecilius Secundus was a Northern Italian from the lands between the Po River and the Alps.* Born about 62 in the town of Comum on Lake Como, Pliny grew up in an area of great natural beauty and retained a love of scenery and rural living all of his life. Though his family was well-to-do, his parents were separated and the boy was raised by his mother. The father-figure in young Pliny's life was his guardian, Verginius Rufus, who had been one of Nero's generals. At Comum, Pliny was educated by tutors, but his schooling was completed at Rome, where he attended the lectures of Quintilian. In the capital, the young scholar had a generous patron in his learned uncle, Pliny the Elder, whose literary output was prodigious. The working habits of his bookish uncle were described by the younger Pliny:

You may wonder how such a busy man was able to complete so many volumes, many of them involving detailed study; and wonder still more when you learn that up to a certain age he practiced at the bar, that he died at the age of fifty-five, and throughout the intervening years his time was much taken up with the important offices he held and his friendship with the emperors. But he combined a penetrating intellect with amazing powers of concentration and the capacity to manage with the minimum of sleep. From the feast of Vulcan [August 23] onwards, he began to work by lamplight . . . to give himself more time for study and would rise half-way through the night; in winter it would often be at midnight or an hour later, and two at the latest. Admittedly, he fell asleep very easily and would often doze and wake

*This area, Cisalpine Gaul, had received the Roman franchise under the dictator Julius Caesar.

up again during his work. Before daybreak, he would visit the emperor Vespasian (who also made use of his nights) and then go to attend to his official duties. On returning home, he devoted any spare time to his work. After something to eat (his meals during the day were light and simple in the old-fashioned way), in summer when he was not too busy he would often lie in the sun, and a book was read aloud while he made notes and extracts. He made extracts of everything he read, and always said that there was no book so bad that some good could not be got out of it. After his rest in the sun, he generally took a cold bath and then ate something and had a short sleep, after which he worked till dinner time as if he had started on a new day. A book was read aloud during the meal and he took rapid notes. I remember that one of his friends told a reader to go back and repeat a word he had mispronounced. "Couldn't you understand him?" said my uncle. His friend admitted that he could. "Then why make him go back? Your interruption has lost us at least ten lines." To such lengths did he carry his passion for saving time. In summer, he rose from dinner while it was still light, in winter as soon as darkness fell, as if some law compelled him. This was his routine in the midst of his public duties and the bustle of the city. In the country, the only time he took from his work was for his bath, and by bath I mean his actual immersion, for while he was being rubbed down and dried he had a book read to him or dictated notes. When traveling, he felt free from other responsibilities to give every minute to work; he kept a secretary at his side with book and notebook, and in winter saw that his hands were protected by long sleeves, so that even bitter weather should not rob him of a working hour. For the same reason, too, he used to be carried about Rome in a chair. I can remember how he scolded me for walking; according to him, I need not have wasted those hours, for he thought any time wasted which was not devoted to work.[2]

As a result of his herculean studies, Pliny the Elder left a body of writings which became a scientific canon in the Middle Ages.

In 79 the adolescent Pliny the Younger and his mother were not far from Pompeii when the resort city was destroyed. The boy was unnerved by the volcanic cloud and showers of ashes from Vesuvius, and he shared the general panic brought on by the quaking earth and the unnatural darkness which fell over the area. During the catastrophe, Pliny the Elder was overcome by curiosity:

My uncle was stationed at Misenum in active command of the fleet. On 24 August in the early afternoon, my mother drew his attention to a cloud of unusual size and appearance. He had been out in the sun, had taken a cold bath, and lunched while lying down, and was then working at his books. He called for his shoes and climbed up to a place which would give him the best view of the phenomenon. It was not clear at that distance from which mountain the cloud was rising (it was afterwards known to be Vesuvius); its general appearance can best be expressed as being like an umbrella pine, for it rose to a great height on a sort of trunk and then split off into branches. . . . In places it looked white, elsewhere blotched and dirty, according to the amount of soil and ashes it carried with it. My uncle's scholarly acumen saw at once that it was important enough for a closer inspection, and he ordered a boat to be made ready, telling me I could come with him if I wished. I replied that I preferred to go on with my studies, and as it happened, he had himself given me some writing to do. As he was leaving the house, he was handed a message from Rectina, wife of Tascus, whose house was at the foot of the mountain, so that escape was impossible except by boat. She was terrified by the danger threatening her and implored him to rescue her from her fate. He changed his plans, and what he had begun in a spirit of inquiry he completed as a hero. He gave orders for the warships to be launched and went on board himself with the intention of bringing help to many more people besides Rectina, for this lovely stretch of coast was thickly populated. He hurried to the place which everyone else was hastily leaving, steering his course straight for the danger zone. He was entirely fearless, describing each new movement and phase of the portent to be noted down exactly as he observed them. Ashes were already falling, hotter and thicker as the ships drew near, followed by bits of pumice and blackened stones, charred and cracked by the flames. Then suddenly, they were in shallow water, and the shore was blocked by the debris from the mountain. For a moment, my uncle wondered whether to turn back, but when the helmsman advised this, he refused.

While the fleet picked up refugees in the disaster area, Pliny the Elder landed near Pompeii at the villa of his friend Pomponianus. There he rested and watched the awesome scene until nightfall:

Meanwhile, on Mount Vesuvius, broad sheets of fire and leaping flames blazed at several points, their bright glare emphasized by the darkness

of night. My uncle tried to allay the fears of his companions. . . .
Then he went to rest and certainly slept, for as he was a stout man,
his breathing was rather loud and heavy and could be heard by people
coming and going outside his door. By this time, the courtyard giving
access to his room was full of ashes mixed with pumice-stones, so that
its level had risen, and if he had stayed in the room any longer, he
would never have got out. He was wakened, came out, and joined
Pomponianus and the rest of the household who had sat up all night.
They debated whether to stay indoors or take their chance in the open,
for the buildings were now shaking with violent shocks and seemed
to be swaying to and fro as if they were torn from their foundations.
Outside, on the other hand, there was the danger of falling pumice-
stones, even though these were light and porous. However, after
comparing the risks, they chose the latter. . . . As a protection against
falling objects, they put pillows on their heads tied down with cloths.
Elsewhere, there was daylight by this time, but they were still in
darkness, blacker and denser than any ordinary night, which they
relieved by lighting torches and various kinds of lamps. My uncle
decided to go down to the shore and investigate on the spot the
possibility of any escape by sea, but he found the waves still wild and
dangerous. A sheet was spread on the ground for him to lie down, and
he repeatedly asked for cold water to drink. Then the flames and
smell of sulphur which gave warning of the approaching fire drove
the others to take flight and roused him to stand up. He stood leaning
on two slaves and then suddenly collapsed, I imagine because the
dense fumes choked his breathing by blocking his windpipe which
was constitutionally weak and narrow and often inflamed. When daylight returned on the 26th—two days after the last day he had seen—
his body was found intact and uninjured, still fully clothed and looking
more like sleep than death.[3]

Since he had cautiously avoided the scene of danger, Pliny the
Younger had to learn the details of his uncle's last day from
survivors.

After inheriting a sizable fortune from his late uncle, Pliny
the Younger soon married and became a successful lawyer at
Rome. The young barrister spent six months on military service
in Syria, where he met the famous philosopher Euphrates, who
had been exiled by Domitian. Returning to Rome, Pliny held
minor magistracies and became a praetor in 93. Like most of his
fellow senators, he was subservient to Domitian and did nothing

Domitian

to offend the tyrant. In later life Pliny claimed that he had been in danger when Domitian purged the Senate of critics and conspirators. Although an accusation against Pliny was later found among Domitian's papers, the cautious senator did not plot against the emperor who elevated him to a treasury post. With diligence and discretion, Pliny carefully advanced his career under Domitian.

Though maligned by senatorial historians, Domitian was a capable ruler before he became obsessed with plots and traitors. According to the historian Suetonius, lack of funds had made Domitian greedy and fear of assassination made him cruel. When he executed his own relatives and servants, the emperor brought about his own death. In 96 the empress Domitia and members of the palace staff decided to kill Domitian and replace him with the aged senator Nerva. The extent of the conspiracy will never be known, but Apollonius and others outside Rome knew the date of the assassination. As soon as his servants had stabbed Domitian, the Senate quickly proclaimed Nerva as emperor, for he was a harmless old man whose poetry had once been admired by Nero. More importantly, Nerva had no sons and would not establish a dynasty. In death, Domitian suffered the same fate that Stalin would in another era, for his arrogance was mocked and his brutality condemned by the very men who had acquiesced in his acts of tyranny. Until restrained by Nerva, the senators prosecuted many former henchmen of Domitian, but some guilty men survived by denouncing the dead despot, and his former secretary now displayed busts of the tyrannicides Brutus and Cassius in his home. After the first outburst of indignation had subsided, the outspoken Junius Mauricus, who had been exiled by Domitian, dryly rebuked the hypocrisy of Nerva's Senate. During a banquet for Nerva, the diners reminisced about a particularly vicious agent of Domitian who had died before the despot: "Everyone at table was talking freely about his villainy and murderous decisions when the emperor said, 'I wonder what would have happened to him if he were alive today?' 'He would be dining with us,' said Mauricus."[4] Like his peers, Pliny made belated attacks on Domitian and basked in the favor of Nerva,* who appointed Pliny's former guardian Verginius Rufus as consul.

In 97 the emperor fell under the control of the army high command, who had not been consulted in his selection and did not intend to allow a senatorial clique to dominate the empire. Encouraged by the legionary generals, the Praetorian guards rioted and demanded that Nerva execute the murderers of Domitian, who had been popular with the army. The frightened emperor handed the assassins over to the Praetorians and turned for protection to the frontier generals, ignorant of the fact that they were behind the disorder in Rome.† On their recommendation, Nerva adopted as heir Trajan, the commander of the legions along the upper Rhine. In 98 the aged Nerva died and a forty-two-year-old career officer from Spain, Trajan, was accepted as emperor by the cowed Senate. In the Year of the Four Emperors (69) the Roman armies had fought each other for the succession, but in 98 the generals cooperated and put a military man on the throne without the waste and bitterness of a civil war. One of Trajan's first acts was the execution of the Praetorian prefect who had served as a cat's paw for the generals.

*In his personal life, Pliny had less cause for happiness, for his first wife had died and death also took his second wife.

†On the role of the generals, see Appendix One.

The hard-drinking military emperor preferred life in the camps but applied himself conscientiously to the duties of his new office. Though he was as thorough a despot as any of his predecessors, Trajan was courteous to the Senate, which ignored his alcoholic excesses and hailed him as a champion of responsible government. The Spanish emperor built extensively at Rome where the huge Forum of Trajan was soon graced by a tall column decorated with scenes of his victories. To encourage farming and large families, Trajan offered low-rate loans to investors in Italian land and used the interest for the care of poor children who otherwise would have been abandoned by their parents.* To communities throughout the empire, Trajan donated public buildings and libraries and expected the upper classes to emulate his generosity. When he conquered Dacia (modern Rumania), the emperor poured the wealth of its gold mines into the Roman treasury, but Dacia would be the last great booty acquired by Rome.

While the empire prospered under his firm benevolence, Trajan preferred the company of generals and Spaniards. Though as an Italian he stood outside the Spanish clique at court, Pliny corresponded with Trajan's chief aide, Licinius Sura, who was more intellectual than the emperor's other Spanish cronies. An able civil servant, Pliny prosecuted Roman officials who had been accused of peculation or misgovernment in the provinces. In 100 the loyal Pliny was rewarded with the consulship and delivered an eloquent and revealing panegyric to the emperor:

Who would willingly take on himself the burden of your responsibility? Who would not shrink from comparison with you? You have experienced in your own person the difficulty of succeeding to a good prince —and you had the advantage of being [Nerva's] adopted son. Is it a small thing, or a thing which is easy of emulation, that nobody now pays the price of security by the loss of honor, or that life and its dignity are now everywhere safe, and men need no longer live in hiding before they can be counted prudent and wise? Clearly, the same rewards attend the virtuous under the government of a prince as they enjoyed in the days of republican liberty. . . . Malleable as

*This program, the alimentary system, was begun in the brief reign of Nerva.

we are, we can be led in any direction by a prince, and we become, so to speak, his shadows. . . . Oh, it is truly the office of a prince and even of a god to reconcile jealous states; to keep proud peoples in order, more by the use of reason than by the exercise of authority; to intervene when officials go wrong, and to undo what ought not to have been done; and finally, in a word, to be like the swiftest of stars, seeing all things, hearing all things, and—from whatever quarter the call may come—always ready, like a god, to act as a present help and comforter. Such, I cannot but believe, is the way in which the Father of the world governs it by His nod, when He lowers His gaze to the earth and deigns to number the fortunes of mortal men among the divine works of His hands. But now, in that field of our human fortunes, He is free from care and engagement ever since He granted you to the world to be His viceregent in dealing with all mankind, and could give His time only to heaven.[5]

While the notion that the ruler embodied the general will was not new at Rome, Pliny's portrait of Trajan as the viceroy of Jupiter was symptomatic of the gradual transformation of the Roman emperors into semidivine beings. So much did the image of Trajan as an ideal monarch impress posterity that centuries later Dante placed the emperor in heaven because a pleasant legend recounted his miraculous and posthumous conversion to Christianity.

In 103 Pliny was appointed to a prominent religious office which greatly increased his prestige. The following year, he joined the commission which supervised the sewer system and flood controls of Rome. Pliny had remarried and was devoted to his third wife Calpurnia. In her absence, he fretted like a young lover:

You cannot believe how much I miss you. I love you so much, and we are not used to separations. So I stay awake most of the night thinking of you, and by day I find my feet carrying me . . . to your room at the times I usually visited you; then finding it empty, I depart as sick and sorrowful as a lover locked out.[6]

When Calpurnia suffered a miscarriage, Pliny wrote to her grandfather:

Being young and inexperienced, she did not realize she was pregnant, failed to take proper precautions, and did several things which were better left undone. She has had a severe lesson and paid for her mistake by seriously endangering her life; so that although you must inevitably feel it hard for your old age to be robbed of a descendant already on the way, you should thank the gods for sparing your granddaughter's life even though they denied you the child for the present. They will surely grant us children later on, and we may take hope from this evidence of her fertility though the proof has been unfortunate. . . . Your desire for great-grandchildren cannot be keener than mine for children. Their descent from both of us should make their road to office easy; I can leave them a well-known name and an established ancestry, if only they may be born and turn our present grief to joy.[7]

Unfortunately, Calpurnia never bore the hoped-for children.

In 111 the emperor sent Pliny on a special mission to Asia Minor to investigate conditions in the province of Bithynia which had been the scene of recent misgovernment. Pliny frequently corresponded with Trajan, and the letters reveal both the methods of the imperial regime and the personalities of the two men. The most famous exchange between Pliny and Trajan concerned the treatment of Christians. In general, the Roman emperors did not approve of private organizations and outlawed most clubs, but exceptions were made for philanthropic associations, craft guilds, and recognized religious groups. In 64 Nero had treated the Christians of Rome with great ferocity and established a precedent that their coreligionists were enemies of the state. Though hostile to Judaism, Domitian had no firm policy against Christianity. However, in the Eastern provinces, individual Christians suffered prison or death for refusing to participate in the imperial cult. Many pagans believed that Christians practiced obscene rites and cannibalism and Jews were quick to point out that Jesus had been executed as a traitor to Rome. Nevertheless, the actual legal status of Christianity in the first century is vague.*

In secular matters, most Christians heeded Jesus' injunction to "render to Caesar what is Caesar's." As a loyal Roman citizen, Paul had defined the civic responsibilities of Christians:

Every person must submit to the supreme authorities. There is no authority but by act of God, and the existing authorities are instituted

*On the legal position of Christians, see Appendix One.

by him. Consequently, anyone who rebels against authority is resisting a divine institution, and those who so resist have themselves to thank for the punishment they will receive. For government, a terror to crime, has no terrors for good behavior. You wish to have no fear of the authorities? Then continue to do right and you will have their approval, for they are God's agents working for your good. But if you are doing wrong, then you will have cause to fear them; it is not for nothing that they hold the power of the sword, for they are God's agents of punishment for retribution on the offender. That is why you are obliged to submit. It is an obligation imposed not merely by fear of retribution but by conscience. That is also why you pay taxes. The authorities are in God's service, and to these duties they devote their energies.[8]

When Paul wrote this passage, the emperor Nero was "God's agent" at Rome. According to the apostle, Christians must obey even a tyrant's whim, for a ruler is answerable only to God.* However, no Christian could compromise with Caesar on one crucial point, the imperial cult, which to pagans was only a gesture of loyalty. To Christians and Jews, the worship of the emperor's *genius* was an act of idolatry, but only Jews were legally exempt from the imperial cult. Earlier, Roman officials had often confused Christians with Jews, but Pliny knew the difference.

When pagans in Bithynia denounced their neighbors as Christians, Pliny was not sure what charges should be brought against the accused individuals. Accordingly, he asked the emperor for a legal decision:

I have never been present at an examination of Christians. Consequently, I do not know the nature or the extent of the punishments usually meted out to them, nor the grounds for starting an investigation and how far it should be pressed. Nor am I at all sure whether any distinction should be made between them on the grounds of age, or if young people and adults should be treated alike; whether a pardon ought to be granted to anyone retracting his beliefs, or if he has once professed Christianity, he shall gain nothing by renouncing it; and whether it is the mere name of Christian which is punishable, even

---

*Throughout the history of Christian Europe, Paul's position has embarrassed countless rebels and reformers and comforted many a tyrant.

if innocent of crime, or rather the crimes associated with the name. For the moment, this is the line I have taken with all persons brought before me on the charge of being Christians. I have asked them in person if they are Christians, and if they admit it, I repeat the question a second and third time with a warning of the punishment awaiting them. If they persist, I order them to be led away for punishment; for, whatever the nature of their admission, I am convinced that their stubbornness and unshakeable obstinacy ought not to go unpunished. There have been others similarly fanatical who are Roman citizens. I have entered them on the list of persons to be sent to Rome for trial. Now that I have begun to deal with this problem, as so often happens, the charges are becoming more widespread and increasing in variety. An anonymous pamphlet has been circulated which contains the names of a number of accused persons. Amongst these, I consider that I should dismiss any who denied that they were or ever had been Christians when they had repeated after me a formula of invocation to the gods and had made offerings of wine and incense to your statue (which I had ordered to be brought into court for this purpose along with the images of the gods) and furthermore had reviled the name of Christ: none of which things, I understand, any genuine Christian can be induced to do. Others, whose names were given to me by an informer, first admitted the charge and then denied it; they said that they had ceased to be Christians two or more years previously, and some of them even twenty years ago. They all did reverence to your statue and the images of the gods in the same way as the others and reviled the name of Christ. They also declared that the sum total of their guilt or error amounted to no more than this: they had met regularly before dawn on a fixed day to chant verses alternately amongst themselves in honor of Christ as if to a god, and also to bind themselves by oath, not for any criminal purpose, but to abstain from theft, robbery, and adultery, to commit no breach of trust, and not to deny a deposit when called upon to restore it. After this ceremony, it had been their custom to disperse and reassemble later to take food of an ordinary, harmless kind; but they had in fact given up this practice since my edict, issued on your instructions, which banned all political societies. This made me decide it was all the more necessary to extract the truth by torture from two slave-women whom they call deaconesses. I found nothing but a degenerate sort of cult carried to extravagant lengths. I have therefore postponed any further examination and hastened to consult you. The question seems to me to be worthy of your consideration, especially in view of the number of persons endangered; for a great many individuals of every age and class, both

men and women, are being brought to trial, and this is likely to
continue. It is not only the towns but villages and rural districts too
which are infected through contact with this wretched cult. I think
though that it is still possible for it to be checked and directed to
better ends, for there is no doubt that people have begun to throng
the temples which had been almost entirely deserted for a long time;
the sacred rites which had been allowed to lapse are being performed
again, and flesh of sacrificial victims is on sale everywhere, though up
till recently scarcely anyone could be found to buy it. It is easy to
infer from this that a great many people could be reformed if they were
given an opportunity to repent.[9]

It is noteworthy that a former consul, who had spent his life in
Roman law courts, had never prosecuted or investigated a
Christian before coming to Bithynia. Since the Christians were
accused of depraved rites and eating food which was not "of an
ordinary, harmless kind," Pliny carefully investigated the sect and
found that its members had not committed any heinous crimes.
Nevertheless, he punished Christians, for they would not participate in the imperial cult. In Pliny's eyes the new sect had grown
because traditional religion had been neglected, and repression
of Christianity would have a salutary effect on temple attendance.
    Trajan's reply to Pliny reveals the attitude of the Roman
state toward Christianity:

You have followed the right course of procedure, my dear Pliny,
in your examination of the cases of persons charged with being
Christians, for it is impossible to lay down a general rule to a fixed
formula. These people must not be hunted out; if they are brought
before you and the charge against them is proved, they must be
punished, but in the case of anyone who denies that he is a Christian
and makes it clear that he is not by offering prayers to our gods, he is
to be pardoned as a result of his repentance however suspect his past
conduct may be. But, pamphlets circulated anonymously must play no
part in any accusation. They create the worst sort of precedent and are
quite out of keeping with the spirit of our age.[10]

While religious persecution is a blight on any society, the policies
of Trajan were far more humane than the vindictive bigotry of
Christian states in medieval and modern Europe. The emperor's

Trajan

refusal to consider anonymous accusations puts some modern democracies to shame.

In the Golden Age of Rome, the supremacy of the state was zealously guarded by the emperors, who were suspicious of local organizations in the provinces. In the pressing matter of fire control, Pliny asked Trajan to authorize a volunteer fire brigade for the city of Nicomedia:

While I was visiting another part of the province, a widespread fire broke out in Nicomedia which destroyed many private houses and also two public buildings (the Elder Citizens' Club and the Temple of Isis) although a road runs between them. It was fanned by the strong breeze in the early stages, but it would not have spread so far but for the apathy of the populace; for it is generally agreed that people stood watching the disaster without bestirring themselves to do anything to stop it. Apart from this, there is not a single fire engine anywhere in the town, not a bucket nor any apparatus for fighting a fire. These will now be provided on my instructions. Will you, Sir, consider whether you think a company of firemen might be formed, limited to 150 members? I will see that no one shall be admitted who is not genuinely a fireman, and that the privileges granted shall not be abused: it will not be difficult to keep such small numbers under observation.[11]

However, the emperor saw dangerous implications in Pliny's proposal:

I have received your suggestion that it should be possible to form a company of firemen at Nicomedia on the model of those existing elsewhere, but we must remember that it is societies like these which have been responsible for the political disturbances in your province, particularly in its towns. If people assemble for a common purpose, whatever name we give them and for whatever reason, they soon turn into a political club. It is a better policy, then, to provide the equipment necessary for dealing with fires and to instruct property owners to make use of it, calling on the help of the crowds which collect if they find it necessary.[12]

Though he was ruler of the world, Trajan feared that a municipal fire brigade would undermine the security of the state and subvert the Roman empire.

While Pliny was in Bithynia, Calpurnia was with him until her grandfather died and she returned to Italy to attend the funeral. Pliny never saw his beloved wife or Rome again, for he died soon after in 113. Although his role in history was minor, Pliny had served the Roman state well and faithfully, and he was fondly remembered for his personal traits. Like Seneca, Pliny had been considerate of his slaves and generous in granting them freedom. Though cagey with money, he lowered the rents of his rural tenants in bad times and toyed with the idea of profit-sharing. Content with simple fare and modest luxuries, Pliny was urbane without being shallow. While never modest about his own works, Pliny conceded the superior talents of his friend Tacitus and hoped to be mentioned in his *Histories*. Conscious of his own personal shortcomings, Pliny was tolerant of the faults of others and was not prone to rancor. Though not a hero himself, he admired the courage of senatorial martyrs who had defied tyrannical emperors. Yet Pliny saw only misguided obstinacy in the Christians of Bithynia. A sincere advocate of paternalism, he believed that the benevolent despotism of Trajan provided the best of all possible worlds. Like Trajan, Pliny donated considerable sums for public buildings and the care of poor children. All in all, the gentleman from Comum was an excellent representative of the sanity and civilization of the second century.

Much of Roman history is a bloody record of wars and conquests, and even Pliny's idol Trajan was an old warhorse who waited impatiently for new conflicts to break out. To many Romans the legendary warrior Gaius Marcius Coriolanus was a worthy hero whose entry into battle was heralded by trumpets:

These are the ushers of Marcius: before him he carries noise, and behind him he leaves tears:
Death, that dark spirit, in 's nervy arm doth lie; Which, being advanced, declines, and then men die.[13]

However, the vain Coriolanus turned on his fatherland and led foreign armies against the walls of Rome. After the Mediterranean nations had been incorporated into the Roman empire, the arts of peace were more valuable than the grim profession of war. Under the emperors Rome needed administrators who were both competent and understanding. Security, peace, and prosperity were the order of the day, and Pliny and his peers labored to achieve the ideals of good government.

Though posterity raised no colossus to Pliny the Younger, the citizens of Comum honored their distinguished neighbor with an inscription:

Gaius Plinius Caecilius Secundus, son of Lucius of the tribe Oufentina, consul: augur: praetorian commissioner with full consular power for the province of Pontus and Bithynia, sent to that province in accordance with the Senate's decree by the emperor Nerva Trajan Augustus, victor over Germany and Dacia, the Father of his Country: curator of the bed and banks of the Tiber and sewers of Rome: official of the Treasury of Saturn: official of the military Treasury: praetor: tribune of the people: quaestor of the emperor: commissioner for the Roman knights: military tribune of the Third Gallic legion: magistrate on Board of Ten: left by will public baths at a cost of [missing sum] and an additional 300,000 sesterces for furnishing them with interest on 200,000 for their upkeep . . . and also to his city capital of 1,866,-666 2/3 sesterces to support a hundred of his freedmen, and subsequently to provide an annual dinner for the people of the city. . . .

Likewise, in his lifetime he gave 500,000 sesterces for the maintenance of boys and girls of the city, and also 100,000 for the upkeep of the library. . . .[14]

There are worse things to be remembered for than philanthropy and public service.

NINE

The Historian—Tacitus

The mind of every man has deep ruts along which his thoughts tend to run. Like all men, historians are prisoners of their personalities and recast the past according to their own lights. Though he may sincerely try to be objective, the historian cannot totally submerge his biases and achieve complete impartiality. From bitter experience the British scholar Lord Acton learned that "a historian has to fight against temptations special to his mode of life, temptations from Country, Class, Church, College, Party, authority of talents, solicitation of friends. The most respectable of these influences are the most dangerous."[1] The scientific historian tries to shake free from his self and his times, but he does not always succeed. In the Roman world historians were frankly partial and quite indifferent to the discipline of scientific history. By any standard, the Roman writer Tacitus was a great historian, but his grim vision of Roman history was evoked by personal agonies of guilt and shame.

Pliny the Younger was proud of his friendship with Tacitus and envied his talents:

I have read your book and marked as carefully as I could the passages which I think should be altered or removed, for if it is my custom to tell the truth, you are always willing to hear it; no one accepts criticism so readily as those who best deserve praise. Now I am awaiting the return of my book from you with your comments: a fair exchange which we both enjoy. I am delighted to think that if posterity takes any interest in us, the tale will everywhere be told of the harmony, frankness, and loyalty of our lifelong relationship. It will seem both rare and remarkable that two men of much the same age and position, and both enjoying a certain amount of literary reputation

(I can't say much about you when it refers to me too), should have encouraged each other's literary work. I was still a young man when you were already winning fame and glory, and I aspired to follow in your footsteps and be "far behind but still the nearest" to you in fact and in repute. There were at the time many other distinguished men of talent, but a certain similarity in our natures made me feel that you were the person I could and should try to imitate. So I am all the happier to know that whenever conversation turns upon literature, our names are mentioned together, and that my name comes up when people talk about you. There may be writers who are ranked higher than either of us, but if we are classed together our position does not matter; for me the highest position is the one nearest to you. You must also surely have noticed in wills that unless someone has been a particular friend of one or the other of us, we are left legacies of the same kind and value. All this shows that our love should be still warmer, seeing that there are so many ties to bind us in our work, character, and reputation, and, above all, in the last wishes of our friends.[2]

Though Pliny's remarks were somewhat ingenuous, the two men had much in common besides sharing legacies. Both writers were outsiders at Rome, both were successful orators and civil servants, and both sat in the Senate under Domitian, Nerva, and Trajan. Their differences lay in intellect and temperament, for Tacitus was more brilliant and more sensitive to the moral dilemmas of politics. While the compliant Pliny bowed easily to the emperors, Tacitus resented the personal indignities of political life and brooded until bitterness poisoned his mind.

Unfortunately, the details of Cornelius Tacitus' family and place of birth are unknown. His first name was probably Publius, and his father may have been the financial agent Tacitus who came from Narbonensian Gaul and was known to Pliny the Elder. In his writings the historian favored men from the Western provinces and was hostile to Greeks, Jews, and other Eastern people. Probably born in Narbonensian Gaul about 56, Tacitus received his higher education at Rome, where he became an accomplished orator. According to Tacitus, his political career was "begun under Vespasian, expanded under Titus, and was further advanced by Domitian." Though he rose from the ranks of the Equites, Tacitus adopted the usual senatorial snobbery toward middle-class upstarts* and social climbing freedmen. To further his career, Tacitus married the daughter of a prominent Roman general from Gaul, Gnaeus Julius Agricola. On his own merits, the efficient young provincial won recognition in various minor government jobs. Tacitus' slow and steady advance in the civil service was reflected in his epigram: "Impatience has ruined many excellent men who, rejecting the slow sure way, court destruction by rising too quickly."[3] On his way up, Tacitus made few enemies.

In 88 Tacitus supervised the religious Secular Games and won the favor of Domitian. In 93 Tacitus was saddened by the death of his father-in-law. According to Tacitus, Domitian was jealous of Agricola's military achievements and had forced the old general into retirement. However, the emperor's alleged hostility toward Agricola did not jeopardize Tacitus' political career. In later life the historian revealed his role under Domitian by praising a courtier from another era:

I find that this Marcus Lepidus played a wise and noble part in events. He often palliated the brutalities caused by other people's sycophancy. And he had a sense of proportion—for he enjoyed unbroken influence and favor with Tiberius. This compels me to doubt whether, like other things, the friendships and enmities of rulers depend on destiny and the luck of a man's birth. Instead, may not our personalities play some part, enabling us to steer a way, safe from intrigues and hazards, between perilous insubordination and degrading servility?[4]

Besides tact, Tacitus had two other virtues, efficiency and loyalty, which Domitian admired in underlings. Since 89, when he had suppressed a serious military revolt, the emperor had become increasingly fearful of conspiracy and suspected treachery everywhere. With ruthless rigor, Domitian purged his critics in the Senate as well as traitors who aspired to the throne. Isolated by suspicion, the emperor became a prisoner of his fears and an object of terror to the aristocracy.

During the reign of terror, Tacitus did nothing to shake

---

*In his *Annals,* Tacitus was indignant that "a small-town adulterer," Sejanus, could seduce a princess and try to marry into the imperial family. Yet Sejanus came from a more distinguished family than did Tacitus.

Domitian's well-placed trust in him. Like the majority of the senators, Tacitus dutifully participated in the treason trials with which the emperor purged real and fancied enemies. Later the historian recalled the scenes with shame:

It was not long before our hands dragged Helvidius to prison, before we gazed on the [sad fates] of Mauricus and Rusticus, before we were steeped in Senecio's innocent blood. Even Nero turned his eyes away and did not gaze upon the atrocities which he ordered. With Domitian, it was the chief part of our miseries to see and to be seen, to know that our sighs were being recorded, to have, ever ready to note the pallid looks of so many faces, that savage countenance reddened with the hue with which he defied shame.[5]

Tacitus' friend Pliny also squirmed under Domitian's watchful glares:

We too were spectators in the Senate, but in a Senate which was apprehensive and dumb since it was dangerous to vote a genuine opinion and pitiable to express a forced one. What could be learned at that time, what profit could there be in learning, when the Senate was summoned to idle away its time or to perpetrate some vile crime, and was kept sitting for a joke or its own humiliation; when it could never pass a serious resolution, though often one with tragic consequences? On becoming senators we took part in these evils and continued to witness and endure them for many years, until our spirits were blunted, broken and destroyed with lingering effect.[6]

To the relief of the Senate, Domitian was slain in 96. Nevertheless, the memory of the treason trials haunted Tacitus, who was tormented by a deep sense of guilt for the rest of his life. In 97 he reached the pinnacle of his career and served as consul under Nerva, but the honor brought Tacitus little satisfaction because the consuls for 97 had been selected by Domitian before his murder.

As consul, Tacitus delivered a funeral oration for Pliny's former guardian, Verginius Rufus, but the speech is no longer extant. One wonders what he had to say about the old statesman who once had tried to save Nero's tottering throne.* Whatever its

*In 68 Rufus suppressed the rebellion of the Gallic governor Vindex and would not permit his own troops to mutiny against Nero. Note the innuendo of Tacitus, *Histories* I 52.

content, Pliny was favorably impressed by Tacitus' speech. Contrary to the sanguine hopes of many senators, the accession of Nerva did not herald an era of senatorial control of the empire. While Tacitus was consul, the aged emperor was terrorized by the Praetorian guards and driven into the hands of the army commanders who demanded that Nerva adopt Trajan as his heir. In Gibbon's words, "the military force was a blind and irresistible instrument of oppression," and Tacitus knew from history how much Roman blood generals had spilled. In 98 Trajan was emperor, but his conciliatory attitude did not relieve Tacitus, who feared the potential for violence in a military ruler. Cowed by Domitian, the Senate did not provide a counterbalance to the absolutism of Trajan. To give the Senate token responsibility for consular elections, the emperor permitted the august chamber to use secret ballots to vote on his candidates, but some senators responded by scribbling jokes and obscenities on their ballots. Despising his peers and wary of their master, Tacitus had no illusions about the imperial system. Like most Romans of his time, Tacitus believed that popular governments were unruly and that the Republic had been a failure, but few would agree with his claim that the last good legislation had been passed in 451 B.C. Neither Republican nor monarchist, Tacitus lacked an ideological crutch on which to lean, for he saw political life as only a savage struggle for power between selfish men. Since it was better to run with the hounds than with the hares, Tacitus served the new regime efficiently, but his heart was troubled by old guilts and new apprehensions.

Had he been only a bureaucrat, Tacitus might have found satisfaction in public service. But he was primarily an intellectual who needed to express the ideas which nagged him. In an early essay on oratory, Tacitus discussed the decay of Roman eloquence in his time. Under the Republic famed orators had goaded men into civil war, but under the emperors conformity had dried up the founts of eloquence. According to Tacitus, great oratory required the open debates of the Republic, but the Roman world needed the mute security which the emperors provided. True eloquence could only spring from great ideas and momentous questions, but contemporary orators could not pursue dangerous subjects. Ignoring the didactic poems of Lucretius, Tacitus argued that poetry was unfit for the expression of ideas. With heavy sarcasm, he depicted the life of a professional poet:

When, with the labor of a whole year, through entire days and the best part of the nights, he has hammered out with the midnight oil a single book, he is forced actually to beg and canvass for people who will condescend to be his hearers and not even this without cost to himself. He gets the loan of a house, fits up a room, hires benches, and scatters programmes. Even if his reading is followed by a complete success, all the glory is, so to say, cut short in the bloom and the flower and does not come to any real and substantial fruit. He carries away with him not a single friendship, not a single client, not an obligation that will abide in anyone's mind, only idle applause, meaningless acclamations, and a fleeting delight.[7]

Disdaining poetry and despairing of oratory, Tacitus took up the writing of history.

Historians too had their share of difficulty. When the emperor Claudius had held the first public reading of his historical work, a bench collapsed and reduced his audience to laughter. However, Tacitus was not interested in public recitals but in private readers. Hoping to win men's minds with rhetoric, Tacitus employed a terse style which bristled with epigrams: "Public opinion is not always mistaken; sometimes even it chooses the right man. . . . It is the singularly unfair peculiarity of war that the credit of success is claimed by all, while a disaster is attributed to one alone."[8] The works of Tacitus are filled with similar acid comments on human nature. He began his career as a historian with two monographs, a biography of Agricola and a description of the German tribes; the latter was a topical subject, for Trajan was campaigning in Germany. For the *Germania* Tacitus borrowed ethnological data from Pliny the Elder and other standard authors. When he moralized on the virtues of primitive life and the vices of civilization, Tacitus merely repeated Hellenistic and Roman sermons on the "noble savage." With more perception, he argued that the Roman empire was safe from invasion only as long as the barbarian tribes remained divided and at war with each other.

In the biography of his father-in-law Agricola, Tacitus inflated the late general into a figure of heroic proportions. The sketch also gave Tacitus an opportunity to exonerate Agricola, himself, and all provincials who had served the tyrant Domitian:

Notwithstanding his irascible temper and an implacability proportioned to his reserve, [Domitian] was softened by the moderation and prudence of Agricola, who neither by a perverse obstinacy nor an idle parade of freedom challenged fame or provoked his fate. Let it be known to those whose habit it is to admire the disregard of authority, that there may be great men even under bad emperors, and that obedience and submission, when joined to activity and vigor, may attain a glory which most men reach only by a perilous career, utterly useless to the state and closed by an ostentatious death.[9]

No doubt, Trajan too was flattered, for he had been one of Domitian's generals. Though anxious to downgrade the image of senators who perished under Nero and Domitian, Tacitus was still rankled by the thought that the theatrics of martyrs do not excuse the guilt of judges and hangmen.

In his monograph on Agricola, Tacitus described his father-in-law's campaigns in Britain and admired the primitive tribesmen who resisted the Romans with courage and tenacity. In praising the brave Britons, Tacitus criticized Romans who expanded the empire for purposes of rapine and glory. As a loyal Roman the historian did not condemn "preventive wars" on the frontier, but he could not condone the relentless march of Roman imperialism. In the late Republic the historian Sallust, whose writings Tacitus admired, had idealized the Spaniards and Asians who resisted Roman expansion. Following in the tradition of Sallust, Tacitus put memorable words in the mouth of a Scottish chieftain:

There are no tribes beyond us, nothing indeed but waves and rocks, and the yet more terrible Romans from whose oppression escape is vainly sought by obedience and submission. Robbers of the world, having by their universal plunder exhausted the land, they rifle the deep. If the enemy be rich, they are rapacious; if he be poor, they lust for dominion; neither the east nor the west has been able to satisfy them. Alone among men they covet with equal eagerness poverty and riches. To robbery, slaughter, plunder, they give the lying name of empire; they make a solitude and call it peace.[10]

Perhaps the historian hoped to calm Trajan's itch for further conquests. More likely, Tacitus could not resist focusing on the evil which lay behind the glory of Rome. The blight in human nature obsessed him.

By 105 Tacitus was well into a major historical work, the *Histories*, which dealt with the Year of the Four Emperors and the Flavian dynasty. According to Tacitus, all historians in the imperial era were warped by servility or hatred, but he claimed to be an exception. However, Tacitus too was hopelessly biased, for he assumed that all men were corrupt and most politicians were drunk with power. In Tacitus' eyes, Vespasian was the only emperor who improved after gaining the throne, and even his accession had revealed the "secret of the empire," that the legions could elevate and unseat emperors at will. To judicious readers in the time of Trajan, the significance of the Year of the Four Emperors was obvious, for Tacitus used the feeble Nerva as a model for his portrait of the ineffective Galba. In the *Histories* an agent of Nero was credited with a speech which could well serve as an apology for Tacitus:

I do not forget the times in which I have been born or the form of government which our fathers and grandfathers established. I may regard with admiration an earlier period, but I acquiesce in the present and, while I pray for good emperors, I can endure whomsoever we may have. It was not through my speech any more than it was through the judgment of the Senate that Thrasea fell. The savage temper of Nero amused itself under these forms, and I found the friendship of such a prince as harassing as others found their exile. Helvidius may rival the Catos and the Bruti of old in constancy and courage; I am but one of the Senate which bows to the same yoke.[11]

The pages of Tacitus are haunted by many figures who could boast—like the Abbé Siéyès—that they had survived. In imperial Rome survival had become a fine art.

Tacitus' account of Vespasian's miracles in Egypt is characteristic of the historian's attitude toward religion:

One of the common people of Alexandria, well-known for his blindness, threw himself at the emperor's knees and implored him with groans to heal his infirmity. This he did by the advice of the god Serapis whom this nation, devoted as it is to many superstitions, worships more than any other divinity. He begged Vespasian that he would deign to moisten his cheeks and eye-balls with his spittle. Another with a diseased hand, at the counsel of the same god, prayed that the limb might feel the print of a Caesar's foot. At first, Vespasian ridiculed and repulsed them. They persisted; and he, though on the one hand he feared the scandal of a fruitless attempt, yet, on the other, was induced by the entreaties of the men and by the language of his flatterers to hope for success. At last, he ordered that the opinion of physicians should be taken, as to whether such blindness and infirmity were within the reach of human skill. They discussed the matter from different points of view. "In the one case," they said, "the faculty of sight was not wholly destroyed and might return if the obstacles were removed; in the other case, the limb, which had fallen into a diseased condition, might be restored if a healing influence were applied; such, perhaps, might be the pleasure of the gods and the emperor might be chosen to be the minister of the divine will. At any rate, all the glory of a successful remedy would be Caesar's, while the ridicule of failure would fall on the sufferers." And so Vespasian, supposing that all things were possible to his good fortune and that nothing was any longer past belief, with a joyful countenance amid the intense expectation of the multitude of bystanders, accomplished what was required. The hand was instantly restored to its use, and the light of day again shone upon the blind. Persons actually present attest both facts, even now when nothing is to be gained by falsehood.[12]

The miracles of Vespasian are as plausible as any in history.

Like most Romans, Tacitus was skeptical of fakirs and foreign cults, but he worried over omens and was troubled by the stars. Though he denounced astrologers as troublemakers who preyed on frightened people and excited ambitious politicians, the historian was uncertain about the role which the stars played in human affairs. According to Tacitus, the ignominious early life of Claudius proved that destiny could be playful: "The more I think about history, ancient or modern, the more ironical all human affairs seem. In public opinion, expectation, and esteem, no one appeared a less likely candidate for the throne than the man for whom destiny was secretly reserving it."[13] As for the baleful influence of Sejanus on Tiberius, the historian felt that the gods had elevated the sinister prefect out of anger toward Rome. The older Tacitus grew, the more he was inclined to believe that a malign force was at work in history.

As governor in Asia Minor in 113, Tacitus may have had contact with Christians. Unlike Pliny, the historian would not have been gentle with the sectarians, for he had great antipathy for the peoples of the East.* His description of Nero's persecution of Christians is a valuable document, which also displays Tacitus' personal bias. Despite Nero's relief efforts for the victims of the great fire of 64, many Romans believed that the emperor had engineered the burning of Rome to make room for a projected palace:

> To suppress this rumor, Nero fabricated scapegoats and punished with every refinement the notoriously depraved Christians (as they were popularly called). Their originator, Christ, had been executed in Tiberius' reign by the governor of Judea, Pontius Pilatus. But, in spite of this temporary setback, the deadly superstition had broken out afresh, not only in Judea (where the mischief had started) but even in Rome. All degraded and shameful practices collect and flourish in the capital. First, Nero had self-acknowledged Christians arrested. Then, on their information, large numbers of others were condemned —not so much for incendiarism as for their anti-social tendencies. Their deaths were made farcical. Dressed in wild animals' skins, they were torn to pieces by dogs, or crucified, or made into torches to be ignited after dark as substitutes for daylight. Nero provided his gardens for the spectacle and exhibited displays in the Circus, at which he mingled with the crowd or stood in a chariot, dressed as a charioteer. Despite their guilt as Christians and the ruthless punishment it deserved, the victims were pitied, for it was felt that they were being sacrificed to one man's brutality rather than to the national interest.[14]

It is noteworthy that the Roman masses felt compassion for Nero's scapegoats. When the city was burning, some excited Christians may have imagined that the end of the world had come, and their joyful hosannas would have evoked surprise and resentment from victims of the fire. Though he considered the sect antisocial, Tacitus did not accept the charge that the Christians were arsonists.

---

*Tacitus' anti-Semitism is particularly evident in Book V of his *Histories*.

In 117 Trajan died in the East and was succeeded by his kinsman Hadrian. Since the death of Trajan and his adoption of Hadrian were announced simultaneously, rumors circulated that Trajan's widow and the Praetorian prefect had forged the adoption on Hadrian's behalf. The new emperor was pro-Greek, and many senators feared that another Nero was on the throne when Hadrian purged four men of consular rank on a charge of conspiracy. Tacitus' suspicions of Hadrian were reflected in his last book, the Annals, which dealt with the Julio-Claudian dynasty.*
As usual, the historian claimed to be impartial, but he portrayed Tiberius as a malicious ogre, Claudius a lecherous buffoon, and Nero a vicious monster. Luckily for Caligula, Tacitus' pages on him have been lost over the centuries. The Annals was a savage study in tyranny, for Tacitus had great contempt for the emperors and their creatures:

It seems to me a historian's foremost duty to ensure that merit is recorded and to confront evil deeds and words with the fear of posterity's denunciations. But this was a tainted, meanly obsequious age. The greatest figures had to protect their positions by subserviency; and, in addition to them, all ex-consuls, most ex-praetors, even many junior senators competed with each other's offensively sycophantic proposals. There is a tradition that whenever Tiberius left the Senate House, he exclaimed in Greek, "Men fit to be slaves!" Even he, freedom's enemy, became impatient of such abject servility.[15]

With gusto, the moralistic historian pored over the partisan literature which had been circulated by enemies of the Julio-Claudian family. Like a master journalist, Tacitus spiced his factual narratives with sly innuendoes and often mentioned an emperor's worthy acts only to impute the ruler's sincerity and suggest some secret mischief. Though he discounted rumors of private vice and sinister crimes, the historian carefully recited the details in order to poison the minds of his readers. For scandalous charges against the imperial family, Tacitus made effective use of a vindictive pamphlet which Agrippina the Younger had written after her fall from power. The aged Tacitus was preoccupied with

*Since an early passage in the Annals refers to the extension of the Roman empire to the Persian Gulf, the bulk of the work can be dated after 116.

death and dwelt excessively on murders and suicides until Julio-Claudian Rome seemed a vast charnel house.

In the *Annals* the historian not only attacked the rulers of the past but also libeled the reigning emperor Hadrian. Without proof Tacitus suggested that the empress Livia had murdered Augustus and concealed his death until Tiberius was secure on the throne—the bizarre tale was a tasteless parody of the events surrounding Hadrian's succession. With his usual ambivalence, the historian also sneered at the enemies of the Caesars and caustically remarked that the Stoic martyr Thrasea Paetus "walked out of the Senate—thereby endangering himself without bringing general freedom any nearer." Yet despite his blinding biases Tacitus was a great historian and filled the *Annals* with valuable data and many sensible comments. Unfortunately, his bitter caricatures of the Julio-Claudian emperors have become more real than the men themselves. Though he once planned to describe the less hectic reigns of Nerva and Trajan, Tacitus changed his mind in his old age and hoped to live long enough to impale Augustus on his pen. However, the historian died about 123 and his study of the Princeps was never written.

The tone of Tacitus' projected work on Augustus may be inferred from a passage in the *Annals:*

Filial duty and national crisis had been merely pretexts. In actual fact, the motive of Octavian, the future Augustus, was lust for power. Inspired by that, he had mobilized ex-army settlers by gifts of money, raised an army—while he was only a half-grown boy without any official status—won over a consul's brigades by bribery, pretended to support Sextus Pompeius, and by senatorial decree usurped the status and rank of a praetor. Soon both consuls had met their deaths—by enemy action, or perhaps in the one case by the deliberate poisoning of his wound, and in the other at the hand of his own troops, instigated by Octavian. In any case, it was he who took over both their armies. Then he had forced the reluctant Senate to make him consul. But the forces given him to deal with Antony he used against the state. His judicial murders and land distributions were distasteful even to those who carried them out. True, Cassius and Brutus died because he had inherited a feud against them; nevertheless, personal enmities ought to be sacrificed to the public interest. Next he had cheated Sextus Pompeius by a spurious peace treaty, Lepidus by spurious friendship.

Then Antony, enticed by treaties and his marriage with Octavian's sister, had paid the penalty of that delusive relationship with his life. After that, there had certainly been peace, but it was a bloodstained peace of disasters and assassinations. And gossip did not spare his personal affairs—how he had abducted another man's wife and asked the priests the farcical question whether it was in order for her to marry while pregnant. Then there was the debauchery of a friend. Finally, there was Livia, a catastrophe to the nation as a mother and to the house of the Caesars as a stepmother.[16]

Tacitus' failure to write a study of Augustus was a loss to literature but not to history.

Under despotism sheep can live in untroubled security, but the introspective intellectual is prone to anxiety. Should he choose to oppose the regime, the intellectual can expect betrayal and death. If he becomes an apologist for the tyrant, the man of intellect loses integrity and does not achieve security, for a sudden policy change may sweep him out of favor. Whether critic or courtier, he lives in fear and frustration. Under Hitler and Stalin, some scholars escaped from reality by burying themselves in either exotic or antiquarian studies. However, men like Tacitus cannot escape into scholarship, for they are trapped by their careers and find it difficult to give up the rewards of high office. Though he scorns the egocentric delusions of rebels and martyrs, the compromised intellectual may eventually turn the torch of analysis on himself. When Tacitus faced the reality of his role under Domitian, the awareness of his guilt permanently scarred his personality. As a historian Tacitus' insights had been sharpened by his experiences under Domitian, and he could see the brutal facts behind the facade of Trajan's Golden Age. Nevertheless, suspicion warped his judgment and Tacitus became like Tiberius, isolated, alienated, and obsessed with the wolfish behavior of men.

Over the centuries many readers have appreciated Tacitus' sardonic comments on men and politics. During the religious wars of the sixteenth century, the French essayist Michel de Montaigne pored over the grim pages of Tacitus:

I have lately been reading without a break the history of Tacitus, which seldom happens to me; it is twenty years since I gave an entire hour to a book. . . . I know no author who connects with a public chronicle so much consideration of private manners and tendencies. . . . He gives us personal judgment rather than a deduction from history; there are more precepts in it than narratives. It is not a book to read, it is a book to study and learn; it is so full of opinions that there are both wrong and right ones; it is a nursery of ethical and political discourses for the purveying and garnishment of those who have some prominence in managing the world. . . . He is more adapted to be of service to a disturbed and disordered state like our present one; you would often say that he is painting us and pinching us.[17]

Though he found much truth in Tacitus, Montaigne also realized that the Roman historian was guilty of prejudice and exaggeration.

Montaigne's criticism of the Renaissance historian, Francesco Guicciardini, could be applied to Tacitus as well:

Of the many minds and deeds he judges, of the many activities and counsels, he never connects one of them with virtue, piety, or conscience, as if those motives were wholly extinct on earth; and of all the actions, however apparently noble they may be in themselves, he ascribes the cause to some sinful opportunity or to some profit. It is impossible to believe that, among that infinite number of actions on which he passes judgment, there may not have been one inspired by the process of reason. No corruption can have infected men so universally that some one did not escape the contagion. This makes me fear that a little vice may have been to his taste; that this may have come about because he judged others by himself.[18]

Though they lived centuries apart, both Guicciardini and Tacitus had bloodied their hands in political purges, groveled before princes at Rome, and later relieved their guilt by libeling rulers who were safely dead. Assessing a kindred spirit, Guicciardini remarked that "Cornelius Tacitus teaches those who live under tyrants how to live and act prudently, just as he teaches tyrants ways to secure their tyranny."[19] Though a major writer, Tacitus is not a safe guide for the study of Roman history because he was hampered by bias and did not comprehend the mentality of despots. However, Tacitus made a valuable contribution to historical sociology with his penetrating studies of opportunists who, like himself, sat in the Senate and survived under tyrants.

TEN

The Emperor—Hadrian

Several times in history Rome has been ruled by great Spaniards. The first Spanish emperors were Trajan and Hadrian, and the family of Marcus Aurelius came from Spain. In the fourth century, the last ruler of a unified Roman empire was a Spaniard, Theodosius I, and in the late fifteenth century, Rome was in the hands of the capable Spanish pope, Alexander VI Borgia. Clever and ambitious, Hadrian would have been appreciated by the Borgias. In 76 Publius Aelius Hadrianus was born in the city of Italica in Spain. His family was senatorial in rank but clannish and provincial in sentiment. When his father died, young Hadrian became a ward of his cousin Trajan, who was at that time a rising career officer. Later, Trajan's friend Acilius Attianus became the boy's guardian. While fond of Greek literature, Hadrian enjoyed hunting, outdoor life, and military service. Though too bookish for Trajan's tastes, Hadrian had pleased his powerful cousin by bringing Trajan the news of his adoption by Nerva. However, Hadrian's brother-in-law Julius Ursus Servianus was jealous of the young man and often maligned Hadrian in Trajan's presence. When Nerva died in 98, Hadrian rushed to announce the good news to Trajan, but Servianus' agents tried to delay him by sabotaging his carriage. Though the vehicle broke down, the young Spaniard continued on foot and was the first person to hail Trajan as emperor. Through such efforts, Hadrian hoped to win the favor of Trajan, but he was disliked by most of the hard-drinking generals who were his cousin's cronies. Even the emperor resented the haughtiness of young Hadrian, who remained aloof during Trajan's drinking bouts. In time Hadrian imitated the bad habits of the emperor, but the two men were never at ease together.

Though often at odds with Trajan, Hadrian had a powerful protector in the military clique which surrounded the emperor. His patron was the Spanish general L. Licinius Sura, who had helped to engineer the bloodless coup which brought Trajan to the throne. Unlike Trajan's other friends, Sura had intellectual leanings and considered Hadrian a bright young man with good prospects. Though Trajan was cool to the proposal, Sura persuaded the emperor to approve a marriage between Hadrian and Trajan's grandniece Sabina. When Hadrian served as a government official and read the emperor's messages to the Senate, the audience laughed at his Spanish accent. Deeply humiliated, Hadrian carefully improved his Latin. From 101 to 106, he campaigned with Trajan in Dacia and gained valuable experience in warfare. Because Hadrian displayed military ability and joined in Trajan's carousing, the emperor looked more favorably on him. When Hadrian was consul in 108, Sura hoped that his protégé would soon be adopted by the childless Trajan. However, Sura died in 110 and left Hadrian with only two friends close to the emperor—the Praetorian prefect Attianus, who had been Hadrian's guardian, and the empress Plotina, who was personally fond of the young man. Though the prefect and Plotina wanted Trajan to adopt Hadrian, the emperor refused to designate an heir. More interested in expanding the empire, Trajan spent his time planning strategy with the Moor Lusius Quietus and other generals who were eager for war. Since the emperor's education had been limited and his speeches needed polish, Hadrian occasionally served as a ghost writer for Trajan, but the ambitious young Spaniard received no assurance that he would ever be adopted as heir.

Since the time of Augustus and Tiberius, Roman foreign policy had reflected a realistic appraisal of the international situation. As long as the barbarian tribes were divided, the Roman empire was safe behind its natural boundaries, the Rhine and the Danube in the north and the wastes of the Sahara in the south. In the east the Roman world stopped at the Euphrates, but beyond lay a major world power, the Parthian kingdom, which had inflicted serious defeats on Roman armies in the past and continued to stir up subject peoples and client states in the Syriac areas. Since neither empire could conquer the other, Rome

and Parthia had accepted a loose balance of power but resorted
to occasional wars over control of Armenia and other buffer
states. To avoid damage to their own territories, the Romans
and Parthians usually fought their battles in Armenia. Unfortunately, Trajan's conquest of Dacia had upset the Augustan
concept of natural frontiers, for the Roman empire now included
areas north of the Danube. In 113 war broke out with Parthia,
and Trajan hurried to the east to win new lands and laurels.
Though he was almost buried alive during an earthquake at
Antioch, the emperor was undaunted and invaded the Parthian
realm. Seizing Mesopotamia, he set up ephemeral Roman provinces in the conquered areas. In 115, when Hadrian was governor
of Syria, Trajan reached the Persian Gulf and talked wildly of
sailing to India. However, his trip to India was only a dream and
his conquests in Mesopotamia soon proved to be a house of
cards. When the Parthians counterattacked, the natives of Mesopotamia rose against the Romans, and Trajan had to withdraw
his legions into Syria. Meanwhile, Parthian agents and Messianic
hopes had excited many Jews throughout the Near East. In Libya
and on Cyprus, Jewish zealots rebelled against Rome and
massacred their pagan neighbors, but the insurrections were
quickly suppressed. After some hesitation, the Jews of Palestine
gambled on Parthian aid and rose against Trajan. However, the
rebels were soon defeated by the brutal Lusius Quietus. Because
of Trajan's lust for glory, Rome had fought an expensive and
fruitless war against Parthia and been forced to crush revolts
in strategic provinces.

In 117 the old emperor was broken in body and spirit. Ill
with dropsy and depressed over recent failures, Trajan suffered a
severe stroke at Antioch and was partially paralyzed. Anxious to
reach Rome, the dying emperor left Syria but was stricken again
in Cilicia. Attended by Plotina, Attianus, and his personal valet,
Trajan died in the small town of Selinus early in August. His
death was kept secret until Plotina and Attianus had sent dis-
patches to Hadrian and the Senate, announcing that Trajan had
adopted Hadrian on his deathbed. The Praetorian prefect also
arranged the quick demise of the valet who had witnessed Trajan's
death. At the news of his good fortune, Hadrian was overjoyed
and may even have been surprised. Since the legions in the east

backed Hadrian, the Senate was compliant and accepted the new emperor.

As ruler, Hadrian's first official act was a drastic reversal of foreign policy—he repudiated the imperialistic aims of Trajan, made peace with Parthia, and gave up any Roman claim on Mesopotamia. In Europe Hadrian retained Dacia and fortified weak spots on the long frontier which stretched from the Black Sea to the North Sea. However, the return to Augustan policies in the East angered the army leaders, who had hoped for continued war. In 118 Lusius Quietus and other generals who had been close to Trajan formed a conspiracy to overthrow Hadrian, but the alert emperor learned of the plot and struck first. In a thorough and unexpected purge, Quietus and three other men of consular rank were executed by agents of Attianus. Though the Senate dutifully approved the executions, its members were troubled by the speed and ruthlessness of the purge. In public the emperor claimed that the Praetorian prefect had been hasty and acted without full authority. But few senators were fooled by Hadrian's hypocrisy or soothed by his promise that in the future, suspected traitors would be tried by their peers in the Senate. To reassure the senators, the emperor forced Attianus to retire and assume the empty role of an elder statesman. As a result of the purge, Servianus and Hadrian's other enemies were cowed and abandoned overt opposition for the present. The wily Hadrian had anticipated Machiavelli's axioms that political murders should be done quickly at the beginning of a regime and that rulers should always repudiate the unpopular acts of their henchmen.

To win over public opinion at Rome, Hadrian burned the records of overdue debts which private citizens owed to the state, and he promised to review such accounts every fifteen years. Since bad debts are uncollectable, the gesture cost nothing and the emperor acquired a reputation for generosity among the common people. Like his predecessors, Hadrian occasionally distributed gifts of cash to residents of the capital and freely granted funds and public buildings to cities throughout the empire. As an imperial philanthropist Hadrian continued state aid for poor children. For greater equity in the courts Hadrian initiated a major codification of Roman law, and many of his own decrees reflected a humanitarian concern for slaves and commoners. Since Vespasian, the middle class had played a significant role in the Roman government, and Equites served on the imperial council, which advised Hadrian on matters of high policy. Senators also sat on the council, but social mobility had made the distinction between the two classes less relevant, for ability rather than birth earned high positions in government, and many able Equites were eventually promoted to senatorial rank. Though he maintained an extensive and efficient secret police, the emperor assured his old enemies that he could no longer indulge in personal hatreds as a private citizen would. In general, Hadrian ruled with restraint and tact, but he remained an object of suspicion and hatred to the senatorial class, who never forgot the purge of 118.

The emperor was a many-sided man with a complex personality. Outwardly friendly, he was suspicious by nature and alienated many with his intellectual vanity. Sporting a curly beard,* Hadrian was a tall and handsome man with a strong physique. Fond of strenuous exercise, he was a dedicated hiker and an amateur mountain climber. Though often outdoors, Hadrian disliked hats and went uncovered in rain or snow. Like Napoleon, the emperor had a phenomenal memory and could remember minute details to the despair of forgetful officials and pompous pedants. An aspiring intellectual, Hadrian wrote excellent poetry and an autobiography which was largely an apology for his career. He admired the contemporary philosophers Euphrates and Epictetus, and the emperor enjoyed discussions with scholars on a great variety of subjects. Opinionated on literature, Hadrian claimed that the Greek epic poet Antimachus was a better writer than Homer. In Latin letters the emperor had archaic tastes and preferred Cato and Ennius to Cicero and Vergil. When court scholars were criticized for tamely accepting Hadrian's biased opinions, the rhetorician Favorinus of Arles explained that no one could argue with a man who commanded thirty legions.

---

*Since the second century B.C., Romans had been clean-shaven like the Greeks, who imitated Alexander the Great. When Hadrian grew a beard to hide a scar or facial blemish, beards became fashionable again.

Hadrian

Like most dilettantes, Hadrian dabbled in many fields. He painted and sculpted, toyed with architecture and engineering, and was fascinated by inventions and intricate weapons. Although his friend Favorinus scoffed at astrology, the emperor firmly believed in astral determinism and was a skilled astrologer. At Rome Hadrian rebuilt the Pantheon as a huge domed structure and built a circular tomb for himself, the present Castel Sant' Angelo. At Tivoli the emperor filled his palatial estate with reproductions of famous buildings which he had admired in his travels. A bizarre private world, Tivoli served as a retreat for Hadrian, whose marriage with Sabina was childless and unhappy. When the ill-tempered empress was slighted by his secretary Suetonius and other palace officials, Hadrian dutifully exiled the guilty courtiers and sent Suetonius off to Gaul.* Though he

---

*A prolific author, Suetonius wrote the *Lives of the Twelve Caesars,* which were lively and disorganized sketches of Roman rulers from Caesar to Domitian. Though fond of spicy anecdotes, Suetonius used valuable documents in the imperial library and described many episodes which Tacitus chose to ignore.

defended Sabina in public, the emperor found distraction in private with a Bithynian youth, Antinous, whose effeminate features have been preserved in many statues. In the belief that his own death would somehow save Hadrian from doom, Antinous drowned himself in the Nile during a visit of Hadrian to Egypt. The grief-stricken emperor deified the dead favorite and built the city of Antinoopolis in his honor. Without Antinous, Hadrian was lonely in the midst of an extremely active life.

A compulsive tourist, the emperor traveled almost constantly and was familiar with most of the provinces in his realm. Acting as his own inspector general, Hadrian often paid surprise visits to provincial officials and frontier posts. While at military camps, the emperor ate with the enlisted men, joined them on forced marches, and participated in spear throwing and sword practice. At the end of a hard day the tireless ruler would spend the night examining the records of adjutants and quartermasters. As a result of Hadrian's harrowing inspections and his insistence on firm discipline, the Roman army reached a peak of preparedness and efficiency under an emperor who disavowed conquest and avoided wars. During his twenty-one-year reign Hadrian's travels kept him away from the city of Rome for a total of twelve years. Visiting Gaul in 121, he was in Britain the following year and inspected Spain in 123. Back at Rome in 124, Hadrian attended the funeral of Trajan's widow Plotina, who had given him the throne but had played no political role in his regime. From 124 to 125 the emperor toured Asia Minor and Greece, and at Athens he was initiated into the venerable Eleusinian Mysteries. Later the imperial tourist stopped in Sicily and climbed the slopes of Mount Etna to view the sunrise from the summit. In 128 Hadrian visited North Africa and spent the following year in Athens. After inspecting Palestine and the Arabian border, he toured Egypt in 130, but his visit was saddened by the unexpected death of Antinous. By 132 Hadrian was back at Rome, but a major revolt soon forced him to return to the east.

In Palestine Hadrian's religious policies had brought on what would be the last great Jewish revolt. The emperor was a fervent Hellenophile and hoped that the peoples of the Near East would abandon their native cultures and embrace Greco-Roman civilization as a totality. Like Antiochus IV centuries earlier, Hadrian commanded his subjects to identify their local Baals as forms of Zeus and did not realize that Yahweh was more than a Baal to the Jews. The emperor had rebuilt the ruined city of Jerusalem, renamed it Aelia Capitolina, and ordered that a shrine for Jupiter be constructed on the former site of the Temple. By Roman standards Hadrian was not narrow-minded, and in Egypt he had insisted that Christians were entitled to due process of law and should be protected from malicious accusers.[1] However, the emperor was probably unconsciously hostile to Judaism because of the Jewish revolt against Trajan. By ordering a pagan temple for Jerusalem Hadrian unwittingly touched off another rebellion in Palestine. Though the severe measures of Titus and Lusius Quietus had broken the spirit of many Jews, some still clung to apocalyptic fantasies and Messianic hopes. In 132 the threat of Hadrian's proposed temple prompted a desperate rising of zealots under a new Messiah, Simon Bar-Kochba, the self-styled "Son of the Star." After Bar-Kochba stormed Jerusalem and defeated a Roman field force, his fanatic followers terrorized Christians and confidently expected victory over Rome. In 134 Hadrian took personal charge of the campaign in Palestine, where both Romans and Jews suffered enormous losses. In 135 the emperor recovered Jerusalem and crushed the last embers of revolt. Furious with the Jews of Palestine, Hadrian outlawed the practice of circumcision and ordered that all copies of the Torah be burned. In the persecution many rabbis refused to surrender the scriptures and were burned together with their books. The law against circumcision was enforced until Hadrian's mild successor Antoninus Pius relaxed the ban and allowed Jews to revive the custom. After the great revolt of 66–70, many Jews in the empire had adjusted to the loss of the Temple, but the rebellions against Trajan and Hadrian brought about the alienation of most Jews from Roman society. No longer a favored or trusted people, the Jews of the Near East slipped gradually into the psychological isolation of the Talmudic era.

When he returned from Palestine the emperor was suffering from dropsy and often bled from the nose. Since he was sixty years old and in poor health, Hadrian decided to adopt an heir, but his choice of a successor was whimsical. In 136 the emperor

adopted L. Ceionius Commodus,* who assumed the official name
of L. Aelius Caesar. An affable playboy, Aelius had served in
the government without distinction and preferred social events
to the duties of state. His sole contribution to Rome was the
invention of a meat pie which was filled with pork and choice
bits of game birds, and his favorite readings were a cookbook
and Ovid's *Art of Love*. Though gossips whispered that he was
a former favorite of Hadrian, Aelius was a notorious ladies' man
and a devoted father. Neither hated, feared, nor respected,
Hadrian's heir tried to rise to his new role and learn the onerous
duties of an emperor. However, it soon became evident that
Aelius was tubercular and would not live much longer. The old
emperor bitterly complained, "I have leaned against a tottering
wall and wasted a fortune on an heir who will not outlive me."
When Aelius Caesar died in January 138, Hadrian chose another
heir, the middle-aged senator T. Aurelius Antoninus, who in turn
was obliged to adopt two boys, his own nephew Marcus Aurelius
and Aelius' son Lucius Verus. Since young Marcus Aurelius was
betrothed to Lucius' sister, Hadrian ensured that Antoninus'
heirs would be the son and potential son-in-law of the late Aelius
Caesar. Though the dying emperor's final choices proved to be
beneficial for Rome, only the death of Aelius had prevented
Hadrian from elevating an incompetent man to the throne. To
the emperor, the best man—Antoninus—had only seemed second-
rate.

The last days of Hadrian were marred by political intrigue and
physical pain. The urban prefect L. Catilius Severus had hoped
to be chosen as Hadrian's heir and was angered by the adoption
of Antoninus. When Severus voiced his opposition, Hadrian removed him from office. The emperor had to take more severe
measures against an old enemy, his brother-in-law Servianus.
For years the Spanish politician had waited to move against
Hadrian, and now that the emperor was dying, Servianus plotted
to seize the throne for his grandson Fuscus. The boy had an
"imperial" horoscope but did not live to fulfill it, for Hadrian

---

*Commodus' father-in-law, Nigrinus, had been a close friend of Hadrian
but had conspired with Quietus and perished in the purge of 118. Perhaps,
the emperor had reconsidered the guilt of Nigrinus and wished to atone
to his family by adopting Commodus who was otherwise unqualified.

learned of the plot, executed Fuscus, and forced Servianus to commit suicide. Depressed by the Servianus affair, Hadrian faced his own death, but his strong physique prolonged the agonies. Helpless and racked with pain, the emperor raged at his attendants and ordered them to kill him, but the servants fled and the doctors feared the consequences of regicide. In a lucid moment, the dying man scrawled a poignant poem on death:

> Little soul, like a cloud, like a feather,
> My body's small guest and companion,
> Where now do you rest, in what places—
> Stripped naked, and rigid, and pallid,
> Do you play as before, little jester?[2]

On July 10, 138, Hadrian escaped from pain and slipped into the dark oblivion of death. Though the vengeful Senate did not wish to deify the late emperor, Antoninus insisted on the conventional honors for the man who had adopted him. Despite senatorial objections, Hadrian became a god and Antoninus acquired the epithet Pius.

Unlike his predecessor, the new emperor Antoninus Pius was frugal, unassuming, and fond of fishing. Unfortunately, he also lacked the grinding efficiency of Hadrian and remained at Rome while his subordinates solved crises in the provinces. Under the gentle regime of Antoninus, Jews and Christians breathed more freely, but the Roman world stagnated. In the *Pax Romana* the general prosperity of the empire had not trickled down to the rural masses, who made up the bulk of the population. Most peasants were not freeholders but tenant farmers, and many urban dwellers suffered from chronic unemployment and lived in squalor in the slums of great cities. The glory of Rome was half submerged in poverty, and the generous social programs of Trajan, Hadrian, and Antoninus Pius did little to relieve the imbalance between the few rich and the many poor. Extensive public and private philanthropy obscured the inequities in the Roman economy and permitted the ruler and the upper classes to indulge in an illusory sense of social responsibility. Camus' epigram is applicable to second-century Rome: "The welfare of the people has always been the alibi of tyrants, and it provides the further advantage of giving the servants of tyranny a good conscience."[3] Though the emperors and most of their agents meant well, their horizons were limited by habit and self-interest. Satisfied with the existing system, the rulers of Rome could not see that changing times would require new techniques for survival. In time Rome would experience a terrifying descent into darkness, but for the present it was the best of all possible worlds in the eyes of the emperors and the well-to-do.

In the reign of Antoninus Pius the attitudes of a self-satisfied age were aptly expressed in the *Roman Oration* of Aelius Aristides. A banal Greek rhetorician, Aristides decked his oration with overblown images of peace and tranquillity. According to Aristides, Apollo gazed down on a happy and prosperous world where all men were brothers and countless cities gleamed like torches at a fete. Fashioned by the hand of destiny, the Roman peace would last throughout eternity, for Rome had solved the problems which had shattered the great empires of the past. Amid his fatuous clichés, Aristides occasionally uncovered the iron and lead which lay beneath the surface of the Golden Age of Rome:

No envy sets foot in the empire, for you yourselves were the first to disown envy when you placed all opportunities in view of all and offered those who were able a chance to be not governed more than they governed in turn. Nor does hatred either steal in from those who are not chosen. For since the constitution is a universal one and, as it were, of one state, naturally your governors rule not as over the property of others but as over their own. Besides, all the masses have as a share in it the permission to [take refuge with you] from the power of the local magnates, [but there is] the indignation and punishment from you which will come upon them immediately if they themselves dare to make any unlawful change. Thus, the present regime naturally suits and serves both rich and poor. No other way of life is left. . . . It is not safe for those to rule who have not power. The second best way to sail, they say, is to be governed by one's betters, but by you now it has been shown to be actually the first best way. Accordingly, all are held fast and would not ask to secede any more than those at sea from the helmsman. As bats in caves cling fast to each other and to the rocks, so all from you depend with much concern not to fall from this cluster of cities.[4]

With his chilling phrase—"No other way of life is left!"—Aristides confessed the complacency and timidity of the urban upper classes in the provinces.

Unlike Aristides, the Greek essayist, Plutarch of Chaeronea, grudgingly bowed to the Romans. Though once a resident of Rome and loyal to the emperors, Plutarch fretted under arrogant Roman governors and took a strange consolation in the notion that "it is often more glorious to pay homage than to receive it." In order to wheedle benefits from the Romans, Plutarch advised his fellow Greeks to accept the reality of their situation:

The greatest blessings which a state can enjoy are peace, liberty, prosperity, a high population, and harmony. As far as peace is concerned, the people have no need for statesmen now, because all war— both foreign and domestic—has been removed from us and has vanished altogether. As for liberty, the people have as great a share in it as our rulers allow them, and perhaps more would not be good for them. Nevertheless, a wise man can still pray to the gods to grant his fellow citizens bountiful crops, a gentle climate, large families, and a secure life for our children.[5]

Since servility robbed the Greeks of pride, Plutarch tried to restore a sense of national dignity by writing moralistic essays on the heroes of the Hellenic past. Even the oracle at Delphi no longer made important prophecies, for the faithful were dwindling in number and only consulted Apollo on trivial or personal matters. A devoted priest of Apollo, Plutarch was deeply concerned that many of his contemporaries had lost faith in oracles and omens. His essays were filled with injunctions to piety and parables of famous men who had come to grief because they had scorned the gods. Plutarch's most moving tale dealt with an event in the reign of Tiberius. A ship was passing an island near Corfu when a voice from the shore suddenly called the name of an Egyptian pilot who was on board. When the astounded sailor answered, the voice cried: "When you reach the next isle, announce that the great god Pan is dead." Worried and puzzled, the pilot was undecided whether or not to obey the mysterious voice, but when they reached the next island, the wind died down and the ship lay motionless offshore. Gathering his courage, the sailor called out that Pan was dead. Before he had finished, the sound of weeping and moaning voices rose from the dark deserted isle. The story, which Plutarch believed had actually happened, reflected the passing of venerable deities who had flourished in the great days of Hellas. Though Pan was dead, other gods and new religions were coming to birth.

An extraordinary example of the religious currents of the second century was Proteus Peregrinus, who was alternately a Christian and a Cynic and finally became a god. Early in the reign of Trajan, Peregrinus was born in the town of Parium near the Hellespont. Since he was impatient to inherit the family fortune, Peregrinus was suspected of having had a hand in his father's death. Whether he killed his father or merely desired his death, Peregrinus was hounded by Oedipal guilt and spent the rest of his life in restless wanderings and religious experiments. Desperate for solace, he found his way to Palestine and joined a Christian group. A sarcastic report of the episode was later written by Lucian, who loathed Peregrinus and the Christians:

He learned the strange lore of the Christians from their priests and scribes in Palestine. Naturally, he quickly made them all look like schoolboys, for he became a prophet, leader of the cult, head of the synagogue, and everything else all by himself. Because he explained and interpreted their books and even composed some himself, they honored him as a god, accepted him as a lawgiver, and submitted to his authority, second only to that of the man whom they worshiped and who was crucified in Palestine when he inaugurated this novel cult into the world. Finally, Proteus was arrested and thrown into prison, which increased his reputation and furthered his career as a charlatan and seeker of notoriety. When he was imprisoned, the Christians considered the affair a catastrophe and tried in every way to rescue him. Failing in this, they showered him with attention. Each dawn, old widows and orphans were waiting at the prison gate to visit him, and the leaders of the cult bribed the guards to spend the night with him. Banquets were brought in, and they read aloud from their sacred books to Peregrinus whom they called the "new Socrates." Even the Christians of Asia sent representatives to console and encourage the great man. They always show amazing speed in such matters and will instantly give everything to the cause. So Peregrinus made a profit from the contributions which were sent to him in prison. These lunatics believe that they are immortal and will live forever, so they do not fear death and willingly accept arrest. Deluded by their original lawgiver, they believe that they are all brothers once they have wickedly denied the Greek gods and worshiped that crucified sophist and accepted his laws. Blindly following such doctrines without rational proof, they despise material goods and treat these as common property. Thus, any tricky charlatan can easily impose himself on these simple people and make himself rich in a short time. However, the governor of Syria was a man of philosophic temperament who saw through Peregrinus and freed him, knowing that he would willingly die to win new fame. The governor did not even consider him worth whipping. . . . Later, Peregrinus again imposed on the Christians in his wanderings and lived very well off them. However, even they turned against him when they saw him eating temple food which was forbidden to them.[6]

Pruned of its hostile tone, Paul would have agreed with Lucian's account of the strength and weakness of the Christian communities. Because of the discerning governor of Syria, Peregrinus was denied the pleasures of martyrdom and did not become a Christian saint. Instead, he returned to Parium, renounced any claims to his father's estate, and tried to live as a mendicant Cynic.

Wandering to Egypt, the Cynic became a disciple of an ascetic hermit who mortified the flesh with bizarre tortures, but Peregrinus soon tired of the strenuous life of a fakir. Moving on to Rome, he won the respect of the lower classes by publicly criticizing Antoninus Pius. Though the old emperor was forbearing, the urban prefect was angered by Peregrinus' tirades and expelled the Cynic from the capital. Insisting that he was a persecuted philosopher, Peregrinus went to Greece and incited anti-Roman riots in some cities. At Athens he assumed the pose of a latter-day Diogenes and baited the millionaire philanthropist Herodes Atticus, because he gratified his vanity by donating public buildings and waterworks throughout Greece. Though Lucian considered Peregrinus a troublemaking fraud, the Latin writer Aulus Gellius was impressed by the Cynic's sincerity and wisdom. Peregrinus' attraction to Christianity and the strange manner of his death suggest that he was a mystic as well as a Cynic anarchist.

At the Olympic games in 161, Peregrinus announced that he would immolate himself at the next Olympic festival. As a Cynic, Peregrinus had learned to respect Hindu holy men who burned themselves to death, and the patron deity of the Cynics, Hercules, had also died in flames. By dying bravely Christian martyrs had won attention and admiration, and Peregrinus too wished to show that his beliefs enabled him to despise pain and death. Lest his sacrifice be in vain, the Cynic instructed his disciples to establish a cult in his honor after his death. In 165 near Olympia, Peregrinus led a large crowd to a pyre, where dressed in white, the Cynic performed religious rites and waited for the moon to rise. When the scene was bathed in moonlight, the pyre was lighted and Peregrinus offered a prayer to his dead parents and leaped into the flames. The audience was deeply moved and began hailing the dead man as a god. Replete with visions and miracles, the cult of Peregrinus spread rapidly through Greece and Asia Minor. Whatever the motives of his bizarre life and fiery death, Peregrinus was not a fraud like his contemporary, Alexander of Abonoteichos.

In an age which hungered for saints, why was Christianity not more successful? To understand the religious climate of the second century, Christianity must be seen through pagan eyes. However, Lucian's sneers will not suffice, for he was a foe of all religion. The average pagan believed in the gods and was shocked when a new cult denounced them as demons or fakes. While parents were hurt when their children renounced the faith of their fathers, respectable Romans were embarrassed when Christian relatives were involved with the police. A representative pagan view of Christianity was embodied in Celsus' tract *The True Word,* which was criticized in the early third century by the Christian scholar Origen. Though Lucian referred to an Epicurean Celsus who debunked magic, the author of *The True Word* was another Celsus, for he was a religious conservative who respected oracles and felt that all gods were aspects of a supreme being. Like Plutarch, the Celsus of *The True Word* was a pious and eclectic Platonist who believed in the immortality of the soul and considered the resurrection of the body ridiculous. Probably an Alexandrian, he wrote some time after the deification of Antinous and at a time when Christians were liable to arrest— perhaps during the persecution under Marcus Aurelius. Well-read in the Old and New Testaments, Celsus pointed out historical contradictions in the Gospels and mythic elements in the Book of Genesis. He also noted that educated Christians did not accept the Bible on face value but explained improbable episodes as allegories. Like most men of his time, Celsus found the divinity of Jesus repugnant and dismissed most Gospel stories as crude legends. According to Celsus, Christianity was a conglomeration of Mithraic, gnostic, and pagan ideas which had congealed around the dubious figure of a Galilean carpenter.

The relationship between Christianity and Judaism prompted Celsus to ask:

If the prophets of the god of the Jews foretold that Jesus would be his son, why did he give them laws by Moses that they were to become rich and powerful and to fill the earth and to massacre their enemies, children and all, and slaughter their entire race, which he himself did, so Moses says, before the eyes of the Jews? And besides this, if they were not obedient, why does he expressly threaten to do to them what he did to their enemies? Yet his son, the man of Nazareth, gives contradictory laws, saying that a man cannot come forward to the Father if he is rich or loves power or lays claim to any intelligence or reputation, and that he must not pay attention to food or to his storehouse any more than the ravens, or to clothing any more than the lilies, and that to a man who has struck him once he should offer himself to be struck once again. Who is wrong? Moses or Jesus? Or when the Father sent Jesus, had he forgotten what commands he gave to Moses? Or did he condemn his own laws and change his mind and send his messenger for quite the opposite purpose?[7]

Though he detested primitive notions in Judaism, Celsus accepted the Jewish religion as a legitimate creed which had the sanction of age and tradition. However, Christianity was a new and radical sect which threatened to destroy both Judaism and paganism.

Though Christianity made some converts among the upper classes, the lowly origins of Jesus were well known, and many missionaries deliberately appealed to the downtrodden lower classes. Christian rhetoric was often anti-intellectual and exalted the poor and the unlettered, who usually bore grievances against society. Christianity also had a great appeal for women, and canny missionaries tried to capture the minds of children. To Celsus Christians were proletarian subversives who undermined the home and the school:

In private houses also, we see wool-workers, cobblers, laundry-workers, and the most illiterate and bucolic yokels, who would not dare to say anything at all in front of their elders and more intelligent masters. But whenever they get hold of children in private and some stupid women with them, they let out some astounding statements as, for example, that they must not pay any attention to their father and school-teachers, but must obey them; they say that these talk nonsense and have no understanding, and that in reality they neither know nor are able to do anything good but are taken up with mere empty chatter. But they alone, they say, know the right way to live, and if the children would believe them, they would become happy and make their home happy as well. And if just as they are speaking, they see one of the school-teachers coming or some intelligent person or even the father himself, the more cautious of them flee in all directions, but the more reckless urge the children on to rebel. They whisper to them that in the presence of their father and their schoolmasters, they do not feel able to explain anything to the children, since they do not want to have anything to do with the silly and obtuse teachers who are totally corrupted and far gone in wickedness and who inflict punishment on the children. But, if they like, they should leave father and their schoolmasters and go along with the women and little children who are their playfellows to the wooldresser's shop or to the cobbler's or the washerwoman's shop, that they may learn perfection. And by saying this, they persuade them.[8]

Disturbed by missionaries who agitated the masses, Celsus was not concerned with the appeal of Christianity to disenchanted intellectuals and world-weary aristocrats. His polemic against popular preachers is as valid as Mencken's sketch of "evangelists of strange, incomprehensible cults whooping and bawling at two or three half-witted old women and half a dozen scared little girls in corrugated iron tabernacles down near the railroad yards, [and] missionaries collecting money from the mill children in Raleigh, N.C. to convert the Spaniards and Italians to Calvinism."[9] Religion is always more acceptable when its proponents bathe often and speak in cultured tones.

Redemption from sin was a popular Christian slogan and frequently meant little more than abandoning idolatry and being born again through baptism. Yet missionaries often dealt with real sinners, and Paul and the other apostles worked among alcoholics, prostitutes, degenerates, and criminals. Though they found comfort in Christ's forgiveness, unsavory and neurotic converts brought a tone of scandal to the Christian community. Celsus was a highly moral man who regarded many Christians as social debris and was furious when they claimed to be God's elect. The arrogance of Christians and Jews prompted Celsus to an outburst of indignation:

When I see these Jews and Christians, I think of a swarm of bats, or of ants coming out of their hole, or of frogs croaking in a marsh, or of worms wriggling about on a manure heap—and saying to one another: "God has revealed to us all that has to be; He cares not for the rest of the world; He lets heaven and earth roll on as they will, He only thinks of us. We are the only creatures to whom He sends his messengers; with us alone He wishes to associate, for He has made us in his likeness. Everything is subordinate to us, the earth, the sea, the air, and the stars; all has been made for us and destined for our use; and because it has happened that some of us have sinned, God Himself will come

An anti-Christian graffito at Rome: "Alexamenos worships God."

or will send his own son to burn the wicked and give us the enjoyment of eternal life."[10]

A creed which condemned Socrates and the majority of the human race to damnation was repulsive to Celsus and other pagans, who could discern no moral superiority in Christians.

In pagan eyes the members of the Christian sect seemed to combine the worst features of the Greek philosophic schools—like Stoics they were a self-righteous elect, like Epicureans they denied the gods, and like Cynics they thumbed their noses at society. In time Christianity would achieve respectability and gain sophistication as it spread among the upper classes. However, intolerance toward other creeds and a high regard for pious ignorance would still characterize Christians in centuries to come. To Hadrian as well as Celsus, Christianity was an Eastern superstition unworthy of serious attention from men who were raised in the venerable religions of Greece and Rome. However, the emperor himself had made a god out of Antinous and personally believed that the stars controlled life on earth. Consistency was never one of Hadrian's virtues.

ELEVEN

The Philosopher—Marcus Aurelius

According to Plato, the world would not improve until society was controlled by a group of philosophers or by a ruler who had been converted to philosophy. Though Plato equated philosophy with Platonism, his notion of government by an educated elite was a feasible concept, for many nations have prospered under mandarin regimes. However, philosophic rulers have been less successful in history. The Egyptian pharaoh Akhenaton and the Babylonian king Nabonidus were impractical visionaries who wrecked their nations, and the professorial Woodrow Wilson unwittingly aborted the League of Nations by treating senators as errant schoolboys. Too often philosophers find it difficult to manipulate men by playing on their distasteful frailties. Generally a philosopher's reaction to error is hemlock for himself and the guillotine for others. The most famous philosopher king was the Roman emperor Marcus Aurelius, who tried to reconcile philosophy and statecraft. Matthew Arnold called him "perhaps the most beautiful figure in history," and Jacob Burckhardt noted "among the imperishable ideal figures of antiquity, the Stoic philosopher seated upon the throne of the world." However, no man should be measured against the image which posterity has imposed upon him. Though he was a conscientious ruler, Marcus Aurelius was cold and aloof and his errors in personal judgment had disastrous results for the empire.

Like most Romans of his class, the career of Marcus Aurelius was advanced through family politics. He belonged to the Spanish clique which surrounded Hadrian, and his grandfather M. Annius Verus was a close friend of the emperor. Marcus' father, also named M. Annius Verus, was married to Domitia

Lucilla, the granddaughter of the urban prefect L. Catilius Severus, who once had hoped to succeed Hadrian. The aunt of Marcus Aurelius married T. Aurelius Antoninus, a millionaire senator of Gallic stock. Born at Rome in 121, Marcus was raised by ambitious Spaniards and learned the arts of success from masters of political intrigue. His formal education was provided by distinguished scholars who awakened an interest in philosophy in the solemn boy. In later life Marcus would reward his old tutors with political appointments. Though he suffered from chest pains and often coughed up blood, Marcus enjoyed hunting and strengthened his frail body with exercise. At the age of twelve, the boy underwent an adolescent conversion and became an ascetic. For a short time he wore a rough cloak and slept on the floor, but his mother disapproved and made him live a more normal life. Though he always dressed well and enjoyed good food, Marcus would revere the ideal of austerity for the rest of his life. When his father died Marcus was still young and was sent to live with his grandfather, who had high ambitions for the boy. In 136 old Annius Verus engineered Marcus' betrothal to Fabia, the daughter of Hadrian's heir Aelius Caesar. When Aelius died in 138, Hadrian chose Marcus' uncle Antoninus as heir and ordered him to adopt both Marcus and Aelius' young son Lucius. Through this adoption, Marcus, who was born M. Annius Verus, became the Marcus Aurelius of history. However, his principal virtue in Hadrian's eyes was his betrothal to the daughter of the late Aelius Caesar. The old emperor favored Lucius, who was soon betrothed to Antoninus' daughter Faustina. As future emperors Marcus and Lucius moved into Hadrian's palace. Marcus was relieved to leave the home of his grandfather, whose mistress had stirred his adolescent interest.

In Hadrian's palace Marcus found much to criticize, for he disliked the emperor's addiction to travel, luxury, and homosexuals. The young prince was singularly handsome and was often teased by Hadrian for his prudishness. In later life Marcus boasted that he preserved his virginity until adulthood. Repelled by the old emperor, Marcus idolized Antoninus and contrasted his calm simplicity with the erratic behavior of Hadrian. Marcus was also grateful to his uncle because, as soon as Hadrian was dead, Antoninus revoked Faustina's betrothal to Lucius and freed Marcus from Fabia. As the older heir and Antoninus' favorite, Marcus was betrothed to his cousin Faustina, whom he married in 145. Though the couple had children, their marriage was unhappy, for the vivacious Faustina was bored with her solemn young husband. For twenty-three years Marcus learned the duties of administration from Antoninus and spent his leisure hours more with books than with his wife. While Marcus was groomed for power, Lucius made friends at court, for he was an outspoken and popular extrovert like his father Aelius Caesar. On the other hand, the reserved Marcus was suspicious and loathed the smiling courtiers who whispered behind his back. His Spanish relatives had taught him pride and a cynical view of human nature, and the years of training and waiting increased Marcus' haughtiness and distrust of others.

Shy by nature, Marcus had few close friends but was at ease with the rhetorician M. Cornelius Fronto, who had been his tutor. The two men shared a fondness for literature and a propensity to hypochondria. A modern historian, Tom B. Jones, has caught the tone of the correspondence between Marcus and Fronto on their favorite subject, illness:

Although he tried hard and protested loudly and often, Marcus could never outdo Fronto in frailty of health. . . . Fronto complains of insomnia, then a pain in his elbow, then his gout. While Fronto is confined to his bed, Marcus Aurelius catches a cold from walking about in his slippers. This develops into a sore throat which is relieved by swallowing some honey water and then ejecting it again. . . . Fronto, however, has the last word because he develops a pain in his shoulder, knee, elbow, and ankle. In a later contest of miseries, Fronto leads off with a pain in the neck. Marcus is forced to confess that he himself got through the night and managed to eat breakfast, but "we will see what the night brings" and "you can certainly gauge my feelings when I learned that you had been taken with a pain in the neck." Fronto was generous: with a pain in his neck, he no longer had one in his foot. Marcus continued to improve and was able to take a bath and drink some wine, but then his daughter saved the family honor by getting the flux. As she recovered, Fronto got a pain in his toe which spread to elbow and neck and finally settled in his groin, first on one side and then on the other. Not satisfied with Marcus' sympathy, Fronto says, "Please acquaint the emperor . . . with my illness." The pious Antoninus, however, had his own troubles: he suffered from migraine although *he* was not given to complaining.[1]

Antoninus added to his discomfort by wearing a painful harness with wooden slats. The device straightened his bent frame into the erect posture which the old emperor felt was proper for his imperial status.

In 161 Antoninus Pius died raving of politics and rival kings. His heirs, Marcus and Lucius, succeeded him as co-emperors with equal authority. As the junior emperor, Lucius married Marcus' daughter Lucilla. A handsome blond dilettante, Lucius could be capable and efficient when the occasion required, but he left policy making to his older colleague. Conscientious and hard-working, Marcus was burdened by his duties and complained that Lucius did not take enough responsibility. In his *Notebooks* Marcus thanked the gods for giving him a colleague who served as an example of what not to be. At heart a bookish man, Marcus had been pushed into a position of great power, which he enjoyed as a challenge but hated as an obligation. Ambivalent towards the throne, Marcus boasted that destiny had appointed him as the "shepherd of the Roman flock," but he also warned himself: "See to it that you do not become Caesarized or dyed with that coloring. For it does happen. . . . Strive to remain such as philosophy wanted to make you. Revere the gods, protect men. . . . Do all things as a disciple of Antoninus."[2] Like his predecessors, Marcus bought the loyalty of the Praetorian guards with a large bonus and often provided the residents of Rome with spectacular shows. However, like Julius Caesar, he was criticized for working on correspondence during the games. A careful administrator, Marcus insisted on accurate state records and kept a strict watch on public expenditures. Though notoriously frugal, he followed Hadrian's precedent and canceled uncollectable debts which private citizens owed to the state. Since he treated the Senate with respect, the emperor was popular with the senatorial class. As a philosopher, Marcus favored Stoicism with its rigid insistence on duty. The troubles of his reign gave him ample opportunity to test his Stoic faith.

In the east, war broke out with Parthia, and on the Danube frontier, barbarian tribes menaced Italy and the Balkans. In

162 Marcus sent Lucius to Syria to direct the campaign against Parthia. Though he enjoyed the urbane pleasures of Antioch, the junior emperor restored discipline in the legions of the east, which had become lax under Antoninus Pius. Under Lucius' command Avidius Cassius and other Roman generals decisively defeated the Parthians. In 166 Lucius returned to Rome and staged a splendid triumph in the capital. However, the victory over Parthia was followed by calamity at Rome, for Lucius' veterans were infected with plague. As the soldiers were reassigned, the pestilence spread through Italy and along the northern frontier. In the afflicted areas, thousands died and the survivors succumbed to religious hysteria. At Rome an imaginative crank climbed up a tree and announced that the world would end when he fell from his perch and turned into a stork. When he dropped to the ground and released a stork from his cloak, the crowd panicked, but the false prophet was quickly arrested for disturbing the peace. Though he pardoned the charlatan, Marcus Aurelius was a deeply religious man who believed in omens and dreams. During the plague the emperor sacrificed so many oxen to the gods that a comic song described the animals as praying that he would cease being so pious. The plague raged for years and broke out again in the reign of Marcus' successor Commodus.

During the years of plague, the Roman masses lived in daily fear and blamed their calamities on the Christians. The emperor shared the common belief that the gods were angry and that Christianity was at least one of the causes of divine displeasure. While Trajan and Pliny had believed that Christian disobedience endangered the social order, Marcus was sure that the sect was guilty of worse crimes, and he slaughtered many Christians in the arena. His close friend Fronto, who was from Cirta in North Africa, had convinced Marcus that Christians indulged in gruesome orgies. The Christian writer Minucius Felix paraphrased Fronto's libels against the Christians:

Details of the initiation of neophytes are as revolting as they are notorious. An infant, cased in dough to deceive the unsuspecting, is placed beside the person to be initiated. The novice is thereupon induced to inflict what seem to be harmless blows upon the dough, and unintentionally the infant is killed by his unsuspecting blows; the blood—oh, horrible—they lap up greedily; the limbs they tear to pieces eagerly; and over the victim they make league and covenant, and by complicity in guilt pledge themselves to mutual silence. Such sacred rites are more foul than any sacrilege. Their form of feasting is notorious; it is in everyone's mouth, as testified by the speech of our friend of Cirta. On the day appointed, they gather at a banquet with all their children, sisters, and mothers, people of either sex and every age. There, after full feasting, when the blood is heated and drink has inflamed the passions of incestuous lust, a dog which has been tied to a lamp is tempted by a morsel thrown beyond the range of his tether to bound forward with a rush. The tale-telling light is upset and extinguished, and in the shameless dark, lustful embraces are indiscriminately exchanged.[3]

Such prurient charges were hoary with age, and the Senate had used them centuries earlier against the Bacchic cult. In the back country of North Africa, Roman officials had recently stamped out a barbarous cult which had practiced child sacrifice. Since primitive pagans could commit such crimes, Fronto assumed that the notorious Christians would surely be guilty of similar deeds. However, Trajan and Pliny had not believed such nonsense; the pagan critic Celsus did not stoop to fanciful calumny; and in the third century, Origen insisted that not even the ignorant mob accused Christians of child murder. Though the horrors of plague and barbarian wars made Fronto and Marcus Aurelius more responsive to wild charges, it is not to the credit of the emperor that he accepted libels without a hearing. Convinced that they were "unbelievers, traitors, and wretches who commit any crime behind closed doors," Marcus watched impassively as Christians were tortured to death in the arena. When some martyrs died with dignity, the Stoic emperor dismissed their behavior as stage-heroics prompted by obstinacy.[4]

Since Italy was ravaged by plague, the barbarians of the North saw an opportunity for pillage, and hordes of Marcomanni and Quadi tribesmen invaded the Po Valley. In 167 the two emperors took the field and drove the barbarians back across the Alps. The fighting was savage and difficult, for neither side gave quarter and many women fought in the German ranks. While the emperors were on their way back to Rome in 169, Lucius died of apoplexy. Since it was rumored that he had poisoned Lucius, Marcus quickly deified his late colleague. Though he had not appreciated Lucius' frank comments on men and affairs, the Stoic emperor probably did not stoop to murder. Nevertheless, Marcus did not regret the passing of Lucius, for Faustina had provided a successor. In 161 she had borne Marcus twin boys, but one later died following a mastoid operation. The surviving twin was Commodus, whom Marcus had made his official heir and planned to appoint as his colleague. Encouraged by Faustina, the philosopher king indulged in family pride and secured the throne solely for his own son.* Like his father, Commodus would be exposed to excellent teachers, but a similar education had not made a philosopher out of Lucius, nor would it succeed with the son of Marcus Aurelius.

The German wars continued without a break, and the emperor spent dreary years fighting the Sarmatians and other barbaric tribes. The plague had depopulated many areas in Italy and destroyed much of Rome's military manpower. To fill his depleted legions the emperor recruited gladiators and bandits, and even slaves were freed to fight for Rome. To pay for the wars Marcus auctioned the treasures of the imperial palace. During one of his campaigns against the Quadi, an opportune thunderstorm broke the morale of the barbarians. Though Marcus gave his magicians credit for the storm, Christians later appropriated the "miracle of the Thundering Legion." Few of Marcus' victories were so easily won, and none gave him pleasure: "A spider is proud when it has hunted down a fly; one man, a hare; another, a sardine in his net; another, piglets; another, bears; another, Sarmatians. Are they not [all] bandits?"[5] When peace finally came in 175, Marcus settled German tribesmen in Italy to replace the farmers and soldiers who had died in the plague. Revitalizing the empire with barbarian immigrants was an enlightened policy appropriate to a ruler whose predecessors had come from the provinces.

---

*If a mature colleague had replaced Lucius, Commodus could still have been Marcus' heir without being exposed too young to the loneliness of power when Marcus died.

Marcus
Aurelius

Faustina

With victory in the north Marcus returned to family squabbles at Rome. While Faustina had never been faithful, her indiscretions increased during Marcus' long absences.* Because her husband was a cold intellectual, the empress was attracted to coarse workingmen and brawny sailors. However, Marcus was a practical Spaniard and did not divorce Faustina, who had powerful friends in the leading families of Rome. The emperor quipped that he did not want to return her dowry, the empire, and even appointed some of her lovers to government posts. Having lost the affection of his wife, Marcus had also alienated his daughter Lucilla by forcing her to marry an aging Syrian senator, Claudius Pompeianus. Both Faustina and Lucilla had bitterly opposed the marriage, but Marcus needed support in Syria.

During the recent war Faustina had feared for the succession of her beloved Commodus, who was too young to protect his interests if his father should die. At a false rumor of Marcus' death, Faustina wrote to Avidius Cassius and asked the Syrian general to take the throne and adopt her boy. The famous commander needed little encouragement, for he had expected to be Lucius' successor and was furious over Marcus' dynastic plans. A strict disciplinarian, Cassius would have made an excellent colleague for the war-weary Marcus, but resentment and Faustina's intrigue lured the Syrian into a desperate gamble. Raising the banner of revolt in 175, Avidius Cassius claimed the throne and seized Syria and Egypt, but loyal troops soon suppressed the rebellion and sent the usurper's head to Rome. Like Caesar viewing Pompey's head, Marcus sighed with relief and expressed regret that he could not pardon a noble foe. Since Cassius had ruled his troops with an iron hand, Rome would not have suffered from Praetorian escapades if he had been Marcus' colleague and watched over Commodus. To stamp out the embers of revolt, Marcus went to the east but kept the purge within reasonable limits. Faustina accompanied him and was accused by Cassius' former followers of complicity in the revolt. In 176 the empress conveniently died of gout or, as contemporaries whispered, by her own hand. Lucius' sister Fabia, who once had been betrothed to Marcus, now hoped to become his empress, but Marcus preferred

*On Faustina's infidelities, see Appendix One.

to remain a widower and took a low-born concubine. The fall of Faustina did not dim the fortunes of Commodus, for in 177 Marcus elevated the sixteen-year-old boy as co-emperor.

The last years of Marcus Aurelius were spent in grim campaigns on the Danube frontier, where the old emperor suffered from the severe winters and gloomy isolation of the wilderness. Ill at his field headquarters, Marcus ate sparingly and eased his pains with theriac, which was a preventive antidote against poison but also contained opium. Earlier, the emperor had worried because the opiate made him sleepy and interfered with his work, but he had become addicted to the drug and was uncomfortable when his doctors mixed theriac without opium. According to his physician Galen, "he was obliged to have recourse again to the compound which contained poppy-juice, since this was now habitual with him."[6] Probably the narcotic helped Marcus more than Stoicism to insulate himself from the unhappiness of life.* Some of his philosophic visions were surrealistic panoramas with great vistas of time and space which suggest the opium dreams of Coleridge and De Quincey. Whatever effect drugs had on him, Marcus worked on a philosophic scrapbook in which he recorded his reveries and thoughts on many subjects.

Neither an apology nor a memoir, the *Notebooks* of Marcus Aurelius was a collection of quotations, comments, and random observations on the human condition. A tireless collector of maxims, the emperor filled his scrapbook with quotes from Epictetus, Epicurus, and other sages whom he respected. Marcus' own musings often reflected his bitterness and frustration, but the *Notebooks* also contained many notable philosophic lines:

Asia, Europe are corners of the universe. The whole ocean, a drop in the universe. Mount Athos, a clod of the universe. The whole of our present age is a point in eternity. All things are small, changeable, vanishing. . . . The maw of the lion, poison, every kind of evil deed, are, like thorns or mud, but incidental accretions on things noble and lovely. . . . He who has seen the present has seen everything, all that from eternity has come to pass, and all that will come to be in infinite time. For everything is akin and the same.[7]

*On the emperor's reliance on narcotics, see Appendix One.

However, behind his philosophic detachment, Marcus was an anguished man who had been lacerated by life and feared the darkness of the tomb.

Like most Stoics, Marcus Aurelius believed that Providence ruled the universe and that most men were crass and sinful. Only a few sages had the intellectual and moral strength to rise above the lures of the flesh and reject the hollow glories of the world. According to Marcus, not even love for a wife or children should distract a sage from focusing his attention on eternity, and sorrow for a dead child was as sinful as wallowing in luxury or delighting in empty honors. To the emperor the gods were real, for he spoke with them in dreams and saw them as stars in the sky. While not obsessed with astrology, Marcus believed that the stars controlled life on earth. Confident that the gods were close to him, the emperor would have been happy by Walden Pond or in a medieval hermitage. Unfortunately, his family had forced Marcus into a life where he was exposed to the endless distractions and fierce intrigues of a court. Every day Marcus awoke in his palace as in a prison: "Say to yourself in the morning: I shall meet people who are interfering, ungracious, insolent, full of guile, deceitful, and antisocial; they have all become like that because they have no understanding of good and evil."[8] Try as he might, the emperor could not hide his distaste for the courtiers who regarded him as "an old schoolmaster silently criticizing us." Like a tired teacher among evil children, he dismissed their hopes and ambitions as "the empty pursuit of triumphal parades, the dramas of the stage, flocks and herds, battles with the spear, a bone thrown to puppies, scraps thrown into fish tanks, the calamities and burdens of ants, the scurryings of excited mice, puppets jerked by strings."[9] From his books Marcus had learned contempt for little men, and his family had taught him to be suspicious of them.

Some men believed that the Roman past had been noble, virtuous, and uncomplicated, but Marcus Aurelius knew better. In his youth he had hoped to write histories of Greece and Rome, and his studies convinced him that accounts of ancient Roman virtue were only noble lies. Closer in sympathy to Tacitus than to Livy, Marcus Aurelius took a bleak view of history:

Consider, for the sake of argument, the times of Vespasian; you will see all the same things: men marrying, begetting children, being ill, dying, fighting wars, feasting, trading, farming, flattering, asserting themselves, suspecting, plotting, praying for the death of others, grumbling at their present lot, falling in love, hoarding, longing for consulships and kingships. But the life of those men no longer exists anywhere. Then, turn to the times of Trajan; again, everything is the same; and that life too is dead. Contemplate and observe in the same way the records of the other periods of time, indeed of whole nations: how many men have struggled eagerly and then, after a little while, fell and were resolved into their elements. . . . Words of old in common usage now sound strange; so the names of men much sung of old are strange today. Camillus . . . a little later Scipio and Cato, too, then even Augustus, then even Hadrian and Antoninus. For all things fade and quickly become legend, soon to be lost in total forgetting. . . . The cause of all things is like a torrent, it sweeps everything along. How puny are these little public men, wisely practical as they believe themselves to be. They are like children with running noses.[10]

The recurrent follies of the past and present depressed the emperor who commanded millions of subjects but felt that his own actions were ephemeral and futile. As a Stoic and a Roman, Marcus stood his ground and tried to achieve justice and order in an unjust and chaotic world.

The futility of public life and high programs often weary great men, but the lucky ones escape briefly into family joys or private pleasures. Unfortunately, Marcus was an austere philosopher as well as a disenchanted politician:

How useful, when roasted meats and other foods are before you, to see them in your mind as here the dead body of a fish, there the dead body of a bird or a pig. Or again, to think of Falernian wine as the juice of a cluster of grapes, of a purple robe as sheep's wool dyed with the blood of a shellfish, and of sexual intercourse as internal rubbing accompanied by a spasmodic ejection of mucus. What useful perceptual images these are! They go to the heart of things and pierce right through them, so that you see things for what they are. You must do this throughout life; when things appear too enticing, strip them naked, destroy the myth which makes them proud.[11]

Robbed of joy by too much analysis, Marcus viewed the pleasures of life with the disgust of a Christian anchorite. However, a monk would anticipate an eternity of ecstasy in heaven, but Marcus could only look forward to a diffusion of atoms and an evaporation of spirit. Though he was not sure what lay beyond the grave, the emperor had glimpsed darkness in the heart of things.

Early in life, Marcus had turned to philosophy and always found solace in slogans of detachment:

In human life, time is but a point, reality a flux, perception indistinct, the composition of the body subject to easy corruption, the soul a spinning top, fortune hard to make out, fame confused. To put it briefly: physical things are but a flowing stream, things of the soul dreams and vanity; life is but a struggle and the visit to a strange land, posthumous fame but a forgetting. What then can help us on our way? One thing only: philosophy. This consists in guarding our inner spirit inviolate and unharmed, stronger than pleasures and pains, never acting aimlessly, falsely, or hypocritically, independent of the actions or inaction of others, accepting all that happens or is given as coming from whence one came oneself, and at all times awaiting death with contented mind as being only the release of the elements of which every creature is composed. If it is nothing fearful for the elements themselves that one should continually change into another, why should anyone look with suspicion upon the change and dissolution of all things? For this is in accord with nature, and nothing evil is in accord with nature.[12]

Occasionally the Stoic mask slipped and the philosopher had to draw support from the aristocratic pride which his Spanish family had instilled in him: "The god within you should be the protector of a being who is a man, of mature years, a statesman, a Roman, and a ruler who has taken up his post as might one who is at ease while awaiting the call to retreat from life, who needs no oath or the testimony of any human witness."[13] Yet even pride could not quiet all doubts, and Stoic dogmas offered only a fragile certainty. Desperate for serenity, Marcus wished to forgive his enemies, love erring friends, and repress his loathing for humanity. Though he needed to believe that all was right and necessary, Marcus was too aware that much in life was absurd and wrong. While he wanted to be a saint, the emperor lacked the necessary aids to sanctity—poverty and anonymity.

As ruler of the Roman world, the philosopher king followed in the administrative footsteps of his imperial predecessors.

Though the Stoic Marcus was a conscientious emperor, Rome had also enjoyed good government under the crafty Augustus, the warlike Trajan, and the sensual Hadrian. Despite his devotion to duty and his tireless defense of the empire, Marcus ultimately failed as an emperor, for his selection of Commodus as heir and colleague was catastrophic for Rome. As a philosopher, Marcus was also a failure, for his view of life was distorted: "Just as taking a bath seems to you a matter of oil, sweat, dirt, scummy water, all of it offensive, so is every part of life and every kind of matter."[14] Hoping to save his soul, the emperor had forsaken the world of reality and became a prisoner of despair.

Early in 180 Marcus Aurelius lay dying in his camp at Vienna. Exhausted by age and illness, he thought of the endless hours he had spent searching for truth in books: "No more vague wanderings. You are not likely to read your memoranda, your histories of Greece and Rome, or the extracts from books which you put aside for your old age. Hasten then to the end, discard vain hopes, and if you care for yourself at all, rescue yourself while you still may."[15] With ill-disguised contempt, the emperor watched his generals and courtiers busily angling for positions under his successor. Disgusted with their behavior, Marcus yearned to escape into the peace of death: "Now, you see how great a weariness there is in living with those who are out of tune with you, so that you say: 'May you come more swiftly, O Death, lest I also may forget myself.' "[16] While he knew that Commodus was a weak young man, the emperor hoped that able advisers would guide the nineteen-year-old prince to maturity and responsibility. On March 17, 180, Marcus Aurelius died gasping to his attendants: "Go to the rising sun. My own sun is setting." The rising sun, Commodus, was an emotionally disturbed young man who dutifully deified his father but hated everything the Stoic emperor had stood for.

Few famous men have had distinguished children, for the household of a prominent man is not always a good environment. Children often resent their father's egotism and rebel against living in his shadow. Like Alexander the Great, some sons try to outdo the deeds of their fathers, but most tire of imitation and sink into mediocrity. To Commodus and Lucilla their father had

been a remote and austere figure who usually wore a look of
pained disapproval. Though he thanked the gods that his children were not ugly or retarded, Marcus confessed that a friend
had to teach him to be "genuinely fond of children." Rejected by
their cold and aloof father, Commodus and his sister had turned
to their vivacious mother and imitated her neurotic search for
pleasure and vulgar companions. Like Faustina, her daughter had
many lovers and gambled in political intrigues. As the widow of
Lucius Verus, Lucilla had once been an empress, but she was
now only a senator's wife and bitterly resented the good fortune
of her brother. Tall, handsome, and vain, Commodus had a strong
physique and heightened his natural blondness by sprinkling gold
dust in his hair. Skilled in archery, the athletic prince was proud
of his left-handedness, though the characteristic had a sinister
connotation in Roman superstition. Since he hated his intellectual
father, Commodus glorified brute strength and idolized gladiators. Though Rome had witnessed peculiar rulers before, public
opinion was not yet prepared for an emperor who wished to
appear in the arena. While not responsible for the excesses of
his children, Marcus had helped to warp their personalities and
was fully aware of Commodus' character when he gave him the
throne.

Freed from his father, Commodus intended to enjoy his new
power. After securing peace on the northern frontier, he
returned to the pleasures of Rome. Lazy by nature, Commodus
left decision making to the Praetorian prefect Perennis and
devoted his own time to sports and chariot racing. Contemporaries noted that the young emperor was neither cruel nor
debauched, but he was easily influenced by his friends and
advisers. To increase his own power, the wily Perennis pandered
to Commodus' every whim and encouraged his public performances as an athlete. The emperor performed in the Circus
and demonstrated his skill as an archer by slaying wild animals
with spectacular shots. In the privacy of the palace, he practiced
swordsmanship with gladiators who used blunt lead weapons.
Unfit to be a ruler, Commodus was a spoiled child who never
grew up. When reality intruded on his childish world, the imperial
athlete responded with violent tantrums and finally withdrew into
total fantasy. Despite his follies the Senate had no quarrel with

the young emperor until his sister put fear in Commodus' heart. In 182 Lucilla conspired with her cousin Quadratus and her stepson Pompeianus to murder Commodus. Since her husband, the elderly Claudius Pompeianus, was ignorant of the plot, Lucilla may have intended to place one of her lovers on the throne. Because a few senators supported the conspiracy, the younger Pompeianus yelled, "the Senate sends you this," as he rushed at Commodus with a drawn sword. However, the emperor's guards disarmed the theatrical assassin before he could stab Commodus. The ringleaders of the plot were executed and Lucilla was briefly imprisoned on Capri and later slain. The abortive conspiracy strengthened Perennis' hold on Commodus, who now viewed the senatorial class with suspicion.

During Commodus' twelve-year reign the extravagant ruler squandered state funds while the Praetorian prefects plundered the treasury and sold official appointments. The empire was still suffering from the aftereffects of plague and war, but Commodus was preoccupied with fears of conspiracy and readily executed senators whom he suspected of treason. In 185 Perennis was involved in a military plot against the emperor, but the bulk of the armies remained loyal and the prefect was slain. As the power behind Commodus, Perennis was succeeded by a corrupt Phrygian freedman, Cleander, who indulged in graft without restraint. Ignoring Cleander's peculations, the emperor surrendered to debauchery, drank heavily, and maintained a harem of both sexes. With casual frankness, Commodus bestowed the name Faustina on one of his concubines. When crowds at Rome rioted over a grain shortage in 189, the emperor blamed Cleander and handed him over to the mob. Continued debauches and morbid fears eroded the weak character of Commodus, who became sadistic and sank into the loneliness of megalomania.

The final years of Commodus were a nightmare of violence and madness. While the prestige of the Antonine family kept the armies loyal, the servile Senate was afraid to oppose the mad ruler, and only his mistress Marcia could restrain the emperor in his wilder moments. Since Marcia favored the Christians, Commodus relaxed the persecution which his father had begun. For years Commodus had been out of touch with reality and now his world dissolved into bizarre fantasies. Insisting that he was

Hercules, the emperor stalked about the palace, dressed in a lion skin and dragging a huge club. Terrified and obedient, the Senate worshiped Commodus as Hercules and renamed the city of Rome Commodiana. Late in 192 the imperial lunatic confided to Marcia that he would execute the consuls on New Year's Day and appear in public with a retinue of gladiators to inaugurate an era of unrestrained violence. When Marcia reported the mad scheme, the Praetorian prefect Laetus and the chamberlain Eclectus decided to end the farce and replace Commodus with a respected senator, Pertinax. On December 31, 192, Laetus and Eclectus directed the murder of Commodus who, like Rasputin, was hard to kill. When Marcia tried to poison him, the husky emperor vomited the potion and had to be strangled by his athletic trainer. Notified by the conspirators, Pertinax sent agents to confirm the death of Commodus. Satisfied that the maniac was dead, Pertinax hurried to the Praetorian camp where Laetus bribed the guardsmen to hail the senator as emperor. At the news of Commodus' murder, the Senate convened in a special night session and gladly endorsed the new emperor. Though the senators wanted to drag Commodus' body through the streets, Pertinax refused to desecrate the corpse and buried Commodus in Hadrian's tomb beside Antoninus Pius and Lucius Verus.

A self-made man, the new emperor Pertinax viewed the imperial office as a grave responsibility. An Italian freedman's son, Pertinax had served in the army under Antoninus Pius and Marcus Aurelius and acquired a fortune as governor of Syria. Despite a reputation for financial sharpness, the portly Pertinax typified the able senators who had served Marcus with distinction but had not rebelled against his son. Had Marcus been as wise as he was learned, the Stoic emperor would have chosen a mature colleague of the caliber of Pertinax or Avidius Cassius, and Commodus could have lived out his days as a do-nothing prince and a popular sportsman. Though he was well aware of Commodus' weakness, Marcus assigned his son a lonely role where he would be exposed to political intrigue and tempted by vice. Oppressed by fear and corrupted by the prefects, Commodus became a pitiful mad child who played at being Hercules. The revered Marcus Aurelius had been too philosophic to understand human frailty.

TWELVE

The Doctor—Galen

The second century A.D. was an age of scientific synthesis. In the fields of astronomy and medicine, the scientific heritage of antiquity culminated in the writings of the astronomer Claudius Ptolemy and the physician Galen of Pergamum. At Alexandria Ptolemy reconciled Greek mathematical preconceptions with centuries of astronomical observations. With great · skill he elaborated the geocentric planetary system which was endorsed by European scientists until the time of Kepler. Even Copernicus did not completely break with Ptolemaic tradition, for he retained Ptolemaic epicycles and the concept of perfect circular motion in the heavens. During the fourteen centuries when Ptolemy was a canon in astronomy, Galen was the supreme authority in medicine. A prolific writer, Galen explained the human body in teleological terms which had great appeal for later Christian readers. In his own time, Galen reached a wide audience because he wrote well and was respected as a practicing physician. Modern doctors are rarely known for their literary accomplishments, and Chekhov won fame as a writer only when he turned away from medicine. However, Galen lived in an era when medical education was broad and the boundaries between science, philosophy, and literature were still undefined. As a medical theorist, Galen is no longer authoritative, but he was a first-rate physician and a representative man of his age.

Greek medicine was closely allied with religion. In the second century the cult of the healing god Asclepius flourished as plague ravaged the Roman empire and piety pervaded all classes. Both Marcus Aurelius and Galen were devoted to Asclepius, and the orator Aelius Aristides was obsessed with the god of medicine. While his *Oration on Rome* reflected the attitude of urban provincials toward Roman rule, Aristides' devotion to Asclepius was symptomatic of the widespread acceptance of faith healing among the upper classes. Though all educated men despised religious charlatans who preyed on superstitious patients, no doctor in antiquity denied the efficacy of miracles and temple cures. Particularly vulnerable to faith healing, Aristides was a hypochondriac who suffered from a variety of real and imagined ailments. A resident of Asia Minor, he won fame as an orator in Greece and Egypt, but his success was marred by asthma and various psychosomatic ills.

With the self-righteous pride of a confirmed hypochondriac, Aristides boasted of his asthmatic affliction:

What man could conceive of the multitude of ills of which I was then a victim? Those who were present on the occasion of each attack know the state of my skin and how sick I was internally. Moreover, my head ran with mucus day after day and night after night; there was fluxion in my chest; my breath would come up to meet the flow of humors in my throat, would be constricted, and become inflamed there. I was so much expecting death from minute to minute that I did not have the courage to call a slave; I thought I should be wasting my time, because it would be too late by the time he came. On top of all this, I had every kind of trouble with my ears and my teeth, and tension round about the veins, and I could neither keep down what I had eaten nor throw it up; for if anything so much as touched my throat or my palate, it closed all the passages, and I could not recover myself. I had a burning pain inside my head and every kind of shooting fits. At night, I was unable to lie down flat; I had to keep sitting up bent forward, my head resting on my knees. In the grip of such ills as these and an infinity of others, I had of course to keep myself wrapped up in woolen blankets and other kinds of covers and be entirely confined with all doors and windows closed, so that the day came to equal the night, and the nights were like days because I could not sleep.[1]

However, Aristides did not spend his life in a cork-lined room like Proust.

At the age of twenty-seven, Aristides had visited Rome. Naturally, his journey was a harrowing odyssey of illness and discomfort. Crossing the Balkans by coach in winter, Aristides suffered from fever, toothaches, and severe attacks of asthma, as well as the inconvenience of the bouncing vehicle and the bitter cold of the weather. In the spring of 143, the orator arrived at Rome but received no relief from the physicians in the capital. Nevertheless, he found strength to deliver his famous Roman oration. Despairing of recovery, Aristides returned to Asia Minor by ship and was sick all the way. At a sanitarium near Smyrna, the orator bathed in hot springs, but the therapy had no effect on his asthma. Though he grumbled that his doctors could not cure him, the invalid was delighted that his illness defied medical science. While he was languishing at the spa in 145, Aristides received help from Asclepius:

That was when the Savior first began to give me revelations. He ordered me to walk barefoot, and I cried out in my dream as if I were wide awake and the vision had been carried out: "Great is Asclepius! the order has been fulfilled!" That was what I dreamed I cried out while walking forward. After this came the god's invitation and my departure from Smyrna to Pergamum to my good fortune.[2]

Apparently cured, Aristides made a pilgrimage to the temple of Asclepius at Pergamum. Though his illness would recur, the sufferer now found relief in the therapy which Asclepius prescribed in dreams—horseback riding, cold baths, and walking barefoot. Marcus Aurelius, who suffered from "spitting blood and vertigo," was also told in dreams to ride, go barefoot, and take cold baths. Since both men were neurotic, the exercise did them no harm and served as a useful ritual for "earning" health.

Through his dreams Aristides prescribed a strenuous regimen for himself. At the direction of Asclepius, the hysterical orator struggled from his sickbed and took long hikes and cold baths. After days of fasting, he would purge himself with strong emetics. In addition, the invalid forced himself to speak and write during asthmatic attacks. Without a supernatural crutch, Aristides could not function as a healthy human being, but with the imagined aid of Asclepius, he escaped from the sickroom and continued a highly successful career. His faith had made him strong, and news of Aristides' cure prompted other invalids to seek the help of Asclepius. Through faith healing Aristides also survived a large

tumor in his groin. To cure the growth Asclepius forbade surgery*
and ordered the sufferer to run barefoot in winter, sail in a storm,
and eat honey and acorns. When the tumor subsided, Aristides
and his friends were exalted. During the dream consultations
Asclepius was not always specific in his instructions, and Aristides often strained his imagination to decipher the symbolism of
the dreams. One particular dream lends itself to a Freudian
interpretation. At a time when his asthma was especially severe,
Aristides dreamed that he was having an asthmatic attack while
on board a ship at sea, when suddenly his foster father appeared
with a horse on the shore. Magically, Aristides was transported
to the horse and experienced a feeling of great joy. When he
awoke in the morning, the invalid went riding. As his steed ran
faster, his asthma vanished and Aristides felt a great sense of
power. In a dream the following night, a voice announced that
the cure was complete.

In the medical regimen of antiquity, cold baths were often
used, and the emperor Augustus was immersed in cold water
while suffering from a major illness. However, when Aristides
plunged into icy streams, his doctors and friends worried over
his health, but the therapy involved more than they could
imagine—as Aristides explains:

It was in the depths of winter. There was a bitter wind from the north
and frost. The pebbles were so glued together by the frost as to look
like a network of crystal, and the water was what one would expect
it to be in such a climate. . . . Still full of the warmth of the vision of
the god, I tore off my clothes and, without even asking for a rubdown,
jumped into the deepest part of the river. Then, just as if I were in
a pool of mild water of just the right temperature, I took my time
swimming and splashing about. When I came out, my skin was fresh
and shining, my body was perfectly light, and the whole crowd . . .
gave forth in splendid volume the famous cry: "Great is Asclepius!"
. . . All the rest of that day and in the evening until I went to bed,
I remained in the state in which I had come out of the bath; I did
not feel my body to be drier or any wetter; the warmth which I felt

---

*In view of the limitations of ancient surgery, it was probably just as well
that Aristides' fear took the form of Asclepius to prevent his doctors from
resorting to the knife.

did not leave me, nor was any added to it; nor did this warmth seem to be such as any human device might have brought about; it was a sort of continuous animal warmth of equal strength throughout all my limbs and over the whole surface of the body. I was in a corresponding state mentally. It was not an obvious pleasure, nor would you have measured it by the standards of ordinary human good cheer. Rather it was a certain indescribable sense of well-being which made all things seem of secondary importance beside the present moment, so that not even when I saw something, did I have the impression that I was seeing it — so wholly close was I to the god.[3]

Even by Greek standards Aristides' euphoria was exceptional, for the ecstatic patient had gone beyond faith healing into the twilight world of mysticism over which the priest and the psychiatrist contend for jurisdiction.

If Aristides had consulted Galen, the great doctor might have suspected that his patient's illness was related to psychological problems, but he would not have doubted that Asclepius appeared to Aristides in dreams. Near Pergamum the god had a famous shrine where Galen often worshiped the medical deity. Born at Pergamum about 129, Galen enjoyed the intellectual stimulation of one of the greatest cities in Asia Minor. Once the capital of the Attalid kingdom, Pergamum was large and cosmopolitan, and its famed library was second only to the great library at Alexandria. The architectural pride of the city was a huge altar of Zeus Soter which was decorated with a 400-foot frieze depicting gods struggling with titans.* A thriving commercial city, Pergamum had a long tradition of sanitation and public health and boasted an excellent medical school. The environment was ideal for Galen, whose father Nicon was a prosperous architect and owned an estate near the city.

Like all men, Galen was greatly influenced by his parents. An only child, he loved his father but hated his mother:

It was my great fortune to have as my father a most good-tempered, just, efficient, and benevolent man. My mother, on the other hand,

---

*The author of the Apocalypse of John (2:13) denounced the Throne of Satan at Pergamum and probably meant the altar of Zeus Soter or possibly a temple which had been erected to Augustus.

was so irascible that she woud sometimes bite her serving-maids, and she was constantly shouting at my father and quarreling with him, worse than Xantippe with Socrates. When I saw, then, the nobility of my father's conduct side by side with the shameful passions of my mother, I made up my mind to love and cleave to the former behavior and to hate and flee from the latter. And besides this enormous difference between my parents, I observed that he was never depressed over any affliction, while my mother became annoyed at the merest bagatelle. You yourself doubtless know that boys imitate what they are fond of and avoid what they do not like to see.[4]

Throughout his life, Galen was revolted by displays of anger. The memory of his shrewish mother also affected his views on love and marriage, for Galen never married and defined love as "a mixture of honey and wormwood." His greatest joy came from the study of medicine, and the scholarly doctor turned out books as rapidly as some people beget children.

When Galen was fifteen Nicon encouraged him to study and compare the four major philosophic schools, the Platonic, Peripatetic, Stoic, and Epicurean. In later life Galen tried to practice the eclectic approach and emotional restraint which his father had recommended:

"You must not," he said, "proclaim yourself in a hurry as belonging to any one school; you must go on for a long time learning and testing them, striving after justice, moderation, courage, and intelligence." These injunctions which I received from my father I cherish to this day. Without proclaiming myself the adherent of any sect, I persevere zealously in the investigation of my father's precepts and continue like him unshaken by the vicissitudes of everyday life. Nor is the loss of anything sufficient to trouble me, unless it might be the loss of all my property—an experience I have never yet had. Reputation and honors my father accustomed me to despise, giving reverence to truth alone. I observe that most men are distressed when they think themselves looked down on by somebody, or when they have lost money. You have never seen me distressed for the former reason, and up to now I have never incurred so great a financial loss as to be unable to attend to the hygienic needs of my body with what remained; nor have I suffered loss of civil rights, such as I see many incur at the hands of the Senate.[5]

Luckily, his serenity was never tested by misfortune, and Galen was free to imitate his beloved father. Since the bickering of philosophers repelled him, Galen was attracted to mathematics and hoped to be an architect like Nicon. However, his father dreamed that Galen was destined to be a doctor, and the son dutifully obeyed the revelation from Asclepius. Though his father warned him to avoid dogmatism, Galen would find absolute truths in the study of medicine.

At the age of seventeen, Galen entered the medical school at Pergamum where he studied anatomy for four years. During his graduate education at Smyrna, Corinth, and Alexandria, Galen also attended courses on subjects unrelated to medicine. A brilliant student, Galen impressed his medical professors and wrote scientific papers which were well received in the profession. To test the theories he had learned in the classroom, Galen converted his family's estate near Pergamum into an experimental farm. There he practiced vivisection on animals and carefully studied their digestive and nervous systems. Since public opinion frowned on the dissection of human corpses, Galen had to infer much human physiology from analogies in the anatomy of apes and pigs. On a hot summer's day, his dissections were messy and dangerous, for the flies were thick and there was always the threat of infection. Later Galen would have ample opportunity to observe human anatomy in the gladiators at Pergamum and Rome. His studies in animal anatomy convinced Galen that every organ had a purpose, which was proof of divine planning. Since the atmosphere of the age was religious, it is not surprising that Galen "looked for God in the entrails of animals."[6] His Egyptian contemporary, Ptolemy, was a fervent astrologer as well as a great astronomer.

Poets have often claimed that the heavens display the handiwork of God, but Galen insisted that men can also see divine intent in the heel of a lowly beast:

I compare the noblest of heavenly bodies to the most modest of all parts of the animal. What is more petty than the heel? Nothing. Yet it could not be placed better anywhere else. What more noble than the sun? Yet neither could this be better situated in any other part of the universe. The universe is the greatest and finest thing that exists. Who denies it? But the ancients who were familiar with nature held that the animal itself was, so to speak, a little universe. In both, you will find the Creator's wisdom equally manifested.[7]

Confident that his teleological notions were true, Galen was deeply religious and loathed Epicureans, who denied astrology and divination and reduced the universe to atoms. Since his philosophic preconceptions overrode his experimental acumen, Galen elaborated the doctrine that spirits dominate the body. Arising in the liver, the physical spirit moved through the veins and controlled growth, reproduction, and nutrition. Mixing with air in the heart, the physical spirit formed the vital spirit which warmed and regulated the body through the arterial system. In the brain the vital spirit was distilled into the psychic spirit which controlled the brain and the nervous system.

Although Hellenistic physiologists had disproved the Hippocratic doctrine of the four humors—blood, phlegm, yellow and black bile—Galen revived the humors to explain the four basic human temperaments—sanguine, phlegmatic, choleric, and melancholic. While the four humors were in balance in a healthy body, an excess of any humor produced temperamental changes and disease. Despite his imaginative theorizing, Galen was an experienced physician and adept in therapy, surgery, drugs, and diet. He not only recommended but practiced moderation, exercise, and good hygiene. Unlike modern physicians, Galen had an unusual consultant, for Asclepius visited him in dreams and even advised on surgical techniques. Apparently the god was a literary critic as well, because Asclepius insisted that Galen add a discussion of the optic nerve to a medical work he was writing.

In 158 Galen received a choice medical post at Pergamum. The high priest of Asclepius, who was also in charge of the games in the arena, hired the young doctor as surgeon for the corps of gladiators. At last Galen could observe the inner workings of the human body as he tended the wounded gladiators. Since many of Galen's charges recovered, the loss of life in the arena was not as great as is often imagined. Managers took care that skilled gladiators were not needlessly butchered, for they were expensive to train and popular fighters always attracted a large crowd of devoted fans. In 161 Galen moved to Rome, where he established a private medical practice and lectured on anatomy. Despite his busy schedule the Asian physician continued to write extensively, and his talents soon became known to the imperial court. Called to the palace for consultation, he scored a personal triumph by curing an ailment which was troubling Marcus Aurelius. After taking the emperor's pulse, Galen asked a few pertinent questions and diagnosed that the great Stoic had overeaten and was suffering from an upset stomach. When the doctor prescribed a homey remedy of pepper and wine, the imperial patient quickly recovered. Impressed with Galen's common sense, the emperor often employed him at court and came to respect his broad learning. Later, Galen would mix the opiate theriac to which Marcus Aurelius was addicted. Despite his success at court, the Pergamene physician was distressed by the controversies and feuds which characterized the medical profession at Rome. Rival cliques of doctors quarreled over theories and personalities, and rowdy physicians jeered at Galen during medical debates. Always sensitive to displays of anger, Galen was hurt by abuse from his colleagues, but in his writings he too engaged in polemics. About 163 Galen abandoned teaching and confined himself to his books and medical practice.

When the plague broke out at Rome in 166, Galen decided to leave the congested city. At the age of thirty-seven, he returned to Pergamum, where he planned to spend the rest of his life in research and writing. However, Galen was recalled by Marcus Aurelius in 168 to join him and Lucius Verus in northern Italy. The physician reached the emperor's camp shortly before the death of Lucius in 169. Since the Roman troops were infected with plague, Galen did not wish to accompany Marcus Aurelius on his campaign against the northern barbarians. Conveniently, Asclepius appeared in Galen's dreams and forbade him to follow the emperor to the frontier. The pious Marcus Aurelius accepted the revelation from Asclepius and sent Galen to Rome to care for Commodus, who was then nine years old. The famous doctor gave the prince excellent medical care and probably entertained the boy with heroic tales of combat in the arena at Pergamum. In 180 Commodus succeeded his father and retained Galen as his personal physician. Though the young emperor and his doctor had little in common, Galen served the imperial athlete loyally

Commodus

and offered Commodus unheeded advice. According to Galen, wise men do not waste their time on strenuous games because the best exercise is really a fast ball game. Unmoved by Galen's warnings, the emperor suffered from a large swelling in his groin which the great doctor was unable to reduce.

Famed as the emperor's physician, Galen became a popular society doctor at Rome. His account of a case of chronic insomnia shows that Galen was aware of the psychosomatic factor in illness:

I was called in to see a woman who was stated to be sleepless at night and to lie tossing about from one position into another. Finding she had no fever, I made a detailed inquiry into everything that had happened to her, especially considering such factors as we know to cause insomnia. But she either answered little or nothing at all, as if to show that it was useless to question her. Finally, she turned away, hiding herself completely by throwing the bedclothes over her whole body and laying her head on another small pillow as if desiring sleep. After leaving, I came to the conclusion that she was suffering from one of two things: either from a melancholy dependent on black bile,

or else trouble about something she was unwilling to confess. . . .
After I had diagnosed that there was no bodily trouble and that the
woman was suffering from some mental uneasiness, it happened that,
at the very time I was examining her . . . somebody came from the
theater and said he had seen Pylades dancing. Then, both her
expression and the color of her face changed. Seeing this, I applied
my hand to her wrist and noticed that her pulse had suddenly become
extremely irregular. This kind of pulse indicates that the mind is
disturbed; thus it occurs also in people who are disputing over any
subject. So, on the next day, I said to one of my followers that, when
I paid my visit to the woman, he was to come a little later and announce to me, "Morphus is dancing today." When he said this, I
found that the pulse was unaffected. Similarly, also on the next day
when I had an announcement made about the third member of the
troupe, the pulse remained unchanged as before. On the fourth evening, I kept very careful watch when it was announced that Pylades
was dancing, and I noticed that the pulse was very much disturbed.
Thus, I found out that the woman was in love with Pylades, and by
careful watch on the succeeding days, my discovery was confirmed. . . .
Now what was it that escaped the notice of previous physicians when
examining the aforesaid woman? . . . They have no clear conception
of how the body tends to be affected by mental conditions.[8]

Through empirical means and insight into the human heart, Galen
solved the mystery of the sleepless woman. With his abiding
interest in psychology, the physician must have been pained by
the mental deterioration of Commodus, whom he had known
since the emperor was a child. In his final madness Commodus
became a classic example of unrestrained sadism with scatophagic
symptoms and a savage joy in the sight of blood.

Like most doctors, Galen avoided political controversy and
remained unscathed through the hectic reign of Commodus.
When the prefect Perennis fell from power in 185, Galen was
impressed by the fortitude of slaves whose owners were purged
with Perennis. When tortured to reveal information which would
incriminate their masters, the loyal slaves refused to confess and
did not make false charges to satisfy the interrogators. From this
episode Galen concluded that nobility of character was not
limited to men who were born free. However, the doctor, who
admitted the courage of the steadfast slaves, did not object to the
institution of slavery. His attitude toward Christianity reflected

the relaxed conditions under Commodus, whose mistress Marcia was sympathetic toward the unpopular sect. As a scientist Galen felt that Christians and Jews relied too much on faith, and he was impatient when they answered his inquiries with "Moses says" or "I believe." Though he scoffed at their dependence on mysteries and miracles, Galen praised the moral behavior of Christians:

Their contempt of death and of its sequel is patent to us every day, and likewise their restraint in cohabitation. For they include not only men but also women who refrain from cohabiting all through their lives; and they also number individuals who, in self-discipline and self-control in matters of food and drink and in their keen pursuit of justice, have attained a pitch not inferior to that of genuine philosophers.[9]

Unlike Marcus Aurelius, Galen respected the virtues and sincerity of the sectarians.*

In educated circles at Rome Christianity was socially unacceptable, partially because too many Christians lacked learning. In the late second century a Christian group at Rome tried to bridge the gap between science and Christianity. Their leader was a wealthy leather merchant, Theodotus of Byzantium, who may have heard Galen praise the morals of Christians while he criticized their ignorance. In religious matters Theodotus and his followers took an Adoptionist view of Jesus and were accused of altering scriptural texts to suit their own views. A contemporary Christian tract, the *Little Labyrinth,* denounced the Theodotus group with great vehemence:

They have tampered with the divine Scriptures without fear; they have dealt treacherously with the rule of the primitive faith; they have not known Christ. They seek not what the divine Scriptures declare but laboriously set out to find a form of syllogism to support their godlessness. And if someone puts in front of them a text of divine Scripture, they try to see whether a hypothetical or a disjunctive form of syllogism can be made out of it. Deserting the Holy Scriptures of God, they pursue the study of geometry, since they are of the earth and their

*For Bar Hebraeus' account of Galen and the Christians, see Appendix Two.

talk is of the earth and they know not Him that comes from above. Thus, some of them make a laborious study of Euclid, they admire Aristotle and Theophrastus, and some of them almost worship Galen. But those who make full use of the arts of unbelievers to establish the opinion of their sect and corrupt the simple faith of the divine Scripture with the craftiness of godless men—how can we say that such are near the faith?[10]

The bishop of Rome, Victor, excommunicated Theodotus and his supporters as heretics, but their fondness for Aristotle, Euclid, and Galen was apparently as offensive to the orthodox as was heresy. Ironically, centuries later the church would approve of Galen and almost canonize Aristotle.

The charge of heresy against Theodotus aborted his attempt to reconcile Christianity and science, and even sophisticated Christians of the next generation felt uneasy when they tried to apply common sense to contradictions in scripture. In North Africa the Christian rhetorician Tertullian met the challenge of reason with a defiant counterblast:

They drag in Aristotle who invented for the heretics dialectic, the art of building up and pulling down, which is so cunning in its statements, so far-fetched in its conjectures, so harsh in its arguments, so productive of contentions—embarrassing even to itself. . . . What indeed has Athens to do with Jerusalem? What the Academy with the Church? What have heretics to do with Christians? Our instruction comes from the Porch of Solomon who had himself taught that the Lord should be sought in simplicity of heart. Away with all attempts to produce a motley Christianity of Stoic, Platonic, and dialectic composition. We want no curious disputation when we possess Christ Jesus, no intellectual inquiry when we enjoy the Gospel! With our faith we desire no further belief. For this is our primary view: that no further belief is required.[11]

Like Fronto, Tertullian was a master of invective and an able distorter of facts. Regretably, his attitude on science was shared by too many Christians. However, the internal problems of Christianity meant nothing to Galen.

The great physician had grown old at the Roman court and had seen Commodus degrade the dignity of the imperial office. In 192 Galen was still in the capital when a fire destroyed the

Temple of Peace and many of his manuscripts which were stored nearby. Subsequently, most of the details of his life are unknown, but the doctor must have witnessed the hectic events which led to the triumph of Septimius Severus in the summer of 193. The Severan regime favored men from the Eastern provinces, and Galen mixed theriac for the new emperor. By the end of the second century, the famed physician was probably dead. Galen's lasting influence was through his books which were cherished by Roman, Byzantine, and Syriac scholars and were reintroduced into Europe by the Muslims after the Dark Ages. As late as the time of William Harvey, Galen of Pergamum was still the greatest authority in medicine.

EPILOGUE

The Severan Triumph

In January 193, Galen and most Romans had expected great things from Commodus' successor Pertinax. Sincere and frugal, Pertinax tried to revive the prestige of the throne and restore discipline among the Praetorian guards. Since the treasury was almost depleted, he raised cash by selling Commodus' treasures and concubines. With some misgiving, the emperor tried to buy the loyalty of the Praetorians, but the prefect Laetus knew that Pertinax would not continue his generosity to the guards. Always practical, Laetus decided to remove Pertinax and sell the throne to another candidate. On March 26, a mob of about two hundred Praetorians broke into the palace searching for the emperor. Though his personal bodyguards were still in the palace, Pertinax tried to shame the soldiers by facing them alone. Only the freedman Eclectus, who had put him on the throne, stayed to defend the elderly emperor. For a brief moment, the mob was awed by the courage of Pertinax and his aide, but then a soldier stabbed the emperor while the others cut down Eclectus. With the head of Pertinax on a spear, the murderers returned to the Praetorian barracks, where the urban prefect was trying to buy the imperial title from Laetus and his officers. However, the wealthy senator Didius Julianus also wanted to become emperor. He hurried to the camp and stood at the gate bidding against the urban prefect. The promises of cash reached astronomical proportions, and the Praetorian guards auctioned the throne to the highest bidder, Julianus. The impertinence of the Praetorians was equalled only by the folly of Julianus, who imagined that the frontier legions would tamely accept the tragic farce at Rome. Backed by the Praetorians, the new emperor intimidated the

Senate and immediately occupied the palace, where he ate the supper which had been prepared for Pertinax. When the news reached the streets, the Roman masses displayed the indignation which their superiors were too cowardly to show. The crowds rioted and denounced Julianus as a usurper. When he appeared in public, the people threw stones at him until they were dispersed by the Praetorians. At the Circus Maximus a large crowd protested the murder of Pertinax and called upon the legions to avenge him. The frontier generals did not need encouragement, for they were well aware of what Tacitus had called the "secret of the empire."

Unrest and apprehension gripped the city of Rome during the brief reign of Didius Julianus, who was a former protégé of Marcus Aurelius' mother and had served with distinction under Marcus. As emperor, Julianus paid his debt to the Antonine family by executing Laetus and Marcia for the murder of Commodus. Meanwhile, news of the death of Pertinax touched off a military revolt in Syria, where the legions elevated their commander Niger as emperor. Soon two other generals followed suit, Albinus in Britain and Septimius Severus on the Danube frontier. The ablest of the three contenders, Severus, was closest to the capital and marched immediately into Italy posing as the avenger of Pertinax. Since the pampered Praetorians had no intention of fighting the Danube Army, Julianus became desperate and offered to share his throne with Severus, who dismissed the proposal with contempt. As the Severan troops neared Rome, Julianus cowered in the palace and tried to avert his fate with magic rites. Late in May the Senate proclaimed Severus as emperor, and a common soldier was sent to kill the wretched Julianus. Outside the city the Severan army was encamped, and the new emperor summoned the Praetorians to account for their crimes. After executing the murderers of Pertinax, Severus disbanded the entire Praetorian corps and formed a new guard of elite troops from the combat legions. The speed and severity of his action was characteristic of the man who now controlled the Roman empire.

Early in June 193 the emperor made a spectacular entry into the capital. The historian Dio Cassius witnessed the colorful scene:

When he entered Rome, Severus rode as far as the gates on horseback and in cavalry uniform, but there he changed into civilian clothes and proceeded on foot. He was followed by the whole army, both infantry and cavalry, in full battle dress. The spectacle was the most brilliant thing I have ever seen. The entire city was decorated with flowers and wreaths and brightly colored banners, and it was ablaze with torches and smoking incense. The civilians wore white robes and happy faces and cheered without stopping, and the soldiers in their shining armor seemed to be on a holiday parade. We senators were also in our finest clothes and on our dignity. The eager crowds surged about to see Severus and hear him speak, as if he had somehow been changed by his success. To catch a glimpse of him, some people held each other aloft. After his entry into the city, he made us some fine promises. Like the great emperors of the past, Severus gave us his oath that he would not put any senator to death. . . . Later, he broke his promise and executed many of us.[1]

When Dio wrote this passage, the joy of liberation had long since faded under the crushing despotism of the Severan regime.

The emperor Septimius Severus was a forty-seven-year-old African general who spoke Latin with a Punic accent. A shrewd, harsh man, he craved power and had married the Syrian beauty, Julia Domna, because she had the horoscope of an empress. To dispose of his rivals Severus adopted Albinus as his heir and defeated Niger in a bloody civil war. Within a few years Severus demoted Albinus and killed him in another power struggle. The ruthless emperor slaughtered senators who had supported Albinus and confiscated their properties. Through the purges, the Severan family acquired great wealth and vast estates throughout the empire. A frank militarist, Severus increased the pay of the armies and ruled the empire as an armed camp. He also insisted on dynastic succession, and his family would hold the throne for half a century. To confirm his dynastic claims, Severus invented a spurious connection with the Antonine family and rehabilitated the memory of Commodus. Orderly and efficient, the Severan regime provided stability and security at the price of extreme regimentation.

Before Severus the emperors had maintained the Augustan pose that their authority was derived from the Senate and the Roman people, even when senators grovelled before the throne.

Stripping away the mask of hypocrisy, Severus openly ruled as a monarch whose strength rested on the legions. Expanding the precedents of earlier emperors. Severus forced Roman society into rigid conformity and mute obedience. The African emperor might well have been the subject of Auden's "Epitaph on a Tyrant":

> Perfection, of a kind, was what he was after,
> And the poetry he invented was easy to understand;
> He knew human folly like the back of his hand
> And was greatly interested in armies and fleets;
> When he laughed, respectable senators burst with laughter,
> And when he cried, the little children died in the streets.[2]

Under Severus the Roman empire became a vast barracks. In the past Roman citizens had the right of appeal to the emperor and were not supposed to be tortured or crucified, but the Severan rulers restricted these privileges to the upper classes and the army. Ironically, the final internationalization of the Roman world took place when Roman citizens no longer had any rights. In 212 Severus' son Caracalla extended citizenship to almost all residents of the Roman empire, but his decree was prompted largely by a desire to increase specific taxes which only citizens paid. The precious citizenship, of which Paul had been so proud, was now only a hollow mockery. Under the Severan dynasty monarchical trends also prevailed in religion, and the emperor Elagabalus tried to elevate the Syrian sun god as chief of the Roman pantheon. Christianity profited from the favor which Severan rulers extended toward Eastern religions, and the enthusiasm of Julia Domna for the cult of Apollonius of Tyana foreshadowed major religious developments in the third century. At all levels of society a new world was taking form.

Though Augustus would not have approved of many Severan policies, the Rome of Augustus was not the city of Septimius Severus. Physically, the capital was larger and decorated with the splendid buildings of Vespasian, Trajan, and Hadrian. Socially, the Italian monopoly on power and rank had been broken by Spaniards, Gauls, and Africans. The Jews were no longer a favored people, and Christianity was slowly winning converts and gaining respectability. Throughout the second century, religiosity had increased and the new age would relish magic, astrology, and mysticism. Politically, the army was in control and the emperors were absolute monarchs, but much of the new era had precedents in the past. Even under the best emperors, the weight of the Roman state had been heavy, because benevolent despots cannot provide both liberty and justice. The developments in the Roman empire were not surprising, for nations must change in order to live and no society is ever static. Yet neither Augustus nor the "adopted emperors" had foreseen the grim Severan world. Only Marcus Aurelius had realized that time is a raging river which carries men from forgotten springs to a dark and unknown sea.

APPENDIX ONE

Sources and Problems

History is a critical discipline, and its practitioners must constantly evaluate the reliability of evidence. In history as in a court of law, not all testimony can be trusted, and historians are as fallible as lawyers and juries. While there is a core of generally accepted facts, the history of antiquity is still productive of lively and fruitful controversies. Because the sources for Roman history are fragmentary and often contradictory, there are considerable differences of opinion among modern historians of Rome. Too often crucial evidence must be drawn from purely literary sources or from late epitomizers who were inept and superficial. Even the major Roman historians obscured facts and issues through their biases and careless errors. With critical methodology and common sense, a modern scholar may reclaim much of the past, but he often has to deal with circumstantial evidence and can only hope for a high degree of probability in his conclusions.

The history of Rome in the first century rests largely on Tacitus, Suetonius, Josephus and Dio Cassius. The reliability of the first three writers is discussed in the text. Born in Asia Minor, Dio Cassius sat in the Senate under Commodus and was a loyal public servant of the Severan emperors. Unfortunately, his history of Rome to 229 does not survive in totality, and much of it exists only in brief Byzantine epitomes. Though his treatment of the first century is uneven, Dio is a fairly reliable source for the second century. Dio's account of the reigns of Marcus Aurelius, Commodus, and the Severans is far superior to the motley *Scriptores Historiae Augustae*, a fourth-century collection of biographies of the emperors from Hadrian to Carinus. Confused and often sensational, the *Scriptores Historiae Augustae* contain many valuable fragments from excellent sources, but the biographies are carelessly written and filled with bias, and the entire work must be used with great caution. About 240 Herodian of Antioch wrote a moralistic history of the emperors from 180 to 238, but Herodian knew little of events in Rome and his book is almost worthless for Roman history before the Severan era. The sources for the lives of Paul and Apollonius are discussed in the text. Seneca, Pliny the Younger, Marcus Aurelius, and Galen provided much autobiographical material in their own writings. For the development of Christianity the *Ecclesiastical History* of Eusebius of Caesarea is a key work, but Eusebius wrote in the fourth century and was often guilty of bias, error, and serious omissions. A few important facts are found only in the fourth-century epitomizers, Eutropius and Sextus Aurelius Victor. Occasionally, a significant episode may be found in a nonhistorical setting—for example, the Jewish response to Herod Agrippa's display of piety in the Mishnah, Sotah 7:8, or Epictetus' statement that Roman policemen would dress as civilians and try to trap strangers into making seditious remarks about the emperor, *Discourses* IV 13:5. Still many gaps remain in our knowledge of ancient Rome.

Since some of the interpretations in the present text deal with matters of scholarly dispute, the reader may find the following selective comments useful:

p. 37.   The sources for the fall of Sejanus are discussed by Ronald Syme (*Tacitus*, Vol. II, pp. 752-754.) According to Syme (Vol. I, p. 406), Sejanus expected to become the emperor's heir, but "the only plot that can be safely assumed and narrated is the plot devised and executed by Tiberius Caesar." Ann Boddington ["Sejanus. Whose Conspiracy?" *American Journal of Philology* (1963), 84:1-16] feels that Sejanus did not have sufficient social status to aspire to the throne. According to Boddington, Tiberius intended to appoint Sejanus as regent for his heirs, but a faction of jealous nobles forced the emperor to destroy the prefect. Nevertheless, the Augustan regime was a revolutionary society, and Sejanus might hope to become Tiberius' heir once he had married into the imperial family, for Tiberius had only been related to the first Princeps through marriage and not blood. As for Sejanus' lowly origin, even Augustus had been only one generation removed from a middle-class background and freely admitted it in his Memoirs (Suetonius *Augustus* 2). Antonia's letter to Tiberius is reported by Josephus (*Antiquities of the Jews* XVIII 180-182), who was close to the son of Antonia's protégé, Herod Agrippa. At the Flavian court Josephus met Vespasian's mistress Caenis, who as Antonia's secretary had written the document and never forgot its contents (Dio Cassius LXVI 14:1-2). Though its specific details can only be inferred, the letter alarmed Tiberius and precipitated the fall of Sejanus.

p. 58. Tacitus' account of the murder of Caligula and the accession of Claudius is not extant, but Josephus described these events in great detail (*Antiquities of the Jews* XIX 17-200, 212-273; *Jewish War* II 204-214). Josephus had two excellent sources, Cluvius Rufus and Agrippa II; Rufus was in the Senate in 41 and later wrote an authoritative history of the Julio-Claudian dynasty. In 41 the conspirators did not agree on Caligula's successor, but Callistus backed Claudius, who was opposed by Chaerea. The German mercenaries killed many of the plotters, and later Claudius executed Chaerea, whose real offense had been opposition and not regicide. The complicity of Claudius in the plot against Caligula and his rescue by the Praetorians is a more plausible explanation than the ludicrous claim that Claudius became emperor through the whims of the guardsmen who found him by chance cowering behind a curtain in the palace (Suetonius *Claudius* 10).

p. 78. The psychological break in Second Corinthians was suggested by C. H. Dodd, "The Mind of Paul, II," pp. 83-128, in *New Testament Studies* (Manchester: Manchester University Press, 1933).

p. 93. The death of Claudius is detailed by Tacitus (*Annals* XII 65-69), Suetonius (*Claudius* 43-45), and Dio Cassius (LXI 34.1-35.4). Both Seneca and Burrus were Agrippina's appointees, and Burrus kept a tight security clamp on the palace in the crucial hours after the murder. It is inconceivable that Nero's adviser Seneca was not involved in the plans of his patroness

Agrippina to replace Claudius with Nero. The Spanish courtier also had a longstanding grudge against the aged emperor who had exiled him to Corsica. According to Dio (LXI 3:1), Seneca prepared a speech for Nero to deliver at the Praetorian camp announcing the death of Claudius and promising donatives. Unlike Nero's address to the Senate, this speech would have been composed before the murder of Claudius.

p. 131.   Apollonius' knowledge of the plot against Domitian was suggested by Michael Rostovtzeff (*Roman Empire*, Vol. I, p. 119) relying on Dio Cassius (LXVII 16:2; 18:1-2).

p. 146.   The role of the army chiefs in the Praetorian mutiny which led to the adoption of Trajan was suggested by Ronald Syme (*Tacitus*, Vol. I, p. 13) who adds: "Indeed, nothing proves that Trajan was not the candidate of the Prefect of the Guard" (p. 35 n.4.). Some significant material regarding Nerva's friends and his successor can be found in Dio Cassius LXVII 15. 1-2,5; Eutropius VIII 1; Aurelius Victor *De Caesaribus* 11-12; Suetonius *Domitian* 23; Dio Cassius LVIII 3:3, 5:4; and Aurelius Victor *Epitome* 13.

p. 149.   There is an extensive literature on the Roman persecutions of Christians, but the best recent discussion of the legal status of early Christianity is G.E.M. de Ste. Croix's "Why were the early Christians persecuted?" *Past and Present* (1963) 26:6-38, with a criticism by A. N. Sherwin-White (1964) 27:23-27, and a rejoinder by Ste. Croix 27:28-33. Ste. Croix believes that the professing of Christianity was a crime, but Pliny the Younger was not sure and Roman criminal law was rarely precise and often arbitrary. Roman courts easily found that Christians did not indulge in depraved rites, but no Roman judge could tolerate a deliberate refusal to participate in the state cult. In Roman eyes Christianity was just another Eastern superstition, but its adherents defied authority and many courted martyrdom.

p. 198.   In his *Notebooks* the emperor devoted pages of praise to his close relatives and intellectual friends but gave Faustina only a brief compliment for her obedience, simple tastes, and affectionate nature (I:17). Like Marcus, the empress avoided ostentation and she had obediently spent a summer at his camp during the war against the Quadi. She was certainly affectionate, more so than Marcus. For dynastic reasons the couple had a number of children, but many queens have bred large families in loveless marriages. Many of the tales of her infidelity are exaggerated, but the basic charge is plausible and based on contemporary reports. Dio Cassius (LXXI 34:3) noted that the emperor did not investigate or punish the offenses of his family "particularly those of his wife." According to the *Scriptores Historiae Augustae* (M.A. 26:5) based largely on the Severan biographer Marius Maximus, Marcus Aurelius "was either ignorant or affected ignorance" of Faustina's behavior. Her posthumous deification proves nothing, for the despised Lucius Verus was also raised to godhood. Marcus' quip about Faustina's dowry suggests that he was both aware of and resigned to her infidelity. On both Stoic and pragmatic grounds, his forbearance was sensible. Many famous men have been cuckolds, and Marcus and his wife retained a common bond in their plans for Commodus. On Faustina's plot with Avidius Cassius, Marius Maximus (A.C. 9:9) and Dio Cassius (LXXI 22:3) are in agreement.

p. 199.   The evidence of Marcus Aurelius' reliance on narcotics is collected and discussed by Thomas W. Africa, "The Opium Addiction of Marcus Aurelius," *Journal of the History of Ideas* (1961) 22:97-102, and Edward C. Witke, "Marcus Aurelius and Mandragora," *Classical Philology* (1965) 60:23-24.

APPENDIX TWO

A Syriac View of Galen

In the thirteenth century, Galen received considerable attention in a brief chapter on Roman imperial history in the *Chronography* of Gregorius Abu'l-Faraj, who is more commonly known as Bar Hebraeus. A major Syriac historian, Bar Hebraeus was a polymath and well versed in science. He was also a Jacobite ecclesiastic and interested in Galen's relations with the Christians. Separated from Galen by a millennium, Bar Hebraeus described the life and accomplishments of the Greek doctor:

In the tenth year of Trajan, Galen the physician was born. . . . [Under Antoninus Pius] Galen flourished. And that he did not live in the time of our Lord, as some men think, is known from Galen's own words. For he saith in the beginning of the First Chapter which treateth of fissures (or wounds), "I composed the first book of fissures when I went up to Rome the first time." And he saith also in his exposition of Plato's Book of Phaedo, "We have seen these men who are called Nazarenes, who found their Faith upon Divine indications (or inspirations) and miracles, and they are in no wise inferior to those who are in truth philosophers. For they love purity (or chastity) and they are constant in Fasting, and they are zealous in avoiding the committal of wrong, and there are among them some who during the whole course of their lives never indulge in carnal intercourse."
. . . Now the total of the years from the Ascension of our Lord to the death of Galen, according to the accurate opinion of chronographers, is one hundred and sixty years. Now this Galen came from the city of Pergamus, and he wrote many books on the craft of the physician, and of these about one hundred works are extant. He revived the Hippocratic system of medicine which had fallen into disuse (or become antiquated). And when he was told about the mighty deeds and healings which Christ our Lord used to do, he said, "I have no

doubt whatsoever that He doeth these things by means of the Divine
Power." And he asked, "Doth any man of His disciples still remain?"
And it was told him, "Such remaineth in Jerusalem," and he rose up
to go to Jerusalem. And when he arrived in Sicily, he died there at
the age of eighty-eight years. . . . Alexander the Aphrodisite . . .
gave Galen the nickname of "mule-head," because of the strength of
his head at the time of disputation and debate.[1]

While not free from error, this account of Galen is an interesting
fragment of the history of science in the medieval Arabic world.
As a Jacobite, Bar Hebraeus has Galen leave Rome to seek the
true followers of Jesus in the east. The tenth century Nestorian
writer Ishaq ibn Hunain (via 'Ubaidallah and Ibn al-Qifti) was
the source for Bar Hebraeus' sketch of Galen. The ultimate Greek
source for the Arabic and Syriac scholars was some *vita Galeni*
composed in late antiquity. Though Galen surely did not make a
pilgrimage to Jerusalem, it is possible that the famous physician
died at an advanced age in Sicily on his way to Asia Minor.

APPENDIX THREE

Genealogical Charts

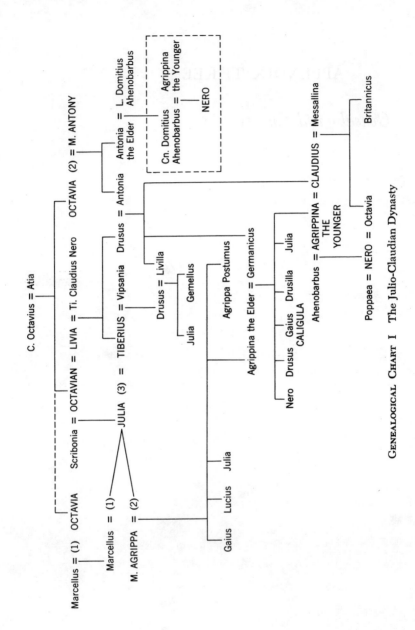

GENEALOGICAL CHART I   The Julio-Claudian Dynasty

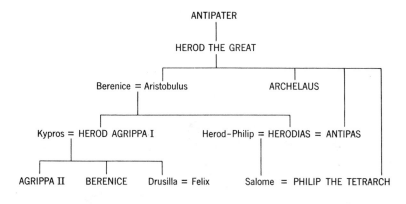

GENEALOGICAL CHART II   The Herodian Family

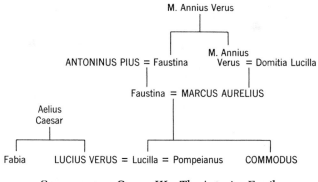

GENEALOGICAL CHART III   The Antonine Family

RECOMMENDED READINGS

There are many excellent surveys and specialized studies dealing with Rome and the empire in the first two centuries A.D. Much valuable material can be found only in learned journals, and the interested reader is advised to consult such periodicals as *Historia, The Journal of Roman Studies, American Journal of Philology, The Phoenix, Classical Philology, Classical Quarterly, Classical Review,* and *Greece and Rome* for recent articles. For readers with "little Latin and less Greek," most of the ancient sources are available in excellent modern translations in the Loeb Classics, the Modern Library, and the Penguin series. The most useful historical sources are the *Res Gestae Divi Augusti,* Velleius Paterculus, Josephus, Tacitus, Suetonius, Dio Cassius, Philostratus, and the *Scriptores Historiae Augustae.* The major literary sources for the period are Lucan, Seneca, Petronius, Martial, Pliny the Elder, Pliny the Younger, Juvenal, Plutarch, Fronto, Lucian, Aelius Aristides, Marcus Aurelius, Minucius Felix, and Galen. The reader may also wish to consult the following books:

Balsdon, J. P., *The Emperor Gaius* (New York: Oxford University Press, 1934).

Brock, Arthur J., *Greek Medicine* (New York: E. P. Dutton; 1929).

The Cambridge Ancient History (Cambridge: Cambridge University Press):
Vol. X (The Augustan Empire 44 B.C.–A.D. 70), 1934.
Vol. XI (The Imperial Peace A.D. 70–192), 1936.

Carcopino, Jérôme, *Daily Life in Ancient Rome* (New Haven: Yale University Press, 1940).

Dill, Sir Samuel, *Roman Society from Nero to Marcus Aurelius* (New York: Meridian, 1956).

Dodd, C. H., *New Testament Studies* (Manchester: Manchester University Press, 1933).

Duff, A. M., *Freedmen in the Early Roman Empire,* 2nd Ed. (Cambridge: Heffer, 1958).

Festugière, André-Jean, *Personal Religion among the Greeks* (Berkeley: University of California Press, 1954).

Frank, Tenney, ed., *An Economic Survey of Ancient Rome,* Vols. II–V (Baltimore: Johns Hopkins Press, 1940).

Gibbon, Edward, *The History of the Decline and Fall of the Roman Empire,* Chapters I–V, any complete edition.

Grant, Michael, *The World of Rome* (New York: Mentor, 1960).

Hammond, Mason, *The Antonine Monarchy* (Rome: The American School, 1959).

Jones, Tom B., *The Silver-Plated Age* (Sandoval: Coronado Press, 1962).

Kähler, Heinz, *The Art of Rome and Her Empire* (New York: Crown, 1962).

Lietzmann, Hans, *A History of the Early Church*, Vol. I (New York: Meridian Books, 1961).

Momigliano, Arnaldo, *Claudius, the Emperor and his Achievement*, 2nd Ed. (New York: Barnes and Noble, 1961).

Nock, Arthur D., *Conversion* (Oxford: Clarendon Press, 1933).

Oliver, James H., *The Ruling Power* (Philadelphia: American Philosophical Society, 1953).

Rogers, R. S., *Studies in the Reign of Tiberius* (Baltimore: Johns Hopkins Press, 1943).

Rostovtzeff, Michael I., *The Social and Economic History of the Roman Empire*, 2nd Ed. (Oxford: Clarendon Press, 1957), 2 vols.

Rowell, Henry T., *Rome in the Augustan Age* (Norman: University of Oklahoma Press, 1962).

Sarton, George, *Galen of Pergamon* (Lawrence: University of Kansas Press, 1954).

Syme, Sir Ronald, *Colonial Elites* (New York: Oxford University Press, 1958).

Syme, Sir Ronald, *The Roman Revolution* (Oxford: Clarendon Press, 1939).

Syme, Sir Ronald, *Tacitus* (Oxford: Clarendon Press, 1958), 2 vols.

Walzer, Richard, *Galen on Jews and Christians* (London: Oxford University Press, 1949).

REFERENCE NOTES

CHAPTER ONE:
1. Ammianus Marcellinus XVI 10:13–15.
2. Edward Gibbon, *Autobiography*, Dero A. Saunders, ed. (New York: Meridian Books, 1961), pp. 152, 154.
3. Henry Adams, *The Education of Henry Adams* (New York: Modern Library, 1931), pp. 90–91.
4. Seneca *De consolatione ad Helviam matrem* 6:2–3, trans. by John W. Basore, *Moral Essays*, Vol. II (Cambridge, Mass.: Harvard University Press, 1932), pp. 429–431.
5. Seneca Epistle 56: 1–4, trans. by Richard M. Gummere, *Epistulae Morales*, Vol. I (Cambridge, Mass.: Harvard University Press, 1917), pp. 373–375.
6. Juvenal III 192–202, 232–258, 268–301, trans. by Rolfe Humphries, *The Satires of Juvenal* (Bloomington: Indiana University Press, 1958), pp. 40, 42–44.
7. Fronto *Principia Historiae* 17, trans. by C. R. Haines, *The Correspondence of Marcus Cornelius Fronto*, Vol II (Cambridge, Mass.: Harvard University Press, 1957), p. 217.
8. Jérôme Carcopino, *Daily Life in Ancient Rome* (New Haven: Yale University Press, 1940), pp. 176–177.
9. Petronius *The Satyricon* 119, trans. by William Arrowsmith (New York: Mentor, 1960), pp. 129–130.
10. Revelation of John 18:5–23, 19:3.

CHAPTER TWO:
1. *Res Gestae Divi Augusti* 34.
2. Naphtali Lewis and Reinhold Meyer, eds., *Roman Civilization, Selected Readings*, Vol. II (New York: Columbia University Press, 1955), p. 35.
3. Suetonius *Augustus* 99, 101, trans. by Robert Graves, *The Twelve Caesars* (Baltimore: Penguin, 1957), pp. 105–106, 108.
4. Velleius Paterculus II 126–127, trans. by Frederick W. Shipley (Cambridge, Mass.: Harvard University Press, 1955), pp. 319–321.
5. Tacitus *Annals* IV 34–35, trans. by Michael Grant, *The Annals of Imperial Rome* (Baltimore: Penguin, 1959), pp. 169–170.
6. Tacitus *Annals* VI 8–9, *ibid.*, pp. 198–199.
7. Juvenal X 61–77, 85–107, trans. by Rolfe Humphries, *The Satires of Juvenal* (Bloomington: Indiana University Press, 1958), pp. 124–125.

CHAPTER THREE:
1. Luke 19:12–27.
2. Luke 3:1–4, 7–16, 18–20.
3. Mark 6:14–28.
4. Luke 23:8–12.
5. Philo *In Flaccum* 6:36–39.
6. Philo *Legatio ad Gaium* 36:277–280, 286–287, 41:326–329, trans. by E. Mary Smallwood (Leiden: E. J. Brill, 1961), pp. 122–126, 134–136.

CHAPTER FOUR:
1. Philippians 3:5–6.
2. II Esdras 8:1; 7:(60–61), trans. by Edgar J. Goodspeed, *The Apocrypha* (Chicago: University of Chicago Press, 1938), pp. 67, 73.
3. Romans 7:7–9.
4. Romans 7:14–15, 17:21–24.
5. Acts 9:3–9.
6. Galatians 1:14–17.
7. II Corinthians 12:2–9.
8. Fyodor Dostoievsky, *The Idiot*, trans. by Constance Garnett (New York: Modern Library, 1935), pp. 213–215.
9. Galatians 3:13–14, 19–20; 4:3–5.
10. Galatians 1:18–2:10.
11. Galatians 2:11–14, 16, 18, 21.
12. I Corinthians 9:25–27.
13. Acts of Paul II 3, trans. by Montague R. James, *The Apocryphal New Testament* (Oxford: Clarendon Press, 1926), p. 273.
14. II Corinthians 11:23–27; 12:11–13.
15. I Corinthians 9:20–22; 10:32–33.
16. I Corinthians 1:20–28.
17. I Corinthians 6:9–11.
18. I Corinthians 14:13–15, 18–20, 23.
19. I Corinthians 14:35.
20. I Thessalonians 4:16–17.
21. II Thessalonians 2:2–4, 6–8.
22. II Corinthians 1:8–9.
23. II Corinthians 4:16–18; 5:16.
24. Acts 28:30–31.
25. Philippians 2:20–21.
26. Philippians 2:15–16.
27. I Corinthians 15:8–11.

CHAPTER FIVE:
1. Geoffrey Chaucer, *The Canterbury Tales* (New York: Modern Library, 1929), p. 231.
2. Saint Augustine *The City of God* VI 10.
3. Seneca Epistle 47:1–2, 4–5, Vol. I, trans. by Gummere, pp. 301–303.

4. Seneca Epistle 47:5–8, Vol. I, trans. by Gummere, p. 305.
5. Seneca Epistle 47:10–12, Vol. I, trans. by Gummere, pp. 307–309.
6. Seneca De otio 4:1–2, Vol. II, trans. by Basore, pp. 187–189.
7. Seneca De vita beata 21:4–22:1, Vol. II, trans. by Basore, p. 155.
8. Tacitus Annals XI 24, trans. by Grant, pp. 236–237.
9. Seneca De consolatione ad Helviam matrem 8:2–5, Vol. II, trans. by Basore, p. 441.
10. Tacitus Annals XII 7, trans. by Grant, pp. 246–247.
11. Tacitus Annals XIII 2, ibid., p. 274.
12. Tacitus Annals XIII 14, ibid., p. 280.
13. Tacitus Annals XIII 42, ibid., p. 294.
14. Seneca Epistle 94:46. Cf. Sallust, Jugurthine War 10:6.
15. Seneca Epistle 105:1–6, Vol. III, trans. by Gummere, pp. 213–215.
16. Seneca Natural Questions VII 30, trans. by F. H. Sandbach, The Cambridge Ancient History, Vol. XI (Cambridge: Cambridge University Press, 1936), p. 693.
17. Seneca Epistle 56:9, Vol I, trans. by Gummere, p. 379.
18. Tacitus Annals XV 63–64, trans. by Grant, pp. 364–365.
19. Seneca De vita beata 17:1–3, Vol. II, trans. by Basore, pp. 143–145.
20. James 2:17.

CHAPTER SIX:

1. Josephus The Jewish War II 254–257, trans. by G. A. Williamson (Baltimore: Penguin, 1959), p. 135.
2. Albert Camus, Resistance, Rebellion, and Death, trans. by Justin O'Brien (New York: Modern Library, 1960), p. 89.
3. Josephus The Jewish War II 258–260, 264–265, op. cit., pp. 135–136.
4. Josephus The Jewish War II 362–364, ibid., p. 146.
5. Josephus The Jewish War II 390–394, 396–399, ibid., p. 149.
6. Josephus The Jewish War III 351–354, ibid., p. 199.
7. Josephus The Jewish War III 387–391, ibid., p. 202.
8. Josephus The Jewish War III 403–404, ibid., p. 203.
9. Josephus The Jewish War VI 257–260, 271–274, ibid., pp. 324, 325.
10. Josephus The Jewish War I 1–2, 4–5, 6–10, 12, ibid., pp. 21–22.
11. Josephus Life 428–430, Vol. I, trans. by H. St. J. Thackeray (Cambridge, Mass.: Harvard University Press, 1961), pp. 157–159.
12. Josephus Contra Apionem II 94–95, Vol. I, trans. by H. St. J. Thackeray, p. 331.
13. Josephus Contra Apionem II 291–294, Vol. I, ibid., pp. 409–411.
14. Josephus The Jewish War V 19, op. cit., p. 264.

CHAPTER SEVEN:

1. A. D. Nock, Conversion (Oxford: Clarendon Press, 1933,) p. 217.
2. Philostratus Life of Apollonius IV 8.
3. Philostratus Life of Apollonius IV 10.
4. Philostratus Life of Apollonius IV 40.

5. Philostratus *Life of Apollonius* IV 44.
6. Philostratus, *Life of Apollonius* V 35. The "man who is outstanding in virtue" refers to Pericles, the uncrowned king of Athens; see Thucydides II 65. Compare the Apollonius-Euphrates debate with the Agrippa-Maecenas debate in Dio Cassius LII 1–41:2.
7. Lucian *Alexander the False Prophet* 12–16, trans. by Paul Turner, *Satirical Sketches*, (Baltimore: Penguin, 1961), pp. 226–228.
8. Lucian *Alexander the False Prophet* 19–24, *ibid.*, pp. 230–232.
9. Lucian *Alexander the False Prophet* 25, *ibid.*, p. 232.
10. Lucian *Alexander the False Prophet* 36–38, *ibid.*, pp. 237–238.

CHAPTER EIGHT:

1. Edward Gibbon, *The History of the Decline and Fall of the Roman Empire*, J. B. Bury, ed. (London: Macmillan, 1909) Vol. I, p. 78. See Thomas W. Africa, "Gibbon and the Golden Age," *Centennial Review* (1963), 7:273–281.
2. Pliny the Younger, Epistle III 5, trans. by Betty Radice, *The Letters of the Younger Pliny* (Baltimore: Penguin, 1963), pp. 88–89.
3. Pliny the Younger, Epistle VI 16, *ibid.*, pp. 166–168.
4. Pliny the Younger, Epistle IV 22, *ibid.*, p. 128.
5. Pliny the Younger *Panegyric* 44, 45, 80, trans. by Ernest Barker, *From Alexander to Constantine* (Oxford: Clarendon Press, 1956), pp. 254–256.
6. Pliny the Younger, Epistle VII 5, *op. cit.*, pp. 187–188.
7. Pliny the Younger, Epistle VIII 10, *ibid.*, p. 218.
8. Romans 13:1–6.
9. Pliny the Younger, Epistle X 96, *op. cit.*, pp. 293–295.
10. Pliny the Younger, Epistle X 97, *ibid.*, p. 295.
11. Pliny the Younger, Epistle X 33, *ibid.*, p. 271.
12. Pliny the Younger, Epistle X 34, *ibid.*, pp. 271–272.
13. William Shakespeare, "Coriolanus" II i 156–159.
14. *Corpus Inscriptionum Latinarum* V 5262, trans. by Betty Radice, *op. cit.*, p. 303.

CHAPTER NINE:

1. John E. Dalberg-Acton, *Historical Essays and Studies*, (London: Macmillan, 1908), p. 505.
2. Pliny the Younger, Epistle VII 20, trans. by Betty Radice, *The Letters of the Younger Pliny*, (Baltimore: Penguin, 1963), pp. 198–199.
3. Tacitus *Annals III* 66, trans. by Michael Grant, *The Annals of Imperial Rome* (Baltimore, Penguin, 1959) p. 147.
4. Tacitus *Annals* IV 20, ibid., p. 163.
5. Tacitus *Agricola* 45, trans. by Alfred J. Church, *The Complete Works of Tacitus* (New York: Modern Library, 1942), p. 705.
6. Pliny the Younger, Epistle VIII 14, *op. cit.*, pp. 220–221.
7. Tacitus *Dialogue on Oratory* 9, trans. by Church, p. 741.
8. Tacitus *Agricola* 9, 27, *ibid.*, pp. 682, 693.

9. Tacitus *Agricola* 42, *ibid.*, p. 703.
10. Tacitus *Agricola* 30, *ibid.*, p. 695.
11. Tacitus *History* IV 8, *ibid.*, p. 598.
12. Tacitus *History* IV 81, *ibid*, pp. 651–652.
13. Tacitus *Annals* III 18, *op. cit.*, p. 125.
14. Tacitus *Annals* XV 44, *ibid.*, p. 354.
15. Tacitus *Annals* III 65, *ibid.*, p. 147.
16. Tacitus *Annals* I 10, *ibid.*, pp. 35–36.
17. Michel de Montaigne, *Essays* III 8, Vol. IV trans. by George B. Ives (Cambridge, Mass.: Harvard University Press, 1925), pp. 129–131.
18. Montaigne *Essays* II 10, Vol. II, *ibid.*, p. 149.
19. Francesco Guicciardini, *Ricordi* C-18, trans. by Mario Domandi, *Maxims and Reflections* (New York: Harper & Row, 1965), p. 45.

CHAPTER TEN:
1. See Eusebius *Ecclesiastical History* IV 9:1–3.
2. *Scriptores Historiae Augustae, Hadrian* 25:9, trans. by Elinor Wylie in L. R. Lind, ed., *Latin Poetry* (Boston: Houghton Mifflin, 1957), p. 305.
3. Albert Camus, *Resistance, Rebellion, and Death,* trans. by Justin O'Brien (New York: Modern Library, 1960), p. 74.
4. Aelius Aristides *Roman Oration* 65–66, 68, trans. by James H. Oliver, *Transactions of the American Philosophical Society,* Vol. 43 (1953), New Series, p. 902.
5. Plutarch *Moralia* 824CD.
6. Lucian, *The Passing of Peregrinus* 11–14, 16.
7. Origen, *Contra Celsum* VII 18, trans. by Henry Chadwick (Cambridge: Cambridge University Press, 1953), p. 409.
8. Origen, *Contra Celsum* III 55, *ibid.*, pp. 165–166.
9. H. L. Mencken, *A Mencken Chrestomathy* (New York: Alfred A. Knopf, 1949), pp. 613–614.
10. Origen, *Contra Celsum* IV 23, trans. by F. A. Wright, *A History of Later Greek Literature* (London: George Routledge, 1932), pp. 254–255.

CHAPTER ELEVEN:
1. Tom B. Jones, *The Silver-Plated Age,* (Sandoval, N. M.: Coronado Press, 1962), pp. 126–127.
2. Marcus Aurelius VI 30, trans. by C. M. Grube (New York: Bobbs-Merrill, 1963), p. 54.
3. Minucius Felix *Octavius* IX 5–7, trans. by Gerald H. Rendall (Cambridge, Mass.: Harvard University Press, 1960), pp. 337–339.
4. See Marcus Aurelius XI 3. Cf. III 16.
5. Marcus Aurelius X 10, *op. cit.*, p. 101. All quotations from Marcus Aurelius in this chapter are from *The Meditations,* translated by G. M. A. Grube, copyright © 1963 by The Bobbs-Merrill Company, Inc., reprinted by permission of the publishers.

6. Galen (Kühn) XIV 4.
7. Marcus Aurelius VI 36–37, *op. cit.*, pp. 55–56.
8. Marcus Aurelius II 1, *ibid.*, p. 11.
9. Marcus Aurelius VII 3, *ibid.*, p. 61.
10. Marcus Aurelius IV 32–33, IX 29, *ibid.*, pp. 31–32, 92.
11. Marcus Aurelius VI 13, *ibid.*, p. 50.
12. Marcus Aurelius II 17, *ibid.*, pp. 16–17.
13. Marcus Aurelius III 5, *ibid.*, pp. 20–21.
14. Marcus Aurelius VIII 24, *ibid.*, p. 78.
15. Marcus Aurelius III 14, *ibid.*, p. 24.
16. Marcus Aurelius IX 3, *ibid* , p. 88.

CHAPTER TWELVE:
1. Aelius Aristides XLVIII 56–58, trans. by André-Jean Festugière, *Personal Religion among the Greeks* (Berkeley: University of California Press, 1954), pp. 90–91.
2. Aelius Aristides XLVIII 7, *ibid.*, p. 90.
3. Aelius Aristides XLVIII 19–23, *ibid.*, pp. 94–95.
4. Galen, "On the Passions," trans. by Arthur J. Brock, *Greek Medicine* (New York: E. P. Dutton, 1929), p. 171. This essay is also available in a translation by Paul W. Harkins, *Galen on the Passions and Errors of the Soul* (Columbus, Ohio: Ohio State University Press, 1963).
5. *Ibid.*, p. 172.
6. George Sarton, *Galen of Pergamon* (Lawrence, Kansas: University of Kansas Press, 1954), p. 59, n. 76.
7. Galen, "On the Utility of Parts," *op. cit.*, p. 155.
8. Galen, "On Prognosis," *ibid.*, pp. 213–214.
9. Richard Walzer, *Galen on Jews and Christians* (London: Oxford University Press, 1949), p. 15. This fragment is found only in an Arabic quotation from Galen's lost commentary on Plato's *Republic*.
10. Eusebius *Ecclesiastical History* V 28:13–15, *ibid.*, pp. 76–77.
11. Tertullian *De praescriptionibus haereticorum* 7, *ibid.*, pp. 79–80.

EPILOGUE:
1. Dio Cassius LXXV 1:3–2:2.
2. W. H. Auden, *Collected Poetry* (New York: Random House, 1945), p. 99.

APPENDIX TWO:
1. Bar Hebraeus *Chronography* 52–54, Vol. I, trans. by Ernest A. Budge (London: Oxford University Press, 1932), pp. 52–54. See the discussion of this passage by Walzer, *op. cit.*, pp. 92–94.

PERMISSIONS

The author wishes to thank the following individuals and publishers for their permission to reprint copyright material:

The World Publishing Company: Edward Gibbon, *Autobiography*, 1961.
Harvard University Press: Montaigne's *Essays*, trans. by G. Ives, 1925.
Seneca, *Moral Essays*, trans. by J. W. Basore, 1932.
Seneca, *Epistulae Morales*, trans. by R. Gummere, 1917.
Fronto, *Correspondence*, trans. by C. Haines, 1957.
Velleius Paterculus, *History*, trans. by F. Shipley, 1955.
Josephus, *Works*, Vol I, trans. by H. Thackeray, 1961.
Minucius Felix, *Octavius*, trans. by G. Rendall, 1960.
University of California Press: A. J. Festugière, *Personal Religion among the Greeks*, 1954.
Routledge and Kegan Paul, Ltd.: F. A. Wright, *A History of Later Greek Literature*, 1932.
Indiana University Press: Juvenal's *Satires*, trans. by R. Humphries, 1958.
American Philosophical Society and Professor James H. Oliver: *The Roman Oration of Aelius Aristides*, 1953.
Penguin Books, Ltd: Tacitus, *The Annals*, trans. by M. Grant, 1959.
Josephus, *The Jewish War*, trans. by G. Williamson, 1959.
Lucian, *Satirical Sketches*, trans. by R. Turner, 1961.
Pliny the Younger, *Letters*, trans. by B. Radice, 1963.
Alfred A. Knopf, Inc.: H. L. Mencken, *A Mencken Chrestomathy*, 1949.
The New American Library of World Literature, Inc: Petronius, *Satyricon*, trans. by W. Arrowsmith, 1960.
E. J. Brill, Ltd: Philo, *Legatio ad Gaium*, trans. by E. Smallwood, 1961.
E. P. Dutton and Company and J. M. Dent & Sons, Ltd.: A. J. Brock, *Greek Medicine*, 1929.
Columbia University Press: Naphtali Lewis, ed., *Roman Civilization, Selected Readings*, Vol. II, 1955.
Coronado Press: Tom B. Jones, *The Silver-Plated Age*, 1962.
Bobbs-Merrill Company: Marcus Aurelius, *Meditations*, trans. by G. M. A. Grube, 1963.
Cambridge University Press: Origen, *Contra Celsum*, trans. by H. Chadwick, 1953. *The New English Bible—New Testament*, 1961.
The Clarendon Press: A. D. Nock, *Conversion*, 1933.
R. Walzer, *Galen on Jews and Christians*, 1949.

M. R. James, *The Apocryphal New Testament*, 1924.

E. Barker, *From Alexander to Constantine*, 1956.

International Authors N.V., Penguin Books, Ltd., and Penguin Books, Inc.: Suetonius, *The Twelve Caesars*, trans. by R. Graves, 1957.

University College, Oxford: Bar Hebraeus, *Chronography*, trans. by E. A. Budge, 1932.

Methuen and Company, Ltd.: E. Gibbon, *History of The Decline and Fall of The Roman Empire*, 1909.

Random House, Inc.: W. H. Auden, *Collected Poetry*, 1945.

Henry Adams, *The Education of Henry Adams*, 1931.

F. Dostoievsky, *The Idiot*, trans. by C. Garnett, 1935.

G. Chaucer, *The Canterbury Tales*, 1929.

A. Camus, *Resistance, Rebellion, and Death*, trans. by J. O'Brien, 1960.

Tacitus, *Works*, trans. by A. Church, 1942.

University of Chicago Press: E. Goodspeed, *The Apocrypha*, 1938.

Yale University Press: J. Carcopino, *Daily Life in Ancient Rome*, 1940.

ILLUSTRATION CREDITS

The fourteen coin photographs are reproduced with the kind permission of The American Numismatic Society.

The two photographs of the model of Rome are courtesy of Alinari — Art Reference Bureau, Inc.

The graffito is reproduced with the kind permission of Professor Michael Gough from his book, *The Early Christians* (London: Thames & Hudson; U.S.A.: Frederick A. Praeger); the drawing was made by Mrs. Mary Gough.

Index

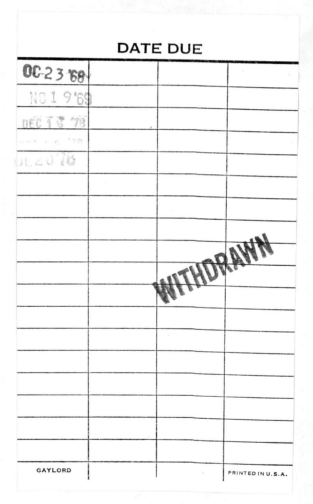

DATE DUE

OC 2 3 '68			
NO 1 9 '69			
DEC 1 8 '78			
DE 2 0 '78			
		WITHDRAWN	
GAYLORD			PRINTED IN U.S.A.